As a student of comparative religion, I believe that Buddhism is the most perfect one that the world has seen.

Carl Jung

I shall say again and again that between Buddhism and modern science there exists a close intellectual bond.

Aldous Huxley

Buddhism has done more for the advancement of world civilization than any other influence in the chronicles of mankind.

H. G. Wells

Contents

Chapter 1
Siddhartha to Vajrayana: The Substance   1

Chapter 2
India to Tibet: The Founding of the
    Karma Kagyu Lineage   41

Chapter 3
Tibet to Texas: The West Inherits the
    Jewels of a Diaspora   78

Chapter 4
A Grassroots History of Karma Kagyu
    Buddhism in Texas: The Texas Sanghas   105

    Austin: Lawrence Wells . . . 105
    San Antonio: Elsa Gonzalez . . . 111
    Houston: Celeste Budwit . . . 116
    Dallas: Joan Klein . . . 119
    Dallas: Beth Condrey Kennan . . . 119
    Dallas: Lama Dudjom Dorje . . . 123
    San Antonio: Jan Puckett . . . 124
    San Antonio: Connie White . . . 127
    Clear Lake: Marilyn Kinsey . . . 128
    Clear Lake: Pattie Hollestein . . . 130

Friendswood: Tore Fossum . . . 133
Houston: Donna Russell . . . 135
Houston: Carol Boethel . . . 138
League City: Bonnie Cooper . . . 140
Houston: Michael Savage and Mary Anne Fields . . . 141
Austin: Dylan Carter and Justin Coody . . . 145
Austin: Sergio Ayala . . . 148
College Station: Nathaniel Rich . . . 148
Houston: Beth Harrison . . . 152
Fresno: Marilyn Kinsey . . . 155

Chapter 5	
The Karmapa War: An Overview	159
Appendix	179
Notes	185
Bibliography	197
Index	201
About the Author	206

Chapter 1

Siddhartha to Vajrayana: The Substance

It is phenomenal that one no longer must journey to the East to study Buddhism. Buddhists are in America—and in Texas—in great variety, offering their profound philosophical and psychological wares to anyone who dares "enter the stream." It is the first time in the history of Buddhism that each of the "three vehicles," Theravada, Mahayana, and Vajrayana, is present in the same country at the same time, competing for practitioners. It is also the first time that the Dharma—Buddha's teachings—has migrated from a third-world country to a more industrially developed society, one far advanced technologically and economically. The dramatic collision between Buddhism and the Western tradition is bringing changes to both cultures.

This numinous breath from the East has deeply affected many who live in Texas, altering for some the very seat of human perception. This is the story of those people who have been touched by the third turning of Buddha's wheel—the Vajrayana school—and more specifically by the Karma Kagyu lineage of Tibetan Buddhism. Texas Kagyu Buddhism is part of a long evolution from Sakyamuni Buddha's original teachings, but it is also part of a new tradition, a new form of the Dharma that is just "getting itself born." Western Buddhism has survived the romantic stage and is now looking soberly at the long haul. A uniquely American form of the Dharma is inevitable.[1]

It is impossible to know who Vajrayana Buddhists are without knowing what they are trying to comprehend and accomplish. Knowing something of the basic philosophy of Buddhism, then, is a must. This story is concerned with more than merely who, when, and where. It is the story, in a modest form, of the Enlightened One, his revolutionary revelations, and the insights that he brought to the world. The story of Texas Buddhism, then, began long ago and infinitely far away.

Siddhartha Gautama, upon becoming Sakyamuni Buddha, taught for 45 years, delivering 84,000 sermons that, when finally fixed in written form, constituted 108 volumes. With all of this information available for more than 2,000 years, it is a little surprising that there was no coherent Western conception of Buddhism until 150 years ago. It is a secondary intent of this chapter to make a small contribution toward healing the effects of this spiritual and intellectual omission by Western civilization.

It is not known exactly when the historical Buddha, Siddharta Gautama, was born, nor when he died. According to Stephen Batchelor, director of the Sharpham College for Buddhist Studies in Devon, England, Gautama probably lived between 560 and 480 B.C.E., passing into total extinction, or Parinirvana, some 543 years before the birth of Christ.[2]

Initially, all of the Buddha's teachings were committed to memory and communicated by word of mouth. A written version was not produced until the first century C.E. in Sri Lanka. This immense body of scripture was called the Pali Canon because it was written in Pali, an ancient, now extinct Indian language, closely related to Sanskrit. The massive collection was divided into three sections, or "baskets," and thus is referred to as the "Tripitaka." The first basket, the Vinaya, includes the code of conduct by which monks are expected to live. The second basket, the Sutra, is the collection of the Buddha's discourses. The third basket, the Abhidharma, is an explanation of philosophical ideas implicit in the Buddha's teachings. Satras are associated commentaries.[3]

Within Buddhist literature, the Buddha wears two faces. First there is the actual person born in Kapilavstu to be king of the Sakya Clan, the gifted man who became the Enlightened One. Then there is the cosmological Buddha, the Tathagata, the one "thus gone." In this latter form, Buddha is a spiritual archetype that from time to time manifests itself in the world in order to give humankind a gentle push along the path toward developing its full potential of mind. Buddha Sakyamuni was just one among many such Buddhas to make an appearance on the world stage—and others will follow.

It will be left to the individual reader to choose between the authenticity of the historical and magical stories or to find some way to integrate the two representations. Even those who have spent a lifetime studying the Buddha often find it necessary to allow for both existences simultaneously,[4] as seen in Gwendolyn Bay's translation of the Lalitavistara Sutra, *The Voice of the Buddha:*

> Unique in history, the Enlightened One stands alone among gods and men alike. Even the Creators and Destroyers of universes revere his matchless knowledge, and acknowledge him as their teacher. The Buddha's omniscience, manifested in all his actions, shows us the limits of our own knowledge. Unlike the Enlightened One, we can never know the outcome of our actions, and we can never be sure that we will attain our goals. As we come to see this, we turn to the Tathagata with a joyful heart, confident that we have found a guide of perfect wisdom.
>
> Yet this is only part of the story, for the Buddha is not a divine messenger or an incarnation, come to earth to offer guidance. Instead, the Enlightened One is himself a human being who has attained the perfection of his human qualities. Through the teaching of pratityasamutpada, which reveals the truths that govern the arising and passing away of all things, he demonstrates that nothing is ultimately beyond our understanding. By teaching that the realm of Enlightenment is inseparable from our own being, he sets us on the path that leads in the end to our also becoming Buddhas. Through his continuing presence, he holds open the door of Liberation for all sentient beings, fulfilling with unending joy the vow that guides this conduct throughout all time and space.[5]

The essence of the primary Buddhist doctrine can be found in the Four Noble Truths, taught by Gautama in the Deer Park in Varanasi (Benares), India, in the fifth century B.C.E. This initial lesson is considered to be the first turning of the wheel, which set in motion the Buddhist Dharma—the teachings, the truth, or the path that leads to liberation and Enlightenment. The basic teaching is that (1) there is suffering in the phenomenal or relative world. (2) This suffering is caused by craving, in the form of grasping at the human personality. This craving, or desire, results in the belief of a separate "self," as well as the longing to perpetuate eternally that nonexistent personality, and incessant suffering results. (3) This suffering can be made to cease. And (4) there exists a method for ending the cyclic round in the world of Samsara (the phenomenal world), the Eightfold Path toward liberation. The path's eight steps begin with Right Understanding and Right Thought (under the category of *wisdom*); next are Right Speech, Right Action, Right Livelihood, and Right Effort (grouped under *morality*). The seventh and eighth steps are Right Mindfulness and Right Concentration, both of which involve the exercise of meditation, an essential activity in any of the three Buddhist vehicles' pathways to awakening.[6]

In the Bernardo Bertolucci film *Little Buddha,* meditation is described as: "Totally relaxed and quiet, separating yourself from everything around you, setting your mind free like a bird. Then you can see your thoughts passing like clouds."[7]

The first step in Buddhist meditation, establishing Right Mindfulness, means to create a space, an emptiness within the mind so that the "infinite" can be approached without fear. Right Mindfulness also requires clarity regarding the meaning and effects of one's actions and perceptions. The next step is Right Concentration, which means developing the knack for pinpoint focus so that nothing can interfere with one's mental work.[8]

In his *Buddhist Handbook,* John Snelling explains:

> Meditation is a specialized activity that helps us to fully realize the Buddha's teachings, to make them an integral part of our being rather than just a new set of ideas to be entertained theoretically in the mind. It weans us away from our usual patterns, particularly our involvement with our thoughts and their emotional sub-themes. At the same time it sharpens and intensifies our powers of direct perception: it gives us eyes to see into the true nature of things. The field of research is ourselves, and for

this reason the laser of attention is turned and focused inwards.[9]

During Shamatha ("dwelling in tranquillity") meditation, one learns to fall into a complete and perfect silence by calming the mind. Peacefulness is the goal. This technique is often practiced in preparation for Vipassana ("Insight" meditation), wherein the meditator's mind is opened and awareness is focused on everything present, regardless of the negatives one is bound to encounter. Understanding is the goal. In the Vajrayana vehicle, the practitioner has the opportunity, through identifying with a Buddha form, of becoming whatever is visualized. Realization is the goal. Within Buddhism, there are many methods of meditating, each representing a successful road to liberation experienced by some master, past or present.

Fundamental to Buddhist beliefs is the principle that at the center of it all, there is no intrinsic entity or god of any kind, but rather vast, luminous space, the clear light that is universal mind. This notion of infinite space, or anatman ("no deity"), was certainly revolutionary when first proposed. It also precludes the existence of an individual self or personal soul. In the place of the self is an aggregate of transitory, changeable parts (skandha), constantly in flux, a pinball-like world where pieces constantly bang into one another and an overpowering sensation of reality arises. This loud, distracting domain is referred to in Buddhist literature as relative or phenomenal. And the human organizational center for this relative or pinball existence is the ego complex. It is the simplest of masks, engendering the illusion of depth and displaying a near-infinite ascendancy in human affairs. It is the perpetually judgmental human being, that breath of air, that work of art formed of matter and energy, by learned behavior, genes, reason, and sometimes, the quiet whispers of intuition. It rankles at the judgment of others, needs "things," swoons at the old songs, loves beauty exceedingly, and shudders with the delight of orgasm. It is paralyzed by fright, a mass of habits, hangovers, and attachments. It laughs and worries, doubts, deceives, and loves. It is the fighter, the hero struggling for a place in the sun. It gives rise to our everyday world, with its hopes, schemes, and hard realities. And it is all there is—or so most of us believe. There is, however, another point of view.

The Buddhist defines personality in terms of the shandha,

or aggregates, which consist of physical forms, sensations, perceptions, thoughts, and consciousness itself. When these aggregates are infused with desire (fear of extinction, and a consequent craving for eternal existence), they are attracted to themselves. Attachment is formed, leading inevitably to the duality of subject and object, and there you have it: the relative world comes into being. Then there is a larger picture having to do with the origin of the origin, which is even more extraordinary.[10]

This entire framework is referred to by Buddhists as *dependent origination*. Buddhists believe that there never was an autonomous entity at all, but only dependent parts, just as a rainbow, though it appears from a distance to be an independent entity, consists of only isolated points of moisture through which light is refracted. For a person who perceives only from the perspective of the relative, the rainbow is altogether real. Buddha, however, emphasized the essential emptiness and impermanence of all elements of existence. All else, according to the Buddhist, is illusion, or *maya*, generated by the original ignorance, the fear that drives the desire for individual, relative immortality. And what keeps the wheel of life in perpetual motion is the law of cause and effect, better known as *karma*, the word itself meaning "action." Every movement in the universe is an effect provoked by some cause and is the consequence of some intended action, however subtle, by the individual.[11]

The Buddhist concept of karma describes a form of reincarnation in which there is movement through the system of death and rebirth, but not by individual souls as in transmigration. Instead, what carries over are the uncontrolled causes that the individual failed to resolve during many lifetimes of opportunity. The closest Western analogue comes from Swiss psychiatrist Carl Gustav Jung (1875–1961): unintegrated archetypes and their presence as the collective unconscious of the next generation.

In Dr. Jung's view, within every individual, below the ego complex, is a personal unconscious mind, a reservoir that holds all forgotten information, including memories so awful one has to repress or suppress them. Beneath this level lie the instincts, which emerge from a collective unconscious common to all humanity. An archetype is an instinct's perception of itself. According to Jung, when a person is born, the entire history of the human race is inherited by the individual consciousness in the form of archetypes, often referred to as "phantoms of the mind" by Eastern psychologists.

There is an individual archetype for every aspect of the life experience. Mythological characters in world literature are said to be archetypal. The war god Mars, for example, represents the urge to experience the violence of battle. From time to time, inexplicably, energy will collect around a single archetype, which itself is a form of energy, and project its essence, present itself to the ego complex. The intent is to force the individual to experience the archetypal energy in the relative world personally so that the archetype itself can come to rest through integration into the individual personality. For instance, as a result of his Vietnam experience, the Robert De Niro character in the film *The Deer Hunter* no longer needed to slay the stag, because the archetype of war had been successfully incarnated. The energy had finally come to rest.

To integrate all archetypes is to discover the self, itself an archetype representing wholeness. The energy of an archetype coming to rest is equivalent to the resting state of energy in the Buddhist vision of luminosity. It is at this point, where energy is perfectly at rest, that Jungian psychology and Buddhist philosophy meaningfully merge and significantly support each other.

Jung explicitly declared his allegiance to Christianity, though he considered himself an outsider. And, unlike the Buddhist, he was God-centered. Also, it should be noted that Jung felt that the ego was the only capital that the human being possesses. It is the ego complex, after all, that has made self-reflection possible. Its evolution has made it possible for energy to reach the point where it can look at itself and say, "I exist." That achievement is truly a miracle in itself, despite the human tendency, by extension, for extreme self-indulgence. After all, there was a time when no ego-consciousness existed on the planet. It is no wonder, then, that this center of consciousness is so protective of itself, so reluctant to relinquish its authoritarian control in the affairs of the individual.[12]

How does all of this relate to karma? In Jungian psychology, individual developments dissolve into a life stream, while unresolved causes, unintegrated archetypes, are passed along as the archetypal structure for the next generation. The Buddhist version is similar.

Reincarnation, without an individual soul or self, is probably the most difficult concept to understand in all of Buddhist philosophy. Let's take a closer look. The new person will be exactly that, brand-new. So, what gets passed along from the old life?

Let's say someone gives a formal dinner. Of course, there are some leftovers, and they are certainly not as fine as the dishes served to the guests at the beginning of the evening. The individual soul at birth is like the dinner originally placed on the table, still untouched by the guest. The leftovers are the fragments that remain at the end of a life's run. A mere fragment is certainly not a complete, individual soul; nonetheless, each of these remnants is looking for a new home. What do these fragments consist of? During a lifetime, decisions are made moment after moment. The ego complex constantly casts out lines of energy with hooks seeking "objects" to attach themselves to, in order to establish subject-object relationships and support its existence and that of the relative world. This attachment happens quickly—in "seventeen thought moments," each moment being shorter than a flash of lightning, according to Buddhist teachings. In that brief timespan, energy is apprehended by the senses and becomes part of the phenomenal world. Futhermore, the original energy becomes conditioned if each individual thought reflects a belief in the independent existence of a self. Ego-complex-centered contemplations are the karmic seeds, the fragments that become one's life stream. This life stream furnishes the energy that ignites the next life, providing momentum, or karma, for the next spin of the wheel of life, or Samsara. At death, the fragments function as pollutants and result in the death-traveler's inability to recognize, while passing through the various bardos ("phases"), what must be recognized in order to "see," experience liberation, and then be absorbed into reality. There is no god sitting in judgment. Karma is a blind force.[13]

The negatives in this formula are manifested by everything, every action and decision made moment to moment while living. Buddhism is a pure form of existentialism in this sense. One is the sum of one's decisions. Without the idea of an individual self or soul, there is no rebirth; the fundamental ignorance can no longer exist, and the mystical equation finds itself in perfect balance. Buddhist scholars point out that if one insists on keeping the idea of self in place through the death process, an infinite number of universes may be created by the karmic order in order to accommodate that concept. As Nyanaponika Thera writes:

> Thus karma is the womb from which we spring, the true creator of the world and of ourselves as the experiencers of the world. And through our karmic actions in deed, word and thought, we increasingly engage in building and rebuilding this world and worlds beyond. Even our good actions, as long as they are still under the influence of craving, conceit, and ignorance, contribute to the creation and preservation of this world of suffering. The Wheel of Life is like a treadmill set in perpetual motion of karma, chiefly by its three unwholesome roots—greed, hatred, and delusion. The "end of the world" cannot be reached by walking on a treadmill; this only creates the illusion of progress. It is only by stopping that vain effort that the end can be reached.[14]

The phrase "stopping that vain effort" insinuates a complete change of perception by paying close attention to what might seem the most insignificant of acts. For example, profanity in itself is not necessarily a bad thing. It becomes negative when the curse finds an object, resulting in a world of duality and securing the longevity of the individual ego complex. Similarly, hatred and anger presuppose an object. Also, these emotions create quite a racket in a person, so that silence and stillness, required in meditation to allow contemplation of the transcendental, are much more difficult to manifest. All negatives are negative insofar as they reinforce the phenomenal world. Seeking revenge, for example, means that one has accepted the relative world as the only reality. Declaring one human being as beautiful and another as not reflects one's attachment to Samsara-based perception. The staunch defense of a political or philosophical point of view creates and sustains the relative. Sitting in judgment of others, whether by flexing a sophisticated, discriminating mind or by reacting violently to another's action, is a sure way to fuel the power source that drives the phenomenal world. A single truth is revealed through any of these ordinary actions: the actor is capable of seeing only through the eyes of the ego complex, not from the reference point of luminosity. It is no wonder that many people consider monasticism essential for spiritual evolution.

There is a starting point for changing behavior and, eventually, the reference point of perception itself. Paul Sherwood, author of *Falling Silent: A Seeker's Journey,* addresses this beginning:

> All that matters is that we not identify ourselves with the person; then, however flawed it may be, [the ego complex] will cause no trouble or heartache for us or others because we will view it dispassionately and thereby be free of its compulsions and weaknesses. Basically, all problems in human relations are due to the fact we take ourselves personally, or believe that we are the person who feels anger and rage and hatred and so on through the whole destructive gamut of negative emotions. So that if we were to cease to take ourselves personally, that is, if we were to realize that we actually are in reality the onlooker looking on at the person impersonating us, personal feelings no longer would have the power to dictate our behavior.[15]

Buddhists teach that we must make the most of our precious lives. The chance of human birth, it is said, is less probable than that of a blind turtle in a vast ocean rising to the surface and accidentally passing its head through an aimlessly drifting yoke. The human being has a greater chance of attaining realization than even a god. Humans are exhorted by the Buddhist masters not to waste such a rare and precious opportunity.[16]

Other religious sects suggest that every experience in a person's life is the "will of God or Allah." This turn of phrase conveniently explains away all of life's horrors. One might assert that in Buddhism, karma is the explanation for every bad thing that happens. But in Buddhism, even though no one, not even a lama, can override the effects of karma, it is the task of the individual to achieve awareness, which in essence puts the "will of karma" and the collective unconscious out of business. This happens the instant one "sees," or turns consciousness around and faces its source. This source and the individual are and always have been one and the same. In Buddhism, there is no scapegoat. The individual is solely responsible, standing alone in an emptiness without end.[17] Reincarnation, then, even without the existence of an intrinsic, individual soul, can be an authentic exercise by the energies that fuse the cosmic realms.

And as for Enlightenment or Nirvana itself, when the great Tibetan sage Tsong Khapa Lo Sang Draka (1357–1419) awakened, he was surprised, it was said, that he found that he was not outside of all that is. Rather, he simply was a part of all, as if inside an infinite, edgeless circle. This circle was actually no circle at all, but a vast space that permeated everything else. The beginningless, endless emptiness is Buddhist Nirvana, all that ever was or is. It is often described as clear space, complete simplicity, the end of cyclic existence, perfect bliss, joyousness, and the end of all suffering. It is seen in a human being as fearlessness, extraordinary patience, honesty, compassion, and tranquility amid the awful turbulence of the frantic world. These qualities or virtues are the manifestation of the Eightfold Noble Path.[18]

Inherent in Buddhist philosophy is the sanctity of all life. One simply does not kill anything. All beings are considered mother or father to all other beings, and taking a life—any life—is tantamount to killing one's parent. Karma is involved even in the act of smashing a mosquito that bombs you in the middle of the night, making sleep miserable to impossible. There is a direct line from the killing to the subject-object relationship and the externalization of the self. And there is the problem of destroying another's life stream, halting their progress toward Parinirvana. No one ever said that being a Buddhist was easy.

The ego complex incessantly seeks justification for its actions and beliefs, at the same time grasping for happiness and pleasure. The inevitable result, Buddhists believe, is a constant emotional swing from the highest highs to the lowest lows and back again, over and over. The aim of Buddhism is to moderate the frantic agitation, establish a foundation for stability, initiate through introspection and intellect the process of spiritual evolution, and ultimately pave the way to Enlightenment.

Traditionally, those who elect to follow this difficult path are supported by and pay homage in their meditations to the Three Jewels: the Buddha, the Dharma, and the Sangha, or monastic order. This conceptual background is common to all forms of Buddhism today. Regardless of which type of Buddhism a believer accepts, all embrace these fundamental concepts. As time passed, however, different schools developed, each having its own interpretations of Sakyamuni's original teachings, different methods of achieving the basic objectives, and, ultimately, even different goals. Some Buddhists feel that all that is taught in Buddhism today was taught by Gautama Buddha himself, and as civilizations matured, they simply realized that what appeared as something new and radically different had been in fact, present all along. There are other theories.

The first turning of the wheel of Dharma, Buddha's sermons, or Sutras, is referred to today as the Hinayana, the Old Wisdom School, or Theravada ("teaching of the elders of the order") Buddhism. In this original Buddhist school, the Buddha is viewed as an actual historical personage. Only monks (bhikshu-beggar) are considered members of the monastic order, or sangha. Gautama certainly served the lay community, ignoring the impenetrable wall inherent in the Hindu caste system, but pursuit of actual liberation was solely the business of the sangha members. The arhat ("slayer of the foe") represents the pinnacle of spiritual evolution as a liberated one. Through an austere code of conduct, the Vinaya, monks privately sought salvation, viewing the world as contaminated and disgusting and the senses as absolute corruption. The relative world and Nirvana are seen as one outside of the other.[19] "The ultimate reality, also called Dharma by the Buddhist, or Nirvana, is defined as that which stands completely outside the sensory world of illusion and ignorance, a world inextricably interwoven with craving and greed."[20]

The late Kalu Rinpoche of the Karma Kagyu lineage characterizes the Hinayana by saying that "The Small Vehicle is based on becoming aware of the fact that all we experience in samsara is marked by suffering. Being aware of this engenders the will to rid ourselves of this suffering, to liberate ourselves on an individual level, and to attain happiness. We are moved by our own interest. Renunciation and perseverance allow us to attain our goal."[21] Wisdom, in the Theravada school, is considered the highest virtue. Wisdom alone is able to chase the illusion of individuality from one's thoughts.

Within a hundred years after Gautama's death, regionalism, growing out of dispersion and isolation, resulted in a laxity of monastic rules, the Vinaya, and some diversity of practices. Concern by those who preferred a strict adherence to the established code of conduct led to an assembly, called the Second Council, or the Council of Vaisali. The offending monks were repudiated for their indulgences by the elders (the Sthaviravada), but even more significantly, as a result of the confrontation, it became apparent that a progressive element in the sangha had developed and would eventually split Buddhism into two major traditions. The new school referred to itself as the Mahasamghikas. This sect asserted the fallibility of arhats, sought to weaken the authority of the monastic elite, and opened the Dharma to the masses of the lay community. In time, the Mahasamghikas paved the way for the foundation of the Great Vehicle, or the Mahayana, the second turning of the wheel, as it is known today.[22]

It is pointed out in *Light of Liberation* that, in reality, there was no clear schism that created a distinct Mahayana school.

> Yet no one school—not even the Mahasamghikas, the most often suggested—appears to have transformed itself into a Mahayana school as such. The Mahayana that emerged between the first and second centuries C.E. disseminated teaching shared by many of the early schools. It may be more accurate to consider that openness to the Mahayana view developed within the Buddhist tradition as a natural unfolding of spiritual capacities, and only later took on distinctive identities.[23]

During this period, other interpretations of the Dharma led to the formation of many new Buddhist schools. Some scholars put the number of sects at eighteen, others as high as thirty-plus. Prominent among these were the Sarvastivadins, who held the view that past, present, and future realities exist simultaneously. This sect gradually migrated to the northwest, including Kashmir and much of Central Asia, providing the Vinaya lineage that still survives in all of the schools of Tibetan Buddhism. Another significant school was the Sthaviravadin sect, known today as the Theravada or Hinayana tradition, and it is prevalent throughout Southeast Asia.[24]

Nevertheless, near the beginning of the common era, a new wave of development asserted itself within the spiritual community that the Buddha had inaugurated, resulting in one of the most magnificent outbursts of creative energy known to human history, one that would sustain itself for five hundred years. The heart of the new Mahayana literature was the Prajnaparamita Sutra, the "transcendent wisdom of the mother of Buddhas." This text began to emerge into prominence in India about 100 B.C.E., four hundred years after the final Nirvana of Sakyamuni Buddha. The Prajnaparamita is the foundation of the Mahayana system of thought.[25]

The Mahayana, the Great Vehicle, or the New Wisdom School embraced a much more socially liberal and spiritually wider vision of the path and goal of Buddhism. This was not a monks-only system. The lay community was accepted as an active participant. Siddhartha Gautama, the man of flesh and bone, was replaced by a transcendental principle, a celestial Buddha, a supernatural being who would manifest in numerous forms in innumerable places, in any time. The cosmological Buddha now made his debut.[26]

Significantly, there is a merging of the relative and absolute worlds, and compassion is the glue that fuses the opposites. In *Mother of the Buddhas,* Lex Hixon writes:

> All living beings suffer, teaches the Buddha. Sentient beings are therefore the inspirers and recipients of heartfelt compassion and are, in this sense, benefactors or even mothers of the bohisattvas who vow to liberate them from suffering. Blissfully awakened bohisattvas come forth from the ranks of sentient beings who are immersed in the terrible dream of suffering.
>
> At issue here is the root principle of Mahayana. The relative truth of existence is that it is an expanse of suffering beings, a condition which is the motivation of the precious Mahayana commitment to universal conscious awakening. This relative truth of suffering must not be swallowed up, even subtly, by the absolute truth that Reality is an inherently selfless expanse, an infinite, empty space, intrinsically peaceful and blissful. Relative truth and absolute truth must remain in subtle balance or even in perfect union.[27]

The relative is now a full partner in mystical union with the absolute. In fact, through the emotion of compassion, the relative becomes more prominent, more spiritually charged than the absolute and becomes a more significant player in the Buddhist system than wisdom. This is the Mahayana.

Such Gnostic Great Compassion permits one to embrace the absolute, which is transparent openness, and the relative, which is the harmonious functioning of all possible structures, at the very same time and with the very same passionate gesture of heart and mind. Selfless love for all beings thus itself becomes the radical wisdom of non-duality.[28]

The spiritual ideal of the arhat who sought, as some felt, a private liberation for his own sake, emphasizing austerity and self-restraint, was thus replaced by the Bodhisattva, "heroic being" as translated in Tibetan, one seeking Buddhahood for the benefit of all beings. The Bodhisattva, with emphasis on the intuitive, will throw himself back into Samsara until all sentient life forms are realized. The individualism of the arhat, one man's solitary struggle for Enlightenment, was replaced by the altruism of the Bodhisattva, and compassion now ranks as an equal with wisdom as the fundamental virtue in one's approach to Buddhahood.[29] The Hinayana emphasizes the humanity of the Buddha, while the Mahayana emphasizes the Buddha-nature of humanity.[30]

The Indian philosopher Nagarjuna systematized the various texts that were being written about 150 B.C.E. into the "Verses on the Middle Way," and the Madhyamaka school became the most prominent among the various Buddhist sects during the age of the "Dharma King" Asoka's reign. Nagarjuna, the first of two important Buddhist personages with the same name, used a ruthless system of dialectical reductionism to prove that one can use neither affirmation nor denial to prove the existence of Nirvana. Truth is somewhere in the catch of the breath, in between. This "between" is Somerset Maugham's *Razor's Edge* and Siddhartha's "Middle Way."[31]

In the history of Buddhism, "Middle Way" has other connotations and connections. For example, when Gautama, during his early years as an ascetic, heard a passing music master tell his pupil that if a string was tightened too much, it would snap, and if left too slack, it would not play, he realized a great truth. The path to awakening could not be that of a self-destructive ascetic nor that of one living in rapacious gluttony. The path to enlightenment was the line between all opposites, the "Middle Way." The term is also applicable to the Mahayana perception that the relative world, though an illusion, is also very real, if only for those still trapped in illusionary dreams.

Nagarjuna, in debates and in writing, would prove the inherent absurdity of all propositions, in turn liberating the audience from all views and leaving debaters with nothing, only emptiness. The Dharma is now referred to as emptiness. The absolute is emptiness and all things are also empty—and emptiness cannot be the object of any belief: "Emptiness is the non-difference between yes and no, and the truth escapes us when we say 'it is,' and when we say 'it is not'; but it lies somewhere between these two."[32]

And as we have seen, in this emptiness, Nirvana and "this world" are no longer different, but the same. All doctrines, even the teachings of Buddhism, must then be false. This is the essence of the New Wisdom School. In order to be awakened, one must reject all philosophical supports one by one and learn to view without fear the emptiness of the soul—which is the ego complex's greatest fear: "When we are thus without any stable support, without any hope of one, then we are said 'to rely on nothing but perfect wisdom,' or emptiness, which is the same thing."[33]

A fascinating and controversial current in the history of Buddhism is that, regardless of in which century a renaissance of thought and literature emerges, the new sutras are attributed to the voice of Sakyamuni. Inevitably, it seems, a prediction by Gautama will be found suggesting the birth of the new philosopher. In this case, the person of note, Nagarjuna, is purported to have received a message from the nagas, serpent kings living in the oceans, that the texts had been stored in their palace beneath the sea until the world matured enough for understanding. The sage was now to visit and make them available for the rest of mankind. It is a fascinating explanation. New schools inevitably appear, it seems, when times get bad for the old.[34]

Indeed, the arrival of the Madhyamaka and its "Middle Way" was a sign of difficult times. Buddhism was in trouble. A new literature said so. Nagarjuna's work of the second century of the common era and the Prajnaparamita literature itself, according to Lex Hixon, signaled a "gentle revolution" in Buddhist thinking. A vast maturing in the Buddhist mind and heart had developed after the five hundred years of intensive meditation that followed the passing of the founder. Arhats were no longer being produced through the mainstream in large numbers. Something was being lost in intellectualizations and discussions in the scholastic setting. A new age, new social circumstances, and new populations inevitably generate the need for a new way of doing things. The Mahayana filled the void.[35]

In their zeal to help others, Mahayana practitioners adopted a method they called "skill in means." This teaching method aims to bring out the spiritual potentialities of different people by adjusting to the variety of needs and adapting to every level of the human being's ability to comprehend. This approach requires profound insight on the part of the teacher. In the Mahayana's requirement of the Six Perfections necessary for movement to Bodhisattvahood, accomplishment of the final perfection, or paramita, wisdom, is obligatory. Therefore a teacher, the interpretation goes, is free as well as wise to say anything, as long as it is useful in the spiritual development of his pupils. Anything goes. Teaching became an art, and fictionalizing became part of the practice. Conze explains:

> It is a series of fictions elaborated to further the salvation of beings. In actual fact, there are no Buddhas, no Bodhisattvas, no perfections, and no stages. All these are products of our imagination, just expedients, concessions to the needs of ignorant people, designed to ferry them across to the Beyond. Everything apart from the One, also called "Emptiness" or "Suchness," is devoid of real existence, and whatever may be said about it is ultimately untrue, false, and nugatory. But nevertheless it is not only permissible, but even useful to say it, because the salvation of beings demands it.[36]

It is impossible to separate the growth of the Mahayana from the absorption and input of the lay community into the New Wisdom School. The original Buddhist communities were all monastic. The normal folk, the poorer castes, were all but left out of the inner circle. With the spread of this popular religion, there was a clamor by the masses for some kind of participation. With the philosophy of "Nirvana is Samsara and Samsara is Nirvana," and the reciprocal relationship of the Bodhisattva and the relative world, laypersons were automatically allowed in. It is the "Middle Way" again. With the masses came the conceptual model of their universe, and with its absorption, a riot of gods appeared. Waiting in the wings was a new Mahayana sect, the Yogacara, geared for this melange of mythologies and some additional mythical surprises of their own. By 500 C.E., this Buddhist sect entirely dominated the philosophical backdrop of Mahayana thought.[37]

While Nagarjuna's contributions to Buddhism's thought are profound, still there remained a residue of nihilism. The Yogacarins, accepting Nagarjuna's philosophy of emptiness or transparency (sunyata) took a more positive approach than the Madhyamikas. John Snelling describes the fourth-century C.E. Yogacara philosophical development introduced by the teaching of Asanga: "All is mind or consciousness, they maintained, hence their central doctrine of *citta-matra:* 'mind only' or 'nothing but consciousness.' According to this view, the objects of the world do not exist per se but are also created from and by the mind."[38]

The Yogacarin's explanation for how this was done was through the process of "Store Consciousness." This was a Jung-like collective unconscious in which seeds of all potential phenomena are stored and from which they ceaselessly pour into manifestation. In fact, these phenomena are only projections of the mind, and everything one could imagine is only a mental projection. Imagining is projecting. Mistaking these projections for something real would be a delusion, and the cure for this sickness is seeing through it by means of meditation. The idea of "mind only" establishes a pure consciousness devoid of all content, which gets one back to Nagarjuna's concept of emptiness again.[39]

Describing the phenomenon of "projection," as well as offering real proof of its existence, is no easy task. Yet there needs to be some sense of what Buddhists mean when they use the term. For example, take the number thirteen. Some skyscrapers do not have a thirteenth floor, because the number is thought to bring bad luck. Collectively and individually, this negative connotation has been a part of the historical mental makeup of the West seemingly forever. The individual projects the content of the belief into the number whenever encountered. For example, a runner is completing a cross-country and has jogged the trail many times before, and thus knows that the next bridge is just down the trail. That bridge is number thirteen. Negative images begin to flood the runner's mind. The negatives do not matter so much, but what does matter is the projection of energy into the approaching event. When the runner is able to cross bridge thirteen with it meaning nothing more than an effort of the legs, then all of those hours of meditation are beginning to have some positive effect.

In the "mind only" school, everything one sees and every event one experiences are merely products of the process of projection. Jung pictured energy gathering around an individual archetype. Why energy gathers around one archetype and not another, he admitted, is inexplicable. Nevertheless, this energy flows from an individual and toward some object. If the energy is intense enough, then the object could function as a trap door. When it opens, suddenly one is dealing with a universal power, the infinite energy of an archetype, rather than experiencing an ordinary reaction to an everyday event. For instance, instead of feeling personal anger when a driver roars up behind you on the freeway and starts flashing his lights to pass, the intensity of the event opens a psychic door, activating an archetype, and there is real trouble. The war god Mars steps through, and road rage emerges in its ugliest, most powerful form. The ego complex becomes inflated with the godlike power of the archetype and even senses itself to be a god, with all the attendant rights and privileges. Clear the road!

When the ego complex identifies with the self archetype, a master inflation can occur, which makes it possible for personal justification of undertakings such as the Crusades, the Inquisition, a jihad, or the actions of Osama bin Laden. The ego complex believes that it has become all-powerful, the eternal atman, and the theistic center makes this all possible. In the name of an absolute, the ego itself is being served, and the godhead is only a projection. The ego complex, in essence, is worshiping itself. In Buddhism, this is simply impossible, for the center is clear, impersonal, luminous, universal mind. There are no extremes, only total awareness.

As Jung saw it, if one can not properly integrate subconscious material, then the energy passes on through the subject, then turns and looks back, becoming the "shadow," or all of the destructive elements in a person's life. Through the shadow archetype, one is capable of projecting the fundamentals of something like pure evil. Couple this with the theistic concept of God, a personal God no less, at the center, and one unconsciously creates a crucible for stewing up absolute evil or a divine antigod. Theism makes the difference. Theism invites duality, and anthropomorphism exalts the ego complex. Though a constant theist, the French philosopher Voltaire contributed to history the consummate statement concerning the human being's anthropomorphic urge and some of its fallout: "If God made man in his own image, we have well repaid him by making him in ours; nothing could better reveal man's conception of himself than his conception of God."[40]

Needless to say, the more intense the dualistic feelings, the more entrenched the opposing forces and antagonisms become, until duality, "them" versus "us," is the reigning principle. Again, in Buddhism there is no hook upon which to hang such an attachment. Unhappy, wild energy forms do exist in Buddhism, but ultimately they are only mental projections. Reality itself is only mind, space, and limitless bliss.

Nagarjuna's system of dialectics offers precious little positive teaching. The Yogacara philosophers did, however, create an entirely new positive perspective in Buddhist thought. The word *emptiness* was replaced by *consciousness* to designate absolute space.[41] Buddhism had always approached its description of Nirvana through the use of negative terminology. Nirvana itself literally means "blown out." The Middle Way constantly makes use of phrases such as "I am not this," or "This is not mine." Meditation itself removes the object by withdrawing from it. But now, practitioners could float in a positive state of mind, free from the morass and hindrances of negatives as they worked their way toward Enlightenment.[42]

The Yogacara school of thinkers also came to the conclusion that consciousness can exist without an object. The philosophical benchmark of the Hinayana school, the Abhidharma, which according to Conze is one of the greatest achievements of the human intellect, classifies consciousness as an object, a skandha—that is, an aggregate as defined by awareness. Just as the physical eye cannot see itself, no one should be able to meet the subject of consciousness, that is, awareness or the absolute, face to face, for as soon as one turns toward the inner subject, it naturally becomes another object, creating the old Buddhist anathema, duality. The Old Wisdom School held that no kind of introspection could regress to the point at which one is absorbed by the infinite. Nonetheless, becoming "subject only" is exactly what the Yogacarins set out to do, and they ultimately managed to harness the technique for both intellectual and practical use.

These philosophers defined the true self as the ultimate subject. Consciousness can create objects out of its own inner potentialities. Mind, they reasoned, can exist by itself without any object whatsoever. The Yogacarins believed that they could achieve salvation by developing the ability to experience an act of cognition that no longer apprehends an object. This would be an act of "thought only," pure consciousness without division between subject and object. That is, there is only a subject. For this school,

> The root of all evil must lie in our proclivity to see anything as separated from, or external to, that inmost self, in the way of an object. In reality, all things and thoughts are but Mind-Only. The basis of all our illusions consists in that we regard the objectifications of our own mind as a world independent of that mind, which is really its source and substance.
>
> The highest insight is reached when everything appears as sheer hallucination. The world is like a dream. A dream is merely an awareness of ideas; the corresponding objects are not really there. Just as one perceives the lack of objectivity in the dream pictures after one has woken up, so the lack of objectivity in the perceptions of waking life is perceived by those who have been awakened by the knowledge of true reality.[43]

With the intimate integration of laymen into mainstream Buddhism, the system automatically accepted new characteristics, among them the use of faith. If there are actually gods out there, then the masses will certainly have faith in their reality, as well as devotion to them. Bhakti, which means loving devotion to deities conceived in human form, eventually invaded the New Wisdom school in full force, resulting in a reference to the Mahayana as a Buddhism of faith.

Such a development brings the danger of instituting duality through the notion that something "out there," outside of "myself" will "save me." Yet if the intellect of the aspirants was meager, then belief in what a teacher suggested, even blind faith, would certainly further learning. Faith, a subordinate virtue in the Hinayana, soon ranked in the Mahayana as equal to wisdom and compassion, the highest virtues.[44] Intellectual strength and acumen of both teacher and student become essential, however, when the meditation process approaches absorption and the time comes to discard the entire apparatus of faith.

The concept of "merit" also became prominent in the

Mahayana. Doing good deeds is viewed as giving some kind of credit that will help with the formulization of karma. In the Mahayana, accumulating merit includes acts like giving gifts and paying homage to and praising Buddha's virtues. This concept developed into the belief that the grace of the absolute alone could carry one across to Nirvana, and that one's own personal schemes and endeavors are quite trivial. This, according to Conze, was all pretty straightforward popular religion, a far cry from the original Theravada notion of a solitary individual's struggle toward liberation.[45] It should be noted that as a Bodhisattva nears complete absorption, all accumulated merit is relinquished.

The new celestial Buddha was invested with a phantom body, or "apparitional body," for his incarnation on Earth, an "enjoyment body" for appearances among the celestial Bodhisattvas, and a "dharma body," as the absolute reality itself. In fact, the one Buddha became many saviors. The Mahayana, in order to meet the needs of the masses, filled the entire universe to the utmost limits of space with Buddhas and Bodhisattvas who were alive and could be treasured by the devoted. Each Buddha has a certain limited field, paradise, or kingdom of influence where he teaches the Dharma to interested creatures, helping them toward Enlightenment. Each field is produced by the mind of the Buddha or Bodhisattva, which means, also, projected by the mind of the teaching lama. Ultimately, all fields are one field, and one field is all fields, and all of this is emptiness. The world, in other words is "a kind of phantasmagoria, in which magically created beings are saved from a magically created suffering by a magically created savior, who shows them the unsubstantiality of all that comes into being. It is no wonder that the conviction began to spread that magical methods alone could deal effectively with such a universe."[46]

The Mahayana was also subject to outside cultural influences. Edward Conze points out that the cult of Amitabha Buddha shows strong Iranian characteristics. Amitabha is the Buddha of Infinite Light, whose kingdom is in the west. He is also known as Amitayus, a Buddha with an infinite life span. Amitabha is still alive and well today.

As noted, within the agrarian communities there was widespread belief in earth goddesses, ghost, sprites, fairies, fiends, demons, ogres, and magical practices of every description. The feminine in nature and spirit was especially revered. In the erotic mysticism of the pre-Aryan Dravidian culture, great emphasis was placed on the female principle, and the cult of the village goddess kept alive the matriarchal traditions surrounding the Mother Goddess. Hinduism was certainly influenced by earlier nature religions, as was the Buddhist system that followed. John Snelling illustrates this influence on the Hindu god Shiva:

> Shiva is the prototype of the dedicated yogi who, in his ardent pursuit of his spiritual ideal, subjects mind and body to the most extreme austerities. But Shiva also has an antithetical erotic aspect and iconographically he is often depicted as coupling with his consort or Shakti. (This sexual union symbolizes the process whereby the passive male aspect of ultimate reality is brought into manifestation by the powerfully creative female aspect.) Indeed sexual symbolism plays a conspicuous part in Tantra, and understandably so, for it is the self-division of the primal unity into the two poles that generates the creation of the ten thousand things; and of course that very process of creation can itself be reversed and a conscious return to unity achieved.[47]

The Yogacarins were more than willing to utilize such popular beliefs when the Great Vehicle itself, the second turning of the wheel, began to lose its initial vitality. This popularization of Buddhism undoubtedly was responsible for real acknowledgment of the feminine principle and a broader acceptance of women in Buddhism.

Just as the Mahayana evolved to balance the scholasticism of the Hinayana, so another tradition emerged from the strange and mysterious voices of the wandering Mahasiddhas (Siddha-Success, in reaching Enlightenment) to balance the intellectualism of the New School. The teachings of these ascetics can be loosely grouped into schools variously known as Tantra, Mantrayana, and later, Vajrayana. Even though the Karma Kagyu in Texas are practitioners of the Vajrayana, the third turning of the wheel by Buddha, an intimate understanding of the philosophical principles of both the Theravada and Mahayana vehicles is considered absolutely necessary and is expected by all Kagyu teachers.

Much more than simply another sect of Buddhism, the Vajrayana was the third turning of the wheel of Dharma. It was a new vehicle to address the imbalances of the previous system. The Vajrayana, a direct descendent of the Yogacara, rejected little that had been preached by its predecessors. Instead, it simply insisted that practitioners practice what they preach and practice with infinitely more primal vitality. [48]

It would be of little use to try to separate Tantrism, Mantrayana, and Vajrayana. It is helpful, however, to note that the Tantric system has two branches, Right-handed Tantra, which stresses the masculine, and Left-handed, which emphasizes the feminine. The Tibetan sect of the Karma Kagyu considers itself a branch of the Mahayana family. The historical line of development then passes through the Yogacara school, the Mantrayana (the use of mantras), and the Left-hand Tantra before it reaches its final home in the Vajrayana system.

Vajrayana is translated as "the Diamond Vehicle," because *vajra* in Sanskrit means "adamantine" or "indestructible": "Nothing can destroy the basic nature of things, because nothing departs from it. Because this vajra nature can never become anything else, it is said to be unborn. Also because it can never become anything else, it is tantra, which means 'continuity.'"[49]

The Vajrayana was founded by a second Nagarjuna, an Indian who, around 750 C.E., systematized the many and varying Tantric teachings into some kind of whole. Its real beginning, however, goes back to the dawn of history, to those agricultural communities pervaded by magic and witchcraft, human sacrifice, the cult of the mother goddess, fertility rites, and chthonic deities. Fakirs roamed the land, astounding people with their wizardry and skills. The hodgepodge that would eventually become the Vajrayana vehicle actually existed before either of India's great theologies: "The Tantra is not really a new creation, but the result of an absorption of primitive beliefs by the literary tradition, and their blending with Buddhist philosophy."[50]

The practice of yoga is as old as civilization itself, in the form of the wandering ascetic, the dedicated yogi who, in pursuit of the spiritual, subjects his mind and body to the most extreme austerities. This is the true individual, one who follows his own insights, often by rejecting the rigidity of existing monastic orders, and certainly by rejecting the expectations of the outside world. His practice is based on personal insight, intuition, direct realization, or apperception and is often expressed through an exotic lifestyle that might appear outwardly shocking. Such a guru may live on what he can beg, as did the Kagyu sage Milarepa, who dined on fish innards, slept in cemeteries, and wore nothing but rags, if such could be found. As L. O. Gomez puts it, these siddhas, or mahasiddhas, represented "a radical departure from Buddhist monkish prudery and an attempt to shock the establishment out of self-righteous complacency."[51] Dr. Reginald Ray, professor of Buddhist studies at the Naropa Institute in Boulder, Colorado, gives this description: "These wild figures, who included men and women of all social backgrounds, mocked, from the pinnacle of their realization, conventionalized spirituality of established monasticism. The essence of their message and example is that the highest spiritual truth is independent of any and all relative conditions, and thus can be manifested and realized instantaneously in any circumstance."[52]

Since the Tantric master is, or hopefully is, a fully realized being, she or he can stand behind the source of the relative and manufacture the projections that create the phenomenal world. The Tantric masters of old were supposed to be able to do anything—magically appear or disappear, walk on water, fly through mountains, change iron into gold, raise the dead, or stop the sun, all the natural results of meditation. Since the phenomenal world is only a set of projections anyway, for the Tantric master, absolutely anything was possible in the relative world.

Behind the façade and low-rent magic, however, these siddhas, who in the Vajrayana replaced the Bodhisattva as the Buddhist ideal, took seriously the implications of the doctrine of emptiness and put the teachings of the Sutras into practice, winning the highest of spiritual attainments—usually in a single lifetime. Because these adepts were able to speak with the wisdom gained from the highest meditations, the power of direct and personal realization, they offered a different perspective from those who relied merely on the wisdom gained by study and reflection.[53]

In *Buddha's Lions: The Lives of the Eighty-Four Siddhas*, one finds that "While the most famous of the siddhas were Buddhist monks, the majority were laymen, an unusual circumstance in a religion that, in India at least, centered upon its monastic element. Furthermore, most of the siddhas had lowly origins and worked in rather menial positions. The fact that they elevated themselves to the highest human possibilities clearly reinforces the teaching that one can find and take up the Dharma from any walk of life."[54]

Nonetheless, members of the establishment did play their part. Gaining momentum between the fifth and eighth centuries of the common era, study of the Tantras was systematized and clarified by siddhas who were also outstanding monastic scholars. "But inevitably, as the Tantric tradition established itself, steps were taken to sanitize and organize it. It was then monasticised and reconciled with orthodox Buddhist philosophy and practice. Eventually integrated systems were evolved which placed the Vajrayana at the apogee of a three-tiered hierarchy and the other traditions of Buddhism—the so-called 'Sutra' traditions—below."[55]

By the tenth century, Tantras had been fully integrated into the curriculae of all Buddhist universities. Supported absolutely through the patronage of the imperial Gupta family, the Vajrayana flourished in northern India. This is where and when the Tibetans found their way into the world of Buddhism. It is possible that Nalanda welcomed its first Tibetan student in the seventh century C.E.[56]

Buddhism, from its very beginning, had accepted and developed the practice of yoga, and there had been a continuous exchange of experiences between Buddhism and other religious systems for two millennia. Gautama warned the bhikshu not to put too much emphasis on the magical aspects of the practice. Only liberation was of any consequence.

So, then, what is Tantrism, anyway? There are a thousand ways to address this question, but it will do to say that Tantra is about energy, sound, the human body, and Enlightenment, the thread that brings all living things together.

In Lama Anagarika Govinda's *Foundations of Tibetan Mysticism,* one finds that:

> The word "tantra" is related to the concept of weaving and its derivatives (thread, web, fabric, etc.), hinting at the interwovenness of things and actions, the interdependence of all that exists, the continuity in the interaction of cause and effect, as well as in spiritual and traditional development, which like a thread weaves its way through the fabric of history and of individual lives. The scriptures

which in Buddhism go under the name of *Tantra* (Tib.:rgyud) are invariably of a mystic nature, i.e., trying to establish the inner relationship of things: the parallelism of microcosm and macrocosm, mind and universe, ritual and reality, the world of matter and the world of spirit.[57]

No one knows what *energy* is; nevertheless, with almost every breath, the word is used in Tantric descriptions. Discussions of its nature seem always to be carefully avoided. But since energy is inevitably the center of everything, some attempt must be made to describe the indescribable.

In any high school textbook one can read that energy is the ability to do work, or it is described as movement. "Working energy" is kinetic, and energy "waiting" or "at rest" is potential. It is never created nor destroyed. Energy certainly exists in the relative world, as both particles and as waves. When one reaches the demarcation line between energy and matter, the word *virtual* is often heard, as in virtual particles, which physics holds sometimes exist and at other times do not, receding into their energy form.

Tracing the phenomenon to its source, to the point where energy disappears into itself, we enter the domain of mysticism, and the terminology begins to change. The word *consciousness* becomes apt, and as the refinement continues, the word *awareness* is found. In the very center of centers, energy is referred to as *suchness,* or *emptiness,* or *mind.* Energy in its potential, it seems, is still present, but the stillness can be perfect. The labels vary with the quality of stillness. Eventually there is only potential. This potentiality for energetic activity is framed in the word *luminous.* The quietness or subtlety can be so perfectly profound that emptiness can seem simply to be inanition, but it is in the nature of mind to be active, to be spontaneously creative. When there is spontaneous activity, waves appear, and the potential, which was luminosity, is expressed as suchness, then awareness, then consciousness, and ultimately can be recognized as energy and matter.

The hackneyed word *spirit* seems to be a generic term that refers to anything beyond the range of detectability by the instruments of contemporary technology. It is energy, even in its nascent form as emptiness, clear limitless space, mind, or bliss, that the Tantric masters recognize and use in their work. It is this force, which is no different from the dynamic forces of the phenomenal universe, that mystics recognize as the essence of humanity's relativistic world. Admittedly, what energy really is remains a mystery. Although, from the relative perspective, it is impossible to define the nature of the phenomenon and words are perhaps only detractors, T. S. Eliot's description, in his "Little Giddings" of the *Four Quartets,* will haunt any thinker. As he so beautifully captured it, energy is "The voice . . . half heard, in the stillness between two waves of the sea."

Eliot's ocean imagery matches the vastness of energy revealed by quantum mechanics scientist Richard Feynman. According to Feynman, particles must be viewed as traveling from one location to another along every path, along an infinity of trajectories. That is, all possibilities do exist simultaneously.[58]

No doubt everyone will agree that everything in the many universes is vested with energy. Einstein showed the world this. The Vajrayana, however, deepens our understanding by adding that "The dynamic forces of the universe ... are not different from those of the human soul, and to recognize and transform those forces in one's own mind—not only for one's own good, but for that of all living beings—is the aim of the Buddhist Tantra."[59]

Let's go back to "suchness," that is, when energy is in its perfect state of stillness. It stirs, and awareness arises. Accompanying awareness is a sense of perfect clarity. If there is perfect clarity, then there must be an object that perception is aware of. Thus the fundamental, original split, the first duality, if formed, and it inevitably evolves into the world, with all its beautiful diversity. The primal separation also provides the opening for the initiation of the projection process. The new "relative" subject, ignorant of its origin and equipped with the capacity for projection, develops pride, and then jealously, anger, and fear, when it senses upon what insubstantial ground its house has been built.[60]

The original separation is viewed by some as a fall from grace, as original sin. The Buddhist, instead of encouraging guilt by making the human race responsible for the fall, views the entire system as merely a process, one to be understood and then worked back through. And there is no eternal hell awaiting the Buddhist whose devotion or meditative abilities fall short. There will always be another chance. In Buddhism, original sin does not exist—only ignorance.

And although ending ignorance may sound easy enough,

the practice of Buddhism is profoundly demanding both intellectually and personally. It is real work, because ultimately there is no savior. The individual is solely responsible. And there can be no once-a-week pretense. Remember, it only takes seventeen thought moments to convert pure energy into conditioned thoughts. One must constantly practice, but take it all in stride while reflecting on the notion that the only difference between Buddha and the practitioner is that Gautama meditated more.

The Tantric masters believe that every human being is already enlightened, now, but simply does not realize it. Since the primal energy of awareness is present everywhere and within everyone, the human body, and even the senses so loathed by the Hinayana, is vested with this cosmic energy. The Vajranaya, then, deify the human body and use its inherent energies to accelerate the process toward Enlightenment. The aim of Tantric practice is to transform one's body, speech, and mind into those of a fully enlightened Buddha by special yogic means and to get it all done in a single lifetime.[61]

The vajra was the mystical thunderbolt of the Indian god Indra and symbolized an instrument for a massive discharge of energy. The Vajrayanists chose this as a symbol and title to represent their spiritual path, their method for blasting away ignorance and delusions in order to inaugurate Enlightenment.

The human body for the Hinayana is corruption, a bag of filth, and an obstacle. To the Mahayana, it is simply an inconvenience, since all is "mind only," a maze of projections. For those who practice Vajrayana, however, the body is a manifestation of the divine, and diving deeply into matter can lead to recovery of the principle of consciousness and a sense of beginningless space.[62]

Even to the Vajrayanist, though, the relative world does not exist. It is no more substantial than the reflection of the moon in a lake. There is only suchness, or the clear limitlessness of mind. Even the body, which the Vajrayana deifies, is not real when compared to true reality. It is impermanent, ever changing, and illusionary as a face in a dream. Yet the real can be found within the relative. The microcosm is the macrocosm, the universe on a small scale. The human body is believed to be a replica of the universe on a small scale. According to Vajrayana psychology, the relative body is comprised of five sheaths, each interlaced by the other, all mutually penetrating forms of energy. First there is the physical body, second is the pranic or ethereal body, then the thought body, and then the body of potential consciousness, which extends far beyond active thought. The fifth and finest sheath, which penetrates all previous ones, is of the highest, universal joy. It can only be experienced in a state of enlightenment, or in the highest states of meditation. Sometimes it is referred as the "body of bliss."[63] "The body is, so to say, the stage between heaven and earth, on which the psycho-cosmic drama is enacted. For the knowing one, the initiate, it is the sacred stage of an unfathomably deep mystery play. And it is for this reason that the knowledge, or what is more, the conscious experience of this body is of such paramount importance for the yogin and for everybody who wants to tread the path of meditation."[64]

The thread of Tantra is the interlacing of all that exists, the intertwining of the celestial and its earthly manifestations. The individual human's mind is considered to be a part of the universal mind. Recognizing its place and function in the totality, and understanding the true nature of luminosity is, in fact, realization. This is the lesson taught by the Tantric masters.

There is a transition from matter-body to spiritual body. Vajrayana teachers envision, 72,000 channels (nadi) through which the primal energies, the subtle winds (prana) can flow. Concentrations of this energy are referred to as *tigles*. The winds move the tigles—all of the goods the mind possesses—throughout the body. This system of channels and energies is not a property of the material body, but a property of an ethereal body from which the visible body has emerged. The yogi, working with the subtle body through which this cosmic energy circulates, aids the student in pacifying the mind. A teacher expects the student to transform conflicting emotions, and obscurations into their positive counterparts. The phenomenal mind, the existential or karmic mind whose organizational center is the ego complex, can then more easily be penetrated by the light of the transcendental, the prajna (wisdom) energies, allowing absorption by reality. The Karma Kagyu lineage works with energy as it flows through the central axis of the body, as opposed to the spinal cord and its nervous system.[65]

In most people, the nadi are all knotted up due to stress, so that movement of the wind energy is impeded. The Tantric master seeks to clear the channels, as well as to direct and dis-

Siddhartha to Vajrayana: The Substance 31

solve the wind energy into tiny "droplets." One such droplet was received from the father, is white, and is located at the crown of the head. The feminine droplet, which is red, is found just below the navel. The yoga seeks to move the two toward each other until there is a union. If this is achieved, conceptual thought automatically and instantaneously ceases, and what remains is nothing less than the primordial state, luminosity itself. When this occurs, one has "turned around."[66]

Are such channels really physically present in the human being? According to Lama Govinda,

> The Tibetan teacher of meditation ... does not make any assertions, which the pupil has to accept as objective facts; he does not say "the nadis are there," but: "create within yourself a vivid mental image, that a current of vital force flows from here to there." In this way he directs the consciousness and the creative imagination of the meditator upon certain functions (for instance, the respiration) and those organs which can be influenced by them either directly or indirectly. Thus he [the teacher] creates the psychic and physical relations and preconditions for the flow of conscious forces. In other words he [the teacher] creates those channels which form the sensitive nerve-system of the spiritualized or "fine-material" body.[67]

Inherent in the Vajrayana system of meditation, as seen before, is the process of visualization, a method of transformative imagination often called deity yoga. The Tantras themselves are meditations, long-tested ritual meditation scripts sometimes referred to as scriptures. In every meditation, a deity is described and the meditator summons mental images of every aspect of the deity, its every gesture, every scrap of action described in the Tantra. The meditator is expected to mentally transform into this deity and the meditation, if not in the first ten thousand attempts, then in the next. This means behaving like Buddha until one becomes a Buddha. It means building up Buddha forms that are meditated upon. These forms mirror the qualities inherent in the individual human being. When these qualities are accentuated, they become a bridge between the practitioner and Buddha. Once these essences are touched, they will stay, and the real qualities can be retained, enabling the meditator to sustain longer periods in a state of bliss.

According to Lama Ole Nydahl, Buddha qualities really become those of the practitioner.[68] Lama Anagarika Govinda further explains how these qualities are assimilated:

> "Thinking is making": this is the fundamental principle of all magic, especially of all mantic science. By the rhythmic repetition of a creative thought or idea, of a concept, a perception or a mental image, its effect is augmented and fixed (like the action of a steadily falling drop) until it seizes upon all organs of activity and becomes a mental and material reality: a deed in the fullest sense of the word.[69]

In these meditations, there can be assistance from the lama as well as celestial Buddhas, Bodhisattvas, and other deities. Dakinis, or skywalkers, for example, are female deities whose function is to integrate the powers liberated by a practitioner in the process of visualization. A dakini is a feminine embodiment of wisdom who appears when she is needed to provoke insight. She is analogous to the anima in Jungian psychology, a guide or transitional element between the individual and spiritual. A yidam is a personal deity, an archetypal image of primordial energy that aids the student in acknowledging the truth as it relates to his or her own personality structure and connects the practitioner to the acknowledged lineage. Yidams are transformed and personified forms of human passions, as well as emanations of a supreme Buddha. There are also many protectors that assist practitioners in difficult times. Like fairies and all other mythological spirits, such entities are concentrated forms of energy that can interact with a person, thus producing effects. The label for the energy packet creates a metaphor—that is, a deity by name. For example, the dakini is an energy packet that manifests inspiration when one unconsciously becomes a seeker. After all, even the human being is only a bundle of energy and matter, and both of these qualities are interchangeable.[70] Since the relative world is a child of projection and to imagine is to project, the existence of anything is possible.

To deal immediately with the threat of identification and attachment to the deities, Tantric visualizations all have a similar closure. The patron deity will inevitably dissolve into the meditator, who then dissolves into the clear, limitless space of

Siddhartha to Vajrayana: The Substance 33

Nirvana. Only suchness, the luminous space of mind, remains. This is of the greatest significance. Without this vanishing, this letting go, the deities would simply be another attachment in the relative world, another object through which to find justification for human actions and keep the wheel of Samsara rolling. With this dissolution into nothingness, however, even the gods are revealed as mere projections. This finality harmonizes the Theravada, Mahayana, and Vajrayana despite the three schools' fantastic array of methods and imagery. Sakyamuni himself described Buddhism as a raft to ferry one across the river. Once across the river, it would be silly to keep carrying the raft on your back. One is required to let go of everything. Even Buddha, then, in the end, could not possibly have been a Buddhist, for as Eliot explains it, Enlightenment is "A condition of complete simplicity Costing no less than everything."[71]

It is worth warning again that, in the Vajrayana, a practical danger always exists. Considering human frailties, foibles, and normal fears, especially of illness, death, and poverty, there is a natural tendency for the practitioner to cling to a god for life. Yet the creation of an object through attachment accomplishes the exact opposite of the meditation's purpose. One must always be vigilant.

Needless to say, the teacher has the pivotal role to play in Buddhism, particularly in the Vajrayana. The knowledge and skill required to work with the subtle force of primal consciousness are rare. They are, in fact, so precious that a cover of secrecy seems to pervade the world of Tantra. Sakyamuni instructed his arhats to teach with an open hand and withhold nothing; secrecy in Tantra comes from the fact that the wisdom is so arcane. As with a difficult subject such as quantum mechanics, no one is trying to keep any secrets, but the challenge of understanding it leaves most people in the dark. Also, the Tantric path has its perils. Working with such energy forms is considered by many to be dangerous physically and psychically, and close scrutiny of the student by a master is advised. Thus the practice is referred to as "guru yoga." Tantric texts are written in an enigmatic language so that the uninitiated will not be endangered.[72]

Secrecy has its own dangers, of course, including the possibility that potentates will consolidate power for selfish purposes. Sexual harassment has occurred in the West, although abuse has no place within the framework of Buddhism.

Despite potential problems, in the Vajrayana, the lama is seen as the embodiment of the Buddha. The student is expected to surrender completely to the teacher and follow instructions unhesitatingly. The student must regard the actions of a lama, however strange, as the enlightened activity of a Buddha, with great faith and perfect devotion. This is difficult for Westerners, who usually have grown up in religious systems that formally discarded an authoritarian Pope and priests, who mediated between the individual and the deity. The Tantric lama assumes a similar prestigious, lofty, and dangerous position for both student and teacher. Still, especially in the Vajrayana, total faith in the guru is absolutely mandatory, not only in the immediate guru, but also in that lama's teacher, and so on through an entire line of siddhas. This line of devotion ends only with a supreme Buddha who taught the first human in the lineage.

The Vajrayana makes use of the mandala, a symbolic model of the cosmos, mudras, sacred hand movements and positions, the vajra (*dorje* in Tibetan), or ritual dagger, used to separate individuals from their attachments, and a bell, or ghanta. The bell symbolizes the female, thus wisdom, and the vajra, the male aspect or skill in means. And then there is the use of sound.[73]

In seeking contact with the gods, or to move energy, sound is of the utmost importance. Mantras are primal sounds that attract such energies. In the Vajrayana, words have power. They are "seed syllables." They possess the power to conjure immediate reality in the form of gods or simply the play of forces. Each word in a mantra is a focus of energies, in which the vibrations of the human voice, the vital expression of the human soul, are transformed into reality. As expressed by Lama Govinda, when language was born, so was humanity. And in the beginning, "Each word was the sound equivalent of an experience, connected with an internal or external stimulus. A tremendous creative effort was involved in this process, which must have extended over a vast period of time; and it is due to this effort that man was able to rise above the animal."[74]

The internal experience was the luminosity of clear, limitless space expressing itself. The sounds or vibrations were expressions of pure reality and became the basis for language.

From time immemorial, in their trance meditations, yogis have had the ability to dissolve into suchness, behind the original revelation of potential, inert energy. Evident to these practitioners are the "seed sounds." These sounds are intimately related to the original vibrations experienced by mankind. The sounds, almost exclusively captured in Sanskrit, are the mantras, which act as attractors of that original energy. These sounds, it is believed, can bring forth the dikinis, the yidams, and the protectors. They open the stillness to the mediator. A word, any word, "in the hour of its birth was a center of force and reality, and only habit has stereotyped it into a mere conventional medium of expression. The mantra escaped this fate to a certain extent, because it had no concrete meaning and could therefore not be made to subserve utilitarian ends."[75]

Mantras, then, express the source of language itself and are symbols of the forces of reality. They are "the audible that clings to the inaudible, the forms and potentialities of thought, which grow from that which is beyond thought":

> The seer, the poet and singer, the spiritually creative, the psychically receptive and sensitive, the saint: they all know about the essentiality of form in word and sound, in the visible and the tangible. They do not despise what appears small or insignificant, because they can see the great in the small. Through them the word becomes mantra, and the sounds and signs of which it is formed become the vehicles of mysterious forces. Through them the visible takes on the nature of symbols, the tangible becomes a creative tool of the spirit, and life becomes a deep stream, flowing from eternity to eternity.[76]

John Snelling says that a mantra works because of its inherent quantum charge. It certainly can be noted that superstring theory, which unites general relativity and quantum mechanics, houses with ease the notion of mantras. In this system, tiny sub-Planck-size vibrating strings are the source of subatomic particles, a phase through which energy passes on its way to becoming matter. Superstrings within oddly shaped containers named Calabi-Yau spaces produce resonant patterns of vibration, sound, or music. Theoretically, mantras would be on the inner side of this physical function. The lama coaxes the resonances through the matrix of strings and the gods tag along to perform the specific function for which their energy was intended. For example, when illness is an issue, one recites the mantra "Teyata Om Bekanze Bekanze, Maha Bekanze, Randza Samudgate Soha" and the Medicine Buddha will emerge from the god realm and offer assistance and perhaps even a cure.[77]

The Tantric teachers want their students to recognize and transform these forces in their own mind, not only for one's own good, but for that of all living beings. This is the aim of the Buddhist Tantras and of those who have chosen the Karma Kagyu path in Texas. They will not cease to exist in the relative world, but the essence of bliss, totality, and wisdom will reside in them. The ego complex will have no avenue for deifying itself, for the origin of perception will no longer be from a source that itself is a mere projection. And thoughts that enter the mind will be like thieves coming to an empty house. There will be nothing to steal.

Teachers of the Vajrayana path do not avoid the worldly. Instead, they embrace it. As in homeopathic medicine, where like cures like, the Vajrayana use the energy inherent in everyday life.

There is the old story of the Hinayana monk who encountered a bush known to be dangerously poisonous; the monk carefully avoided the plant. On the other hand, the Mahayana monk simply ignored it, realizing that all is merely projection. The Vajrayana practitioner, however, tore into the bush and ate every leaf. Everything in the relative world, all of the energy that is present in any form, is bound to be of some use.[78]

The Vajrayana look at the emotion of desire in the same way. It is merely something to accelerate the way to enlightenment, and transformation is the key. Tantra seeks to transform every experience, no matter how irreligious it may appear, into the path for fulfillment.

The sexual instinct and its worldly form of desire is a most powerful emotion and a paramount source of energy. This energy, captured and rechanneled through meditation, can result in infinitely powerful and penetrative awareness and an enhanced ability to concentrate. In the use of desire, one is in essence unifying one's own male and female energies. By manipulating the energies within the body, a practitioner is empowered to expand the range of consciousness and experience advanced levels of blissful wisdom.

Whenever any one of our sense organs contacts a pleasure-giving object, instead of descending into our habitual pattern of grasping, attachment, dullness and disappointment, we will be able to channel the desirous energy that is aroused so that it embraces our entire nervous system. And at the time we will be able to allow this emerging, blissful consciousness to become absorbed indistinguishably into the clear space of non-duality. All the old problems associated with desire will have been solved; instead of being the cause of dissatisfaction, desire is now fuelling the experience of totality.[79]

Within the Tantric system, there is present a form of Buddhist practice that is outside of the world of celibacy. Maranda Shaw, author of *Passionate Enlightenment,* made the following comments in the magazine *What Is Enlightenment?*

Tantrics would already have familiarized themselves with the philosophy of emptiness, the understanding that all phenomena are devoid of intrinsic identity, of permanent, independent selfhood. So in that sense, there's an understanding that the world is illusory and thus is not capable of providing satisfaction or ultimate bliss. What tantric partners do in the midst of the experience of bliss is to take this specific insight and apply it to the experience of bliss itself and to deconstruct it, to see that there is no self that is experiencing the bliss. The bliss has arisen in a kind empty space. There's no owner of the bliss. There's no source of the bliss. The combination of bliss with this insight into its emptiness should then lead each partner into vast, sky-like awareness, a decentered awareness—in essence, an experience of universal Awareness.[80]

Desire is not the only emotion utilized by the Tantric masters. The energy of possessiveness will be transformed into generosity; anger becomes clarity, pride gives way to the perception of the absence of "me," jealousy is transformed into peace, desire-attachment into empty felicity, hatred-aversion into empty clarity, and blindness into knowledge. All of this is accomplished through meditation, using the energy found in the emotions. The process is something like the Stanislavsky school's method acting. One remembers the emotion from the experience in the relative world, projects the feelings, and captures its energy in images visualized during meditations.

While Mahayana insists on the emptiness of all phenomena, Vajrayana insists on the union of manifestation (the relative) and emptiness, emphasizing clarity. With the metamorphosis of the coarser negative human emotions into their positive form, the resulting tranquil outcome aids in quieting the mind, making further transformations possible. In fact, the more primitive the emotions, the more intense the energy, and thus the quicker the solutions.[81]

The power needed to infuse the meditation process with energy enough for reaching Enlightenment in a single lifetime is to be found in the relative world. After all, if one sees the human body as well as the mind at all its levels as forms of energy, then confluence with energy of a more refined, peaceful nature is not inconceivable at all. Nirvana *is* Samsara, remember? The Tantric teachers take full advantage of this fact.

There are those who insist that Buddhist Tantrism was only an outgrowth of its Hindu counterpart, and, because of its sensual content, a defilement of the original teachings of Sakyamuni. Lama Thubten Yeshe writes that, without any doubt, the Buddhist Tantra predates the Hindu and, if anything, the Hindus drew from the Buddhists. Each new turning of the wheel was merely an outgrowth of its predecessor—and should a beautiful, ancient oak denigrate the acorn that brought it into the world?

The Mahayana, certainly a minority in its beginnings, chose the disparaging term *Hinayana,* small vehicle, for the elders, the old conservatives, to emphasize their own broadness through inclusion of the lay community, their compassionate stance as possible Bodhisattvas, and the ultimate goal of Buddhahood rather than liberation alone. Theravada is nonetheless still the foundation of all Buddhist philosophy. Its Abhidharma is still considered one of the greatest creations by the human mind in the history of literature. The Theravada exists today as a thriving community in Southeast Asia, as well as in the United States. As a result of contact with the American way of life, the Hinayana is making a place for the lay community in their system. Vispassana, or insight meditation, was originally a Theravada practice. It was transformed into and became the traditional Tibetan meditation technique of Shamatha and is now a part of the Vajrayana Karma Kagyu practice. This same meditation system is the foundation for the Theravada lama S. N. Goenka, who has many practice centers in Texas. The Buddha taught that there must be many paths to enlightenment, for there are so many different kinds of people. Each turning of the wheel of Dharma has its place. What's right for one may not be appropriate for another. There is a Buddhism for everyone.

The Karma Kagyu student believes in, practices, and absorbs every tenet of what has been explained in the preceding pages. These practitioners have worked their way from the foundation of Buddhism, the Hinayana, through the "Middle Way" of the Mahayana, and the "mind only" approach of the Yogacara, to reach their home base of Vajrayana. Seeing and understanding what the Texas people are attempting to comprehend philosophically and accomplish spiritually is the only way of knowing who they are as human beings. They have fallen in love with the clear light of mind and are attempting a total inner transformation. This metamorphosis involves shifting perception from the ego-based relative to that of boundless luminescence and, ultimately, to no point at all. With this new point of perception, the person finds that he or she is and was always energy at perfect rest. With this recognition, the individual becomes all possibilities, with all illusions destroyed. The person is absorbed by and becomes luminosity. Enlightenment has happened, and a new Buddha has been born. These Texas men and women have chosen a path of unbelievable philosophical complexity and challenge.

*   *   *

It was prophesied by the Indian Tantric master Padmasambhava in the eighth century C.E. that "When the iron bird flies, and horses run on wheels, / The Tibetan people will be scattered like ants across the World, / And the Dharma will come to the land of the Red Man."[82]

Perhaps Buddhism was predestined to reach America. But first, it had to travel from India to the Land of Snows, Tibet. Rick Fields, in his book *How the Swans Came to the Lake*, describes the movement this way:

> From its home in Magadha, Buddhism traveled northwest to the Iranian border, Pakistan, and Central Asia, and

then to China along the Silk Route, carried not only by bhikshus (monks) but by merchants, caravaners, and foreigners—worldly, cosmopolitan men attracted to Buddhism by its practicality (traders could understand the ethical accountability of karma) and its transcendence of caste, race, and nation.

In the third century C.E. the Mauryan Emperor Asoka sent Buddhist missionaries as far west as Greece (where they had little, if any success), and south across the Indian ocean to Sri Lanka. Sri Lanka, followed by Burma, Siam, and Cambodia became the home of the Theravadins, the one surviving school of the elders of the Second Council.

Buddhism entered China during the first century C.E. Both Mahayana and Hinayana scriptures were translated into Chinese, and the monastic sangha established.

From China, Buddhism traveled to Korea and Vietnam. Buddhism first reached Japan in 550 C.E. when a Korean king sent Buddhist images and sutras as gifts to the Japanese imperial court.[83]

Tibet would become the last of the great Asian nations to receive the Dharma.

Chapter 2

India to Tibet: The Founding of the Karma Kagyu Lineage

The year 333 c.e. marks the dawning of the Sacred Doctrine and the beginning of Dharma history in Tibet. In this year something extraordinary came into the view of King La-tho-tho-ri, who, in his seventy-ninth year, was residing at the summit of the Palace Yam-Bu-la-gang – a chest, appearing to descend in a ray of light, fell from the sky. When the King raised the lid, he found two Sutra books, the Six-syllable Mantra, Om Mani Padme Hum, a golden Stupa, and a Wish-fulfilling Gem with its base cast for impressing. The texts, however, were written in a language that neither the King nor his ministers could read, and, since they had fallen from the sky, it was first thought that the chest and its mysterious contents were the gifts of a Bon sky god. In a dream, the King received a prophecy which revealed that the significance and meaning of this magnificent gift would not be known for five generations. Nevertheless, these objects were honored as something portentous and very precious. Through their powerful influence, the King was rejuvenated into a youth of sixteen, lived to be 120, and his whole kingdom flourished. To this day, King La-tho-tho-ri is revered as an emanation of the Bodhisattva Samantabhadra.[1]

Buddhism pervades Tibetan culture so completely that the country's historical events are overlayed with Buddhist significance and Buddhist deities have been written into all important occasions, regardless of the original facts. This practice is so pervasive in historical works that even the pre-Buddhist history of Tibet has been cast as a story of the preparation of the country for dissemination of the Dharma. So again and again, one is forced to differentiate between or integrate the supernatural and the mundane, to balance romantic and prosaic possibilities in some rational way.[2]

For example, the story of the Dharma's arrival in Tibet has a less fantastic counterpart. In the Blue Annals, the gifts from the sky were actually brought to Tibet by an Indian pandita (pundit) and his translator. When it was discovered that the king could not read Sanskrit and would never understand the meaning of the books, the scholar returned to India.[3]

Nevertheless, as predicted, the fifth successor to the throne following King Lhatotori, Songtsen Gampo, assumed the throne in 582 C.E.. In Crystal Mirror IV, it is stated that out of respect for the Buddhadharma, this Tibetan king sent an emissary to India to obtain a very valuable statue of Avalokitesvara and two priceless representations of Sakyamuni Buddha. However, the latter two statues had already been given as gifts to potentates in Nepal and China. Demonstrating his boldness and tenacity, King Songtsen Gampo proposed marriages with princesses in both neighboring countries in order to secure the sacred objects. The king of Nepal readily agreed, as did the Chinese emperor, but only after 200,000 Tibetan troops arrived in the Chinese province to force the issue.

This event reveals that religious zeal was not solely responsible for Tibet's contact with the Buddhist world. This was a period of massive political expansion by the Tibetan ruling elite. The Yarlung dynasty brought most of the warring tribes under its control and built a formidable military power. The empire began to expand. The kingdom of Shangshung, which is today western Tibet, was quickly annexed. By the sixth century, the Tibetan army had also annexed large areas of Central Asia and in 635 C.E. attacked China itself. The Chinese emperor was required to pay yearly tribute to the Yarlung kings. In 763 C.E., the Tang emperor was forced to flee his kingdom, and the Tibetans set up a puppet ruler in the Chinese capital of Chang-an. During this era, Tibetans dominated Nepal, sent military expeditions as far east as Burma and southward into India, and penetrated west as far as Afghanistan, Tajikistan, Turkmenistan, and Uzbekistan along the route of the Amu Darya River (Oxus River) nearly reaching the Caspian Sea. The success of this military expansion from the seventh to the ninth centuries C.E. is emphasized by the fact that the caliph of Baghdad felt threatened enough to forge an alliance with the Chinese emperor in the face of the Tibetan advance. In light of Tibet's present total immersion in the Dharma ideal, it is a great irony that Tibetan invasion forces attacked many Buddhist institutions in neighboring countries of Central Asia, killing, pillaging, and thus fulfilling karma for many a dedicated monk.[4]

Considering Tibet's military exploits and that Buddhist missionaries had long established themselves in the Katmandu Valley of Nepal, in Kashmir, along the Silk Route to China, throughout Central Asia, and beyond, the Dharma clearly had no trouble finding its way to the Land of Snows without the intercession of the gods.[5]

Tibetans had no written language or common grammar as late as the mid-seventh century. Dharma texts were still finding their way to Tibet, and still no one could read or interpret them. During the reign of King Songtsen Gampo, translators were invited to Lhasa from India, Nepal, China, and Kashmir, and the king ordered a Tibetan scholar, Tonmi Sambhota, to create an alphabet and grammar based on the Indian system. This choice to use the Indian model was critically important. It aligned the Tibetan culture with its southern neighbor rather than its northerly neighbor, China. Eventually, this would orient Tibet toward the West instead of the East. Sambhota's linguistic contribution to Tibetan culture resulted in his annunciation as an incarnation of Manjusri, a Bodhisattva, the manifestation of wisdom.[6]

Just before his death, Songtsen Gampo, "Protector of the Doctrine," wrote an inscription on a copper plaque prophesying that in five more generations, a great-grandson of his would usher in the golden age of the Dharma. This king ruled for sixty-nine years, instructed his people in the arts of meditation and healing, spent years in perpetual samadhi, or deep trance, and initiated the construction of 108 temples throughout the country. At eighty-two, with his two queens, while together embracing a statue of Chenrezig, the three dissolved into the Abode of Joy.[7]

The reign of Songtsen Gampo marks what is known as the First Transmission of the Dharma in Tibet, which John Snelling dates circa 640 to 838 C.E. This period in Tibetan history is referred to as the era of the Three Great Religious Kings. Trisong Detsen (704–97 C.E.) is the second of the three kings, followed by Ralpachen, who lived from 805 to 838 C.E.[8]

Viewing history from a down-to-earth perspective, Per Kvaerne writes of Songtsen Gampo's national policy in *The World of Buddhism*:

> There are no signs of the king himself having adopted Buddhism, nor in fact any mention at all of Buddhism in contemporary literary sources. On the contrary, the king seems to have been loyal to his ancestral religion, a religion in which the cult of the king, regarded as a divine being, played a crucial part. In particular, complicated rituals on a vast scale, involving animal as well as human sacrifice, took place in connection with the burial of the kings, and Srong-btsan was buried in the traditional way in the Yarlung valley. In fact, recent research indicates that the cult of royal divinity was considerably developed during the reign of Srong-btsan.
>
> In introducing Buddhism, the true motives of the Tibetan king were certainly not religious. It is far more likely that he wished to acquire for his government certain elements of culture, so prominent in neighboring civilizations, without opening the country to foreign influence. For this purpose Buddhism, with its universalistic perspective, must have seemed the ideal instrument.[9]

The popular folk religion in Tibet prior to the arrival of Buddhism was Bon (pronounced "Bern"). This religious and cultural system was a vaguely defined collection of shamanistic and animistic practices that professed the belief that living souls and spirits inhabited every aspect of nature's creation. These life forms, it was believed, dwelt in trees, in the stars, and even in the stones of the earth. Demons and other aboriginal powers that lived in the obscure recesses of the country possessed the relentless capacity to unleash earthquakes, floods, and other natural catastrophes. The pre-Buddhist Tibetans believed their kings to be divinely empowered and, like the Buddhists, traced their ancestry to the heavenly realms. As long as a king served as intermediary between the world of man and the world of the gods, man and the mysterious powers of a seemingly impersonal nature might live together in some degree of harmony. Bon also denotes a particular type of priest (bonpo) who performed rituals to propitiate local spirits and ensure the well-being of the dead in the afterlife: "The folk religion is a rich and varied system, with a large pantheon, elaborate rituals and ceremonies, local shamans with special powers who can propitiate and exorcise, and divinatory practices that allow humans to predict the influences of the spirit world and take appropriate measures."[10]

This old religion of Tibet continued to develop into a coherent whole after the arrival of Buddhism and, though a distinct system, it absorbed much of the Buddhist liturgy. From the Bon prospective, Buddhism tends to focus on final liberation, and the bonpo concern themselves with the pragmatic world. Bon is alive and well today and seems to have an especially intimate relationship with the Buddhist Nyingma tradition.[11]

And as with any product of civilization, there was a fusion of pre-Buddhist society and religion into a cultural fabric that intertwined the bonpo, the financial elite, and royalty, with actual importance, status, power, and the avenue of ascendancy. Any disturbance was bound to cause an ocean of waves. Trisong Detsen, the second great religious king, created a tidal wave of turbulence and change.

Creators of the Nyingma Crystal Mirror series conclude that the bonpos were not the principal opponents of the introduction of Buddhism into Tibet. The Nyingmas believe, rather, that the unsympathetic families of the old Tibetan aristocracy, those who saw the Dharma as a threat to their power and political positions, were the real foes of Buddhism.[12]

When Trisong Detsen ascended the throne, his first order of business was military in nature. With a well-disciplined army, the young king soon controlled more than one-third of the then-known world, and trade spread, creating great prosperity throughout the land. Now it was time to advance the Dharma, but how? Two envoys, Sangsi and Salnang, were sent to the Chinese imperial court to ask for advice. The ministers returned with a thousand Buddhist compositions and the advice that they should find a certain Indian upadhyaya (professor of spiritual philosophy), Santaraksita, and with his gift, the Doctrine would blossom in Tibet.

Salnang was immediately dispatched to India to find Santaraksita, who was known to be in his eighties and, according to John Powers, was abbot of one of the greatest seats of learning in the country, Vikramasila. But there was a problem back in Lhasa.[13]

A non-Buddhist minister, Mazhang, was busy planting seeds of conspiracy against the Buddhist royalty. He was powerful enough to order the deportation of all Buddhist monks and the banishment of the sacred image of Buddha of Lhasa to Nepal. The viharas (monastic centers) were transformed into butcher shops, and the king was powerless to intercede. The minister Mazhang was poised to seize the throne and, with the aid of a portion of the nobility, destroy the Holy Doctrine.[14]

During this confusion, Salnang returned with the news that Santaraksita was willing to make the journey to the Land of Snows. Fearing for both his envoy and the Dharma, the young king acted swiftly and decisively. He called upon his military for assistance. To Mazhang's dismay, the army supported its legitimate king, and the minister ended up confined for life in a tomb for the dead.[15]

Even though there was still opposition, the king and the Buddhist party now had the upper hand, and the task of providing the people of Tibet with the Dharma could begin. Santaraksita selected Samye, a few miles southeast of Lhasa, as the site for Tibet's first Buddhist monastery.

Strangely, a series of natural disasters occurred at this time, including lightning strikes of the royal palace, and terrible earthquakes. Bon-inclined ministers contended that the Indian scholar was responsible, for he and his alien doctrine had offended the native deities. Santaraksita was forced to leave the country, but before his departure he advised Trisong Detsen:

> Do not be dismayed, I shall go to Nepal! The Bon spirits are surely displeased at my presence and my powers are not sufficient to subdue them. Some spiritual force of superior capabilities is needed to subjugate the many nonvisible and mountain spirits who defy the Lamp of the Doctrine and who play upon the wrathful nature of men's minds. However, Oh Great King, in the country of

India to Tibet: The Founding of the Karma Kagyu Lineage   47

Uddiyana there resides a great and learned Bodhisattva who is more than human. his name is Padmasambhava, the Lotus-born. Only through the gift of his exemplary compassion and power of mantra will these demons, manifestations of man's collective mind-projections, be completely transmuted. Invite this Master to Tibet, and the Dharma will most certainly succeed."[16]

The Buddha said in the *Sutra of Predictions in Magadha:* "I will pass away to eradicate the view of permanence. But in twelve years from now, to clear the away the view of nihilism, I shall appear from a lotus in the immaculate Lake Kosha as a noble son to delight the king and turn the Dharma wheel of the unexcelled essential meaning."[17]

There is nothing about Guru Rinpoche, as Padmasambhava is often called, that is not fantastic and wondrously miraculous. For example, Stephen Batchelor gives this account of his birth in his *Awakening of the West*:

Bodhisattva Avalokiteshvara, upon seeing that Uddiyana was suffering severe famine and drought, appealed to the Buddha Amitabha for help. Amitabha spontaneously projected a beam of red light from his tongue, which struck a lake from whence a lotus blossomed unfurled. He then projected the mystic syllable HRI from his heart which appeared as a golden *vajra* or scepter in the center of the lotus, which then transformed into an eight-year-old boy enveloped in a haze of rainbow light. Thus Padmasambhava, the "Lotus Arisen One," came into the world.[18]

In 770 C.E., Padmasambhava, omnisciently aware that the king of Tibet was to invite him to the Land of Snows, flew on the winds to the Afghan-Tibetan border, defeated the opposing demonic forces and turned them into protectors of the Buddhadharma, and subdued most human opposition to the Doctrine. Santaraksita was asked to return. In 779 C.E., Tibetans celebrated the founding of Samye, as well as the investiture of its first indigenous bhikshus (monks), called the "Seven Elected Ones," establishing Tibet's first monastic sangha.[19]

No story of Guru Rinpoche would be complete without the

description of his departure from Tibet: "When the time came for Padmasambhava to leave the country, he was escorted to the border by a great throng of disciples. Having exhorted them to devote themselves to the Dharma, he 'mounted a winged horse which appeared from out of the sky, and, rising upwards in a mist of rainbow radiance, he vanished on the rays of the sun.' "[20]

While Santaraksita was a representative of the traditional Theravada-based monasticism and the Sutra-inspired philosophical tradition in Mahayana, Guru Rinpoche was a Tantric siddha of the Vajrayana. These two masters represented two different forms of Buddhist practice, one of a scholastic, philosophical nature, and the other unconventional and of a mystical cast. These two very different techniques have, over the decades, been practiced side by side and even interlaced, a custom that remains a fundamental characteristic of Tibetan Buddhism. The Tibetan Buddhists who chose the monastic life for the most part followed the same disciplinary code as the Hinayana schools, while their philosophy was unquestionably that of the Mahayana. Yet their meditative ritual practices were mainly those of the Tantric Vajrayana school. The term *lamaism* is often applied to describe the entire melange, and the lama certainly is unique in Tibetan society:

> The lama in Tibet is not necessarily a fully ordained monk and consequently the monk does not monopolize the Dharma as he does in other Buddhist countries. A host of quasi-or semi-monastic priestly types is found with overlapping aims and conventions. Whether living in settled communities or not, these yogins, spell-binders and meditators are broadly considered to belong to the Sangha and are treated as such even if married. . . . The diversity of professional types found in Tibet, each sanctioned either by scriptural authority or by historical precedent, is in turn a reflection of the belief that all human activity can be directed to achieving Enlightenment on the interim level where "relative" and "ultimate" truths are seen as dualities.[21]

There is a dramatic gulf between the two "ways" of Buddhism as represented by the different styles and approaches of Santaraksita and Padmasambhava. One epitomizes monasticism, with its emphasis on intellectualism and scholasticism, and the other a Tantric path with its solitary and intuitively mystical yogic practices. The clash between these two very different systems is a constant and recurring theme in Tibetan religious history. The eventual resolution of the two into a single system through the sufferings of Gampopa, a Kagyu lineage holder, was a long time coming and reflects the influence of the Vajrayana school in the history of Tibetan Buddhism. The practical and philosophical settlement was emphatically fundamental in the development of the Karma Kagyu order. The story of this collision of practices is one of individual human beings, decisions they made about their own lives, and the best way to reach the goal of Enlightenment. It is an issue that will repeatedly emerge throughout the early history of the Karma Kagyu sect. But there were other basic philosophical problems that required an immediate and lasting solution.

    The arrival of one Hoshang Mohoyen to Trisong Detsen's court, and his subsequent declaration that his Chinese Chan school of Buddhism, with its concept of sudden Enlightenment, was superior to that of the traditional Mahayana school of gradual Realization, is of significance. Both sides had popular support. As one story goes (and there are many versions), beginning in 792 C.E., Kamalasila, a student of Santaraksita, representing the gradualist, met Hoshang in debate for two years in the presence of the king and the court, probably in Samye. The gradualist faction eventually emerged victorious, but Chinese assassins murdered Kamalasila, and Hoshang committed suicide because he was so upset by the degeneration of the Dharma in Tibet. Regardless of the historical loose ends, it is important to our story that there was a decline in the popularity of the Chinese system, assuring the continual growth of the Indian version of Mahayana and Vajrayana systems of thought.[22] And as John Powers states, "Tibetan relations with India were generally amicable, but Tibet and China had a long and bitter history of conflict. Both were major powers in Central Asia, and both were involved in armed competition for supremacy in the region. Given their history, it was unlikely that the king would have ruled in favor of the Chinese faction."[23]

    Since Padmasambhava was the incarnation of Sakyamuni Buddha, an emanation of Maitreya, the future Buddha, his wisdom was beyond the comprehension of most mortals, and his teachings were incomprehensible for even a generation. To deal with this difficulty, many of his writings were sealed and hidden away for decades, waiting for those who were emotionally and cognitively mature enough to appreciate, comprehend, and teach the texts.[24]

Trisong Detsen's son, Mune Tsenpo, was poisoned by his mother at seventeen, and a second son was banished from the country because he killed the chief minister's son in an argument. A regent ruled until the "Long-haired One," Ralpachen, who lived from 815 to 841 C.E., assumed the Tibetan throne. During his reign, as well as during the short rule by his two immediate predecessors, so much progress was made in developing the Dharma, especially in translating Indian texts, that Ralpachen is remembered as one of the three most important Dharma kings in the history of Tibet. Every technical Buddhist term was indexed with perfect grammar and syntax, and the intended meaning of the original text was preserved so that any intelligent person could understand the meaning clearly. Earlier texts were revised and edited. Ralpachen decreed that each monk and lama would be supported by seven households. His translator, Vairocana, one of Padmasambhava's twenty-five disciples, mastered over three hundred dialects and attained many psychic powers, though he used them sparingly and in private. Vairocana saw the practicality of the Vajrayana tradition and recognized that this deeply inspired tradition would link the future of Buddhism to the rest of the world.

The work undertaken by the translators was of great importance. Translations were made of Chinese as well as Indian texts, but ultimately, it was decided to copy only the Sanskrit versions exclusively. There were revisions, and revisions of revisions, by both Indian and Tibetan scholars. In the end, a Tibetan literary language was created, and it has remained more or less unchanged to this day, making Tibetan Buddhism heir to the immense Buddhist literature of India.[25]

With all of the Dharma accomplishments, Ralpachen appears to have been content to leave affairs of state in the hands of chosen monks. Court intrigue eventually resulted in his murder, along with that of this chief minister, allowing his brother Langdarma, an enemy of the Dharma, to ascend the throne. Thus ended the era of the First Transmission, and a spiritual dark age ensued, lasting until 1000 C.E.

Langdarma's brief but devastating persecution virtually obliterated Buddhism from central Tibet. Monasteries in Lhasa were boarded up and sealed with plaster. Monks and nuns were forced to return to lay life, and those who refused were executed. Contact was halted with India, and texts were ordered destroyed.[26]

The Dharma, however, had become so widespread and revered by the Tibetan population that it managed to survive the onslaught. It simply went underground. Many moved west, out of the sphere of Lhasa's influence, among isolated hermits and communities. Lay Tantrics, it is recorded, managed to hide most of the translations made up to the time of King Ralpachen, thus preserving the majority of the ancient heritage, including the esoteric teachings transmitted orally and through hand and body gestures known as mudra by Padmasambhava, Vairocana, and Santaraksita. It is written in the Crystal Mirror that because Langdarma feared the guardian goddesses who were watching over the sacred texts at Samye Monastery, the teachings of the Vinaya, Sutra, Abhidharma, and Tantras were preserved.[27]

All of the original teachings and practices continued in some form. The practice remained unbroken and still remains unbroken from the time of Guru Rinpoche to the present. This line of Tibetan Buddhism is referred to as "The Ancient Ones," or the Nyingma school. But other systems would eventually find their way into Tibet and into the religious fabric of Tibetan life. One of the new lines would develop into the Karma Kagyu and eventually find its way to the West and thence to Texas, but it will take us a while to get there.

Langdarma was eventually assassinated by an avenging monk. This led to a collapse of the Yarlung dynasty, ushering in a period of political chaos. The disintegration also marked the end of the Tibetan empire in Central Asia. For a short period, China was able to regain control of the areas it had lost to Tibet in the seventh century, until its empire also disintegrated, leaving a no-man's-land between the two once-great kingdoms. The Mongols would eventually fill the void. The role played by the Khans eventually had major consequences for the Karma Kagyu lineage in Tibet.[28]

In spite of the severe religious suppression by the Langdarma royal court, something was happening out in the wastelands of western Tibet, the domain of nomads, freebooters, and mahasiddhas. Padmasambhava represented the Tantric tradition, no doubt, but an independent wave of the yogic heritage was to manifest and find its way, through the "trickle-in effect," to the Land of Snows, creating a brand-new tradition of Tibetan Buddhism.

King Tsenpo Khore of the Kingdom of Guge renounced his throne, relinquishing it to his nephew, and became a Buddhist monk, taking the name of Lama Yeshe O. Through his intervention, twenty-one Tibetan monks were sent to India to study the Dharma, of which only two survived. These two, Rinchen Sangpo and Lekbe Sherap, returned to Tibet in 978 C.E., the date marking the inauguration of the Second Dissemination, better known as the Second Transmission.[29]

Yeshe O became aware of the existence of Diamkara Srijnana (982–1054), one of the directors of Nalanda University and a teacher in Vikramasila, the second greatest center of learning in India, just south of Nalanda on the Ganges. Historically referred to as Atisa, this master of Buddhist philosophy, including Tantric yoga, was at the time the most famous practitioner of the Dharma in the known world. Yeshe O, while gathering gold as a gift and incentive for Atisa's traveling to Tibet to teach the lama, was captured and imprisoned by a neighboring king. A ransom was demanded. Lama Yeshe chose to die in prison rather than forfeit the gold and thus the Tibetan people's chance to grow through Atisa's gift of the Dharma. The Indian, though advanced in years and warned by the goddess Tara that if the trip was undertaken his life would be considerably shortened, accepted the challenge. The great teacher arrived in Guge in the year 1042 C.E. David Snellgrove and Hugh Richardson write in their account of Atisa that

> From this time on the Tibetans clearly began to subordinate everything else to the propagation of their holy religion, even though their practice of it might not always be particularly holy. At all events Atisa's authority and prestige gave a new direction to the thinking and practice of other religious teachers in Tibet, and he certainly attracted the attention and devotion of ordinary people to such an extent that the dominance of Buddhism over the whole range of Tibetan life was never thereafter seriously challenged.[30]

Atisa sought to integrate Tantric techniques, the practices of those like Padmasambhava, with those of the Mahayana's more traditional and strenuous path of the Bodhisattva. He was able to demonstrate that the vehicles of Sutra and Tantra formed an integrated whole. In this sense, Atisa was a great reformer. What he did not do, according to W. Y. Evans-Went, however, was to emphasize with any marked degree of burning zeal the practical application of Buddhism by means of the yogic ideal. What he did emphasize was the moral self-discipline required to practice the Vajrayana successfully. Atisa in essence took a middle road between the monastic and Tantric systems. Those strictly inclined toward Tantric practices would pick and chose from older teachings or gather momentum from other sources, evidence that the schism between the two "ways" in Tibetan Buddhism, in spite of Atisa's efforts, still existed.[31]

From Atisa stems the mainstream of Tibetan Buddhism, particularly of Buddhist monastic religion in the centuries to come, as well as the first Tibetan order of the New School system.[32]

Dromton, one of Atisa's disciples, founded the monastery of Reting, north of Lhasa in 1056 C.E. This sect was eventually known as the Kadam, which translates as "bound by command." This religious order eventually evolved into the Gelugpa school of Buddhism, the domain of the Dalai Lama. The appearance of the Kadam order marks the first of the New Schools of Tibetan Buddhism, or Sarma, as opposed to the Old School or "Ancient Ones," represented by the Nyingma, all Vajrayana in nature. New translations of the original Sanskrit texts were carried forth by the Sarma, while deemed unnecessary by the Ancient Ones, who considered the old translations superior. The Sakya school, named after its principal monastery in southern Tibet, founded in 1073 C.E., represents another of Tibet's New Schools of Buddhism. The Sakyapa, thanks to their Mongol connection, was the first Buddhist entity to rise to political prominence and power in the Land of Snows.[33]

While Atisa was accomplishing his miracles in Guge, a completely different kind of Buddhist practice was introduced into Tibet from Bihar and Bengal in India. These practices were Tantric, stressing a certain meditative procedure involving extraordinary yogic powers as the approach to voidness or shunyata, rather than seeking Enlightenment through intellectual means alone. So again we encounter the mahasiddhas, those eccentric wanderers who spurned the world, who inhabited graveyards and caves seeking only the truth and sacrificing everything for that truth. And again, one cannot help but sense the conflict that inevitably develops when the Tantric and monastic want to occupy the same space and time.[34]

To know a Kagyupa, even those of the Texas variety, one must be intimately familiar with the persons who make up the living lineage. Indeed, all Kagyupa know the stories of their lineage founders; such is the importance of a tradition that is guru yoga. The Tibetan princes laid the initial groundwork for Buddhism in the country. Lamas such as Santaraksita, Guru Rinpoche, and Atisa, and thousands of other practitioners, made the Dharma happen in fact. But for the success of the specific order of the Karma Kagyu, five men were immediately and personally responsible. Their stories expand into what will eventually become the Kagyupa odyssey.

So who were these five Tantric masters, and what did they actually do? Such a narrative begins neither on Earth nor in the phenomenal realm of being. To historically trace the Karma Kagyu lineage, it is appropriate to start at the very beginning, which in this case would be with "suchness," the "pre-force," energy at perfect rest, the clear, limitless light of mind from whence everything emanates. The Kagyus refer to this as Vajradhara, or in Tibetan as Dorje Chang, the Dharmakaya aspect, or simply the primordial Buddha, the essence of Enlightenment, the ultimate source. Sakyamuni Buddha is an emanation of Dorje Chang who appeared on Earth. *Dorje* means "indestructibility," and *chang* translates as "permanently possessed." To make an analogy, Vajradhara would be the sun, while Sakyamuni Buddha would be the sun's light. Vajradhara does not actually appear on Earth but is the full realization and stabilization of the Enlightened quality within all sentient beings. Ultimately, Vajradhara is nothing separate or different from "ourselves." The information that permeates clear, limitless space must find some way to make itself manifest on Earth in order to enter human consciousness. The recipient of Vajradhara's communiqué, Tilopa (988–1069 C.E.), was, according to Stephen Batchelor, a Buddhist tutor in a king's court, but other sources state that he was born to be a king in India. Either way, he is the first human in the line that eventually becomes the Karma Kagyu tradition of Tibetan Buddhism.[35]

According to the royal version of the many biographies, Tilopa possessed everything that a man could want—wealth, power, leisure, and security—but felt an overwhelming need for something else. That "something else" seemed to define itself as Buddhism. While still a young man, Tilopa began his search for a teacher of the Dharma. Unknowingly, he helped the great siddha Nagarjuna cross a dangerous river. In time, dakinis appeared, to aid the wanderer in his search for Vajradhara. For twelve years he meditated in a single cave with his ankles chained so that there would be no temptation to leave. Because of his noble background, though, and the pride and arrogance that often accompany such an exalted position, Tilopa's spiritual progress stalled. To remove the psychological impediment, a dakini appeared and instructed Tilopa to seek out a certain prostitute in a nearby village and become her business assistant. During the day, Tilopa ground sesame seed into oil for her, and at night he solicited customers. One day while preparing the seeds, through no intellectual instruction, but rather through the process of direct apperception, he realized the Vajradhara aspect of Enlightenment. When Tilopa spoke with a spiritual mentor, he would appear to be engaged in conversation alone with himself. Witnesses must have considered him insane. Nevertheless, with pride vanquished, Buddhahood was not only possible but also immediate. Villagers witnessed the metamorphosis, seeing Tilopa levitating at the height of "seven royal palm trees" while still holding his mortar and pestle.

> With everyone assembled below, Tilopa sang a song of the Dharma, using the example of the sesame seed in his teaching. In his song, Tilopa explained that although a sesame seed contains oil, it cannot produce oil by itself; without the hard work of grinding the seed, the oil cannot be extracted. So although Buddha nature is within every living being, without the hard work of practicing the Dharma, there is no way to realize our inherent Buddha nature.[36]

The prostitute, who was in the crowd, asked Tilopa if he would accept her as a student. He immediately made a flower fall from the sky and come to rest on her shoulder, resulting in complete Realization.

The Indian siddha Tilopa stands first in the line of mortals who founded the Karma Kagyu lineage. Tilopa took only one disciple, Naropa, a thirty-three-year-old scholar with an aristocratic background. Naropa (1016–1100 C.E.) was abbot of the greatest Buddhist university in India, Nalanda, and was a brilliant man in the process of having a nervous breakdown.[37]

One day while Naropa sat quietly alone in his room, reading a sutra, a leper, a frightfully ugly, toothless old woman appeared before him and asked if he understood what he was reading. Naropa answered with pride that he indeed did understand every word of what the Buddha had taught. The old woman giggled and danced as if crazy and exclaimed that it was most fortunate that a scholar like this existed on the earth. She then said that there was nothing difficult about grasping the literal meaning of things, and she continued her interrogation by asking if he understood the "real" meaning of the work.

So Naropa replied, "Yes." As he replied yes, the expression of the face of the ugly old woman turned from one of joy to one of sadness, and she fell to the floor and beat it with both her hands and cried, "To think that such a great scholar as you knows how to tell lies!" This embarrassed Naropa, who inquired, "Is there anyone who really understands the inner meaning of the Dharma?" The old woman replied, "Yes, my brother, Tilopa."[38]

Because of the spiritual impurities that still existed in Naropa's psyche, in this case attachment to conceptuality and the cold joy of the rationality of his own intellect, he could not recognize the Vajrayogini for what she actually was. Nor could he penetrate the inner meaning of the teachings of the Buddha. (One cannot help but notice the similarities in the characters of Herman Hesse's *Narcissus and Goldmund*). Herbert Guenther points out in *The Life and Teachings of Naropa* that the dakini had to appear as an ugly old crone, because she stands for that part the total person that has been rejected, that has never been allowed to come alive, or has done so in only an underdeveloped or distorted way. The anima, the integrating, nurturing feminine, was frowned upon and unfavored by the ego complex. And right out of the C. G. Jung school of depth psychology, Dr. Guenther explains:

> Lastly she is a deity because all that is not incorporated in the conscious mental make-up of the individual and appears other than—and more than—himself is, traditionally, spoken of as the divine. Thus he himself is the old, ugly, and

divine woman, who in the religious symbolism of the Tantras is the deity Dor-je phag-mo (Vajravarahi) and who in a psychological setting acts as "messenger" (phona).[39]

With his vision of the leper, a subtle change was beginning to stir within the scholar. Unconsciously, Naropa was becoming aware of a new truth and the futile and fleeting character of the relative world. There were hints of the reality, but the house was still divided against itself. As a result, the abbot sensed that he must get rid of the ordinary occupations, the daily rituals and habits, that had dominated his life for so many years. Naropa resigned his exalted position, abandoned his worldly honors, and began the search for his guru, for the integrity of his own being as represented by the old woman. It was a nightmarish search, a process of psychological purification that, due to its lack of success and to many strange encounters, nearly ended in his death.

Naropa's road was a long and difficult one. His trial lasted twelve years, and during the first year, Tilopa refused to even speak to his pupil at all. When at last he did speak, it was to explain that if he had a true disciple, he would not hesitate if asked to jump from the top of a building, regardless of the consequences. Naropa made the leap and was rewarded with a load of broken bones and a simple lesson. Tilopa said that he had nothing to show his student and then pointed to the empty sky, saying, "Here is the primordial wisdom of self-awareness that transcends words and mental objects." Suddenly, Naropa's eyes were opened, the veils of delusion were lifted, and he truly, for the first time, understood the pure nature of mind.

Na in Tibetan means "pain," *ro* means "killing," and *pa* makes the word a noun. Naropa, as the name indicates, suffered infinitely during his education, but it was all necessary because of his negative karma. In his case, intellect alone was no road to the truth. Tilopa knew that for his disciple, it was only through personal hardships that a personal or direct experience with reality was possible. Thinking would open no doors. The intellect itself was the wall, artfully disguised as pride, that blocked every avenue of direct Realization. But the master assured his charge that even though harshness and roughness are essential in a teacher, the guru and the student are always one and the same.[40]

Naropa's slow understanding that manufactured knowledge, book learning, was his tragic flaw reveals a constant in the Kagyupa narrative: the conflict between intellectualism, and the direct and personal illumination of Tantrism. Every time a reformer reforms, it is a resolution, some kind of assimilation of these two divergent approaches to Realization that is being sought.

The greatest contributions Naropa made to the world of Buddhism, and especially to the Karma Kagyu lineage, was his lesson of Six Perfections, the qualities in which a bodhisattva must be trained in order to create the matrix of an Enlightened personality, and his practice of the Six Yogas. These are instructions, still practiced today, that teach students to use visualization and breathing methods to utilize their 72,000 energy channels, to harness and direct the energy current called "Mind of Enlightenment" into the central channel to produce (1) inner heat, the first yogi. (John Powers points out that the yogin actually develops the ability to experience directly the luminous nature of consciousness which is then manifested in the form of heat and light.) The same source of energy can be used to create (2) an illusory body, revealing the emptiness of all inherent existence of the relative world, and (3) to take control of dreams, or practice dream yoga. The third yoga instructs one in how to (4) transfer consciousness from a living organism to that of any available life-form body, but more importantly the disciples learn how to transfer themselves to a pure Buddha Land upon death. This system is referred to as Phowa and is a distinctive feature of the Kagyu practice, even for beginners. (5) Learning to negotiate the transition between death and rebirth, the bardos, is the purpose of the fifth yoga. (6) In the yoga of clear light, the practitioner becomes aware of the nature of mind, which is radiant emptiness. One enters a trance through meditation and remains in this state, contemplating emptiness, and this causes the vital energies to enter the central channel, remain awhile, and then dissolve. This gives rise to the wisdom of clear light.[41] John Powers captures the practical side in this exercise of pure Tantric yoga:

> All of these yogas serve to undermine our fixed attachment to the phenomena of ordinary experience as being fixed and immutable. They give the successful meditator a measure of control over the unfolding of experience and allow him or her to manipulate it in ways that are

thought to be impossible by people still bound by the conceptual limitations of ordinary beings. Even death is no longer the inevitable cessation of existence, but rather a doorway of opportunity for spiritual progress.[42]

The supreme of all Kagyu teachings is the Mahamudra, the Great Seal or Great Sign, a practice that is designed to lead one to a personal realization of "being-in-itself," the unoriginated truth. The term "Seal" is used because at the moment that Mahamudra is understood, one receives a seal or stamp, a mudra formed by Buddha Sakyamuni that looks like an "ok" configuration of the fingers, meaning, "That's It. You've got all there is to get."[43]

Mahamudra is the path of self-realization that integrates authentic vision, contemplation, and action into one perfect insight where seer, the thing seen, and the seeing are one and the same. When one enters the Karma Kagyu lineage, the "forever goal" is to reach the point where the Mahamudra is fully appreciated. During this practice, one can reach Enlightenment at any moment through directly experiencing the clear, luminous nature of mind. It took Naropa twelve years of constant struggle to realize Mahamudra. Passed down continuously from Mahasiddha Tilopa to the present, this practice is the essence, the very heart of the Karma Kagyu system of Buddhism. The Great Perfection or Maha-Ati of the Nyingma school and the Great Middle Way or Madhyamika of the Gelugpa both express essentially the same teaching as that found in their Kagyu counterpart.[44]

In the words of the third Karmapa, Mahamudra is to add nothing to mind's nature: "Since in the view of mahamudra, analysis does not apply, cast mind-made knowledge away. Since in the meditation of mahamudra there is no way of fixating on a thought, abandon deliberate meditation. Since in the action of mahamudra there is no reference point for any action, be free from the intention to act or not. Since in the fruition of mahamudra there is no attainment to newly acquire cast hopes, fears and desires far away."[45]

Before approaching the Mahamudra practice, a student is expected to undergo an unbelievable amount of training, a process of purification known as the Ngondro. This preparation requires 111,111 prostrations in honor of one's own Enlightened nature, and endless repetitions of the Tantric meditation Dorje

Sempa, in order to dissolve the disturbed feelings that lie beneath the surface of the conscious mind. This is followed by Mandala offerings, to build up positive impressions after wrestling with all of the negatives. The final preparatory step before the big show is guru yoga, which is designed to accumulate wisdom, through integration into the Karma Kagyu transmission lineage and through the absorption of its full blessing. Completing the Ngondro itself is an incredibly formidable process, and yet it is only a preparation. Consider the degree of difficulty facing one when approaching the realities of the Mahamudra, including mastery of Naropa's Tantric skills of the Six Yogas. But it can be done. There have been others before, and the guru is the key that turns the lock in the Vajrayana system. As John Powers writes: "There are others who have successfully traversed the path to enlightenment and thus acquired the ability to look directly into the minds of students and skillfully guide them past the pitfalls they will encounter on the path. The successful student must have a strong desire to transcend the suffering of other sentient beings, a high level of intelligence, and most importantly, an intense and unwavering faith in the lama."[46]

The Karma Kagyu refer to their order as those of the "teaching or oral-transmission lineage," as "the transmitted" or "ear-whispered command." Such descriptions denote the acceptance of only a finite number of disciples, with an extraordinary personal closeness between teacher and pupil. It is a grassroots system, teaching and spreading the Dharma through personal contact, in its most pure form. Both Tilopa and Naropa accepted only a single student, unlike Jesus, a profoundly evolved Bodhisattva in the Buddhist view, who required himself to go public. Paul Sherwood took on no more than three or four pupils during his time. "Ear-whispered" not only indicates the secrecy involved in the Tantric system, but again denotes the closeness of student and teacher, like a body and its shadow. Herbert Guenther describes it this way in his *Life and Teachings of Naropa:* "Tilopa is Naropa's total-self, which summons him to find himself."[47]

The lama must be seen as the embodiment of the Buddha, and the student must surrender completely to the teacher and follow his advice unhesitatingly. Without such a commitment by the disciple, there will be no Enlightenment. If things are not working, the student must make an honest effort to discover what he or she is doing wrong. If there is nothing to discover, then a search for another teacher begins. If a student accepts the authority of the teacher, then the student will inevitably be led to his own inner authority. The guru is the power, the gate, the source from which seekers discover and gather their strength for the greatest of all human and spiritual tests. The guru is the sun, the disciple his or her light. The position and importance of the lama cannot be overstated. It is considered paramount. The guru must never be conceived of as merely human. To do this would only serve to feed and support the disciple's ordinary attitude, which both student and teacher are trying so hard to overcome.[48] Such is the role of the lama in the Karma Kagyu tradition, and such was the importance of Naropa in the life of his only disciple, Chogi Lodro of Mar: "Marpa was in the world, but not of it, since his perception was developed to a point where he could view the world as a completely purified Buddha land and all beings as fully Realized deities."[49]

Marpa (1012-97 C.E.) was the first Tibetan member of the Ear-Whispered Lineage, thus father of the Karma Kagyu order in Tibet. While a common householder with wife and family with all of the obligations and responsibilities thereof, Marpa was still able to achieve a level of Enlightenment equivalent to that of Vajradhara. He developed the astounding ability to gather belongings without having any attachment to these possessions. He was like a Buddha, acting and living in the world while still perceiving the nondifference between Nirvana and Samsara. He was and still is an inspiration for all nonmonastic Buddhists, especially in Texas, where virtually all Kagyu members are laypersons.

Always an aggressive and voracious student, Marpa studied to be a translator of Sanskrit for fifteen years and then sought out Naropa in India as his chosen teacher. In all, there were three grueling trips to India, during which Marpa stayed and studied for sixteen years.[50]

When he returned to Tibet, Marpa married and settled down to the life of what appeared to be an ordinary family man and joined no monastic order. (The Kagyu school does not require strict celibacy nor membership in a religious institution of its followers, obviously a great boon for all contemporary lay Buddhists.) Yet Marpa was an accomplished Tantric master capable of conferring initiations into the most esoteric practices.

He had the ability to transfer his consciousness into the body of any dead being and then actually become that living entity. It was to Marpa whom Naropa confided his Six Doctrines.

Because of the hardships that Marpa was willing to go through, all the Karma Kagyu traditions and teachings became available and are available in the same way to this day. Without Marpa, the Kagyu tradition would not exist. It is Marpa, "The Translator," who, though he was never ordained nor lived in a monastery, is respected as the Tibetan founder of the Karma Kagyu lineage.[51]

One of the best-known and most popular Buddhists, revered it seems by all Tibetan schools, is the yogi Jetsun Milarepa (1052–1135 C.E.), who sought out Marpa to be his guru. His story, captured and easily followed in his songs, is one of immense pain and misery, but also one of ultimate victory through complete Realization.

Seeking revenge as a youth through the use of the black arts for the theft of his mother's property by an aunt and uncle, Milarepa wrought horrible damage upon innocent people as well as the land. Realizing from a Buddhist perspective that his magical powers were being utilized only for selfish purposes, he became terrified that his life would end in the hell realms if there was not some radical change in a spiritually ameliorative direction. With, ironically, the help of his teacher of sorcery, he was directed to a teacher of the Nyingma sect. Pride in his past accomplishments in sorcery made his meditations impossible, so the lama said to the young man,

> I see quite well that I shall not be able to convert thee. Now there is a monastery called Dowo-Lung (Wheat Valley), in Lhobrak, wherein liveth at present a faithful disciple of Naropa, the great Indian Saint. He is the worthiest among the worthiest of men, a very prince among translators—one who hath obtained supernormal knowledge in the new Tantric Doctrines, unequalled in all the three worlds; he is called Marpa the Translator. Between thee and him there is a karmic connection, which cometh from past lives. To him you must go."[52]

Milarepa was accepted by the lama but from the moment of encounter was treated with detachment and scorn. Rechung Dorje Tagpa's description of Marpa's ill treatment of his student can be troubling for any reader. The shishya (student-devotee) was directed to build numerous towers, as well as a nine-story house, but before the completion of any of them was ordered to tear down what had been done, return every stone to its original resting place, and begin another project. His body covered with gaping sores, suffering from utter exhaustion, and sinking into deep depression, Milarepa entertained suicide more than once. He eventually ran away and found another teacher, only to find his way back to his destined guru, more torture, and ultimate triumph.

Marpa, in the end, gave his pupil the transmission, explaining that his vile treatment of Milarepa was required if his karmic legacy accumulated through the use of the black arts and the harm it had wrought was ever to be balanced by accumulated merit. Marpa explained, "Now I am going to care for him and give him those Teachings and Initiations which I hold as dear as mine own heart. I myself will provide him with food while he is in retreat, and with mine own hands will enclose him in the place of meditation. Henceforth rejoice."[53]

Milarepa lived in solitude as a hermit for the rest of his life in meditation, the ideal life of a Kagyu devotee, dying at the age of eighty-four, poisoned by a jealous lama. Like Marpa before him, he was never ordained, nor did he ever become a member of a monastery. Hunger was a constant foe, his diet often consisting of pine-needle broth because of his seclusion from the world. Nevertheless, the reward was won. Milarepa became the perfect yogi while converting humans and tutelary gods alike, helping those who were inclined to defeat the demon of egotism. He gained the power to reproduce his physical body in countless numbers simultaneously in all parts of the world or upon other worlds. He learned to fly, to transfer consciousness, and developed completely Naropa's yoga of "inner heat," which served to keep him warm though he dressed only in simple cotton clothing (*Milarepa* means "cotton-clad") in fireless, freezing caves through the harsh Himalayan winters.

In Tantric terms, the yoga that produces this heat in essence is the untangling of subtle nervous obstructions or energy knots in the central nervous system that keep humans locked in a spasm of self-delusion.[54]

Herein, Milarepa justifies the life of ascetical seclusion from the world. Unknown to the worldly multitude, who regard the yogi as a useless member of society, he is, in fact, the most useful; owing to his thought-force, broadcast like silent and invisible arrows which fall among all nations, virtue and goodness are kept alive in the world, and the pathway leading to the Olympus of the Gods is guarded and kept open.[55]

While in the midst of flames upon his funeral pyre surrounded by disciples and followers, it is reported that the great yogi rose

> in the Indestructible Body, into which are merged both the spiritual body and the phenomenal body. The flames of the funeral pyre assumed the shape of an eight-petalled lotus, and from the midst of this like the stamens of the blossom, Jetsun sat up, one of his knees half raised and his right hand extended in the preaching attitude pressing down the flames. "Listen," he said, "to this old man's last testament." Then, both as a reply to Rechung's prayer and as his final teachings to his disciples, with his left hand placed against his cheek, he sang this final hymn concerning the Six Essential Commandments for the mist of the funeral pyre, in a divine voice issuing from the Indestructible Body:
> "Gurus, Devas, Dakinis—Combine these in a single whole, and worship that; the goal of aspiration, the meditation, and the practice—Combine these in a single whole, and gain Experimental Knowledge; This life, the next life, and the life between [in Bar-do] Regard these all as one, and make thyself accustomed to Them [thus as one]."[56]

The Doctor of Takpo, Dvagpo Rinpoche, better known in the West as Gampopa (1079–1153 C.E.), proved to be Milarepa's most influential disciple. He was originally a student of medicine, as well as of the teachings of the Kadam tradition, the severely austere monastic lineage founded by Atisa's disciples. After his wife and children died, Gampopa took initiations from a variety of orders before pursuing the Tantric path with Jetsun Milarepa. When Gampopa first approached Milarepa's cave, the master met him at the entrance and announced that the doctor's coming had been prophesied and offered his new disciple a skull cup of chang (beer).

Gampopa at first was reluctant to drink it, since doing so would conflict with this monastic vow, which expressly forbade him to drink liquor. Milarepa, reading his mind, ordered him to drink it, which he did. This act began a process of weaning him from attachment to monastic vows, which, although they are designed to help people to escape from the cycle existence, may prove to be a hindrance if one fails to realize that even Buddhist teachings can become an object of negative attachments.[57]

Tension between monastic life and Tantric practices continued throughout Gampopa's life. He stayed in Milarepa's presence for thirteen months, absorbing and mastering the Tantric teachings. In the end, the teacher told his student that he would be a "colossus" and cautioned him that he should abandon the world and just practice meditation, keeping to retreats and solitary places. Contrary to his guru's advice, Gampopa resettled in a Kadam monastery, of all places, and joined in their religious practices. It did not work, so he isolated himself within the grounds and practiced Milarepa's teachings. During this work, he realized that his Tantric master existed as the absolute body (Dharmakaya), even though the world at large could only see the siddha. At this point, Gampopa left the monastery and sought out lonely places, eventually settling in central Tibet's Gampo region, from whence he became known as the Man of Gampo, or Gampopa. While there, his understanding of the Mahamudra reached perfection.[58]

This master produced several literary works of great importance, one of which was the "Union with the Innate," a Tantric piece, and another a treatise on the Kadam doctrine. These two works brought the two streams—Kadam, the lineage founded through Atisa's disciples, and the Tantric Mahamudra tradition—together. Gampopa thus succeeded in combining the Tantric teachings transmitted by Marpa and Milarepa with the already established strict monastic traditions of the Kadam order, successfully bringing to an end the difficulty of the Tantric-monastic schism. Without this event, scholars believe that there would be no Kagyupa religious schools of Tibetan Buddhism today, because there would never have been any organized community life with a broad, eclectic curriculum and universal appeal. Neither Tilopa nor Naropa had any interest at all in monasticism or the community. They were free-roving Tantric yogins. Marpa, on the other hand, embraced the world and its senses, dwelling in a community and in perfect "suchness" simultaneously. Milarepa was a pure Tantric practitioner who wanted "his disciple to live in permanent solitude, avoiding all ordinary people, lest their exhaled breath disturb his mental equilibrium. This is certainly not the way a Bodhisattva should act, avoiding the very people whom he is supposed to be helping, and there need be no shortage of quotations from Mahayana sutras, fully justifying Gam-po-pa in his eventual return to monastic life."[59]

It is interesting that the Tantric masters are challenged here with the same negative charges of selfishness and self-absorption that the Mahayana flung at the Theravada arhats centuries before. Monastic centers no doubt allowed for more interaction with the masses than yogins could possibly experience in their isolated and solitary existences. Thus one sees the intense psychological split that confronted Gampopa. John Powers writes:

> Someone visiting the great Kagyu monasteries of present-day India and Nepal might wonder how a lineage that began with ascetic, iconoclastic teachers developed into one of the major schools of Tibetan Buddhism, with large monasteries and centers all over the world. The period of transition begins with Gampopa, who received the teachings of Milarepa and incorporated them into a system of institutionalized monasticism. Gampopa combined the yogic practices and meditational techniques of the early Kagyu teachers with the monastic structures of the Kadampas (the lineage founded by Atisa's disciples), and the result was a new school that could transmit the yogic teachings of Milarepa and his predecessors and preserve them within a monastic framework.[60]

The Tantric, though not tamed by any stretch of the imagination, was in effect institutionalized. Gampopa's immediate students founded the six sects of the Karma Kagyu Order, in which both non-Tantric teachings and the esoteric Tantric teachings were practiced within the monastic framework. The distinctive unifying feature of these six groups was the established spiritual lineage of Dorje Chang, Tilopa, Naropa, Marpa,

Milarepa, and Gampopa; also, all six embraced the Mahamudra as the school's ultimate expression.[61]

Gampopa's inspiration made it possible for the Kagyu to develop training centers, monastic universities, and curricula that could meet the needs of spiritual seekers of different levels of spiritual attainment and with different interests and abilities. This innovation effectively addressed, it seems, that eternal conflict between the intuitive mystic and the intellectual, scholastic-minded monk.

> Anyone who wishes to become a teacher [in the Kagyu Order] must have completed a three-year meditative retreat, a practice that severely tests the fortitude of even the most strong-willed person. This combination of monasticism and solitary retreats has served the Kagyu order well, allowing it to transmit its teachings and practices to successive generations of students while maintaining a spiritual continuity with the Tantric yogins who were its founders.[63]

The subsects of the Karma Kagyu order are divided into two divisions or groups, four greater and eight lesser schools. First of the "Four Great Schools" is (1) the Pakmo Kagyu sect. The first great monastery of the Kagyu school was Densatil, founded by Gampopa's disciple Pakmodrupa Dorje Gyelpo (1110–70 C.E.), and the school was named Pakmo, after its founder. This is usually the way it went. A master would build himself a simple hut, students would gather around him, building their own dwellings, and eventually a monastery would evolve from the seemingly inauspicious beginning. In the case of Densatil, due to the patronage of a wealthy family named Rlang, the numerous student buildings rapidly grew into a large and powerful monastic complex. This Kagyu school no longer exists. (2) Tselpa Kagyu, founded by Shang Tselpa, derives its name from the district of Tsel. (3) Baram Kagyu, founded by Darma Wangchuk. (4) The Karma Kagyu, or Karma Kamtsang, founded by Tusum Khyenpa (1111–93). David Snellgrove refers to this school as the Karmapa sect, which he says derived from the succession of Lama Dusum Khyenpa (1110–93), who founded the Tsurphu Monastery in 1185. He indicates that this suborder was probably named after the monastery of Karma Dansa, which Lama Dusum had founded earlier in his homeland in eastern Tibet. The Eight Lesser Schools originally were the (1) Drikung, (2) Taklung, (3) Tropu, (4) Drukpa, (5) Mar, (6) Yerpa, (7) Shuksep, and (8) Yamsang. Of these eight groups, the Drukpa school, centered in Bhutan today, is still active. The Drikung and Taklung schools still survive. However, two newer schools of the lesser variety have come into existence, and they are called Shangpa and Ugyen Nyendrup Kagyu.[63]

Tsurphu Monastery was in central Tibet, but the Karma Kagyu had a considerable following in Kham Province, to the east. The head Kagyu lamas became famous for the time they spent traveling between their monasteries. Traditionally, Karmapa had a guard that provided protection during the long tours, known as the Garpa, referred to as the Karmapa Garchen in the *Buddhist Handbook*. The lineage had no single patron, but rather enjoyed the support of a wide range of landed and nomadic families.

The spiritual fountainhead of the Karma Kagyu lineage today is the Karmapa, originally the head lama of the Karma Kagyu lineage seated in the Tsurphu Monastery.

The title Karmapa translates as "man of action." Karma itself means "action." The working translation, then, is "a master of karma" meaning master of past, present, and future. This in itself means that for this master, linear time does not exist. The Karmapa is Buddha living on Earth. He is considered an emanation of the compassionate Bodhisattva Avalokiteshwara, that is, Chenrezig in Tibetan. The Karmapa is considered to be a form of energy and light. Space that is the clear light of mind and the Karmapa are one and the same. Dorje Chang is Karmapa's mind, and the Karmapa is Dorje Chang's body. The Karmapa holds every living transmission and carries the unbroken Enlightenment of all Buddhas even to the present. He is considered the king of yogis. It is through this deity form, the compassionate spirit that expresses itself through the Karmapa, that members of the Karma Kagyu Order have access to Realization. Identification with the Karmapa, even in contemporary Texas, is the central essence of the lineage practice.[65] There have been sixteen Karmapas up to the passing of Rangjung Rigpe Dorje in 1981. The story of the seventeenth is complex and contentious, and will be treated in a later chapter.

Karmapa's equivalent in the Gelug Order, the Dalai Lama, from the Kagyupa point of view, though certainly respected for his spiritual relevance as another emanation of Avalokiteshwara, is seen for the most part as a political figure only. The intertwined history of the two camps, the Gelugpa and Kagyu, has at times produced a difficult relationship. For some Kagyus, the relationship remains problematic. Still, Jonathan Landaw and Andy Weber, in the text of *Images of Enlightenment,* are quick to point out that

> It is important to bear in mind that the four extant lineages, or schools, of Tibetan Buddhism—the Nyingma, Sakya, Kagyu, and Geluk—are not self-contained, independent or opposing entities. They are equally rooted in the teachings of Shakyamuni Buddha and, despite differences in approach and emphasis, each school preserves and transmits the insights and inspiration capable of guiding sincere practitioners to full enlightenment. Further, if we examine the guru-disciple lineages of any one school we almost always find that they are inextricably intertwined with the lineages of one or more of the other schools.[65]

The first Karmapa was Dusum Khyenpa, who lived from 1110 to 1193 C.E. He was a student of and initiated by Gampopa. The coming of the Karmapa fulfilled a prophecy made by Lord Buddha, in which he predicted that sixteen hundred years after his own passing that "There would be born a man of great spiritual attainment and infinite compassion. This man would spread the Buddhist Dharma for many successive incarnations and would be known as the Karmapa, 'Man-of-Karma.'"[66]

Gampopa and two other great masters of the time recognized Dusum Khyenpa as the Karmapa as foretold by the prophecy. The founder of the Karma Kagyu sect and the first of the Karmapa lamas, even though this recognition came after the fact, are, then, one and the same.[67]

It must be noted that upon Gampopa's Parinirvana, Dusum Khyenpa had a vision of his master in the sky and then engaged himself in extensive rites for the propagation of the Kagyupa line. Fifty miles west of Lhasa, the Karmapa arranged for the building of a monastery named Tsurphu, the same referred to previously in reference to the founding of the Kagyu subset, the first of the Karmapa lamas. This monastery became and remains the principal seat of the Karmapa incarnates.[68]

Dusum, the man, acquired a deep knowledge of religious texts, withdrew to solitary places for mediation, and acquired the height of spiritual power by means of special techniques of yoga. He established the Kampo Nesnang Monastery in 1165 C.E., near which is an enormous rock on which the Tibetan letter "Ka" manifests when a new Karmapa incarnates into the world. During the time that he was establishing what was to become the largest and most important Kagyu center, Karma Gon, it was reported that he healed many who were sick and was able to bring sight to the blind. Once he miraculously transported himself instantly to Ceylon for practice, and again to another realm altogether when he met with Maitreya, the future Buddha, from whom he received many important lessons.[69]

Dusum Khyenpa himself made a prediction containing the place and all of the details of his next birth. Since the Karmapa lives in all "three times," such an ability should not seem so strange. The idea is based on the notion that one as spiritually advanced as the Karmapa is able to consciously choose his reincarnation vessel, time, and place. Such a pre-announced reincarnation is called a tulku, and the Karmapa was the first such entity in history, a practice which eventually became common throughout Tibet's other Buddhist orders.

Within the Kagyu system there are other tulkus. The second Karmapa predicted that future Karmapa lamas would manifest in two forms, separate and distinct, yet not totally unrelated. This "other" Karmapa was called the Shamarpa and was given a ruby-red crown. He was referred to as the Red Crown Karmapa. Other reincarnated lamas of great significance in the Kagyu order include the Chogyam Trungpa, Tai Situ, Goshir Gyaltsap, and Jamgon Kongtrul tulkus. Interestingly, each of the current tulkus is presently a critical player in an international struggle for power. This story will be discussed in a later chapter.[70]

The Karmapas became figures of wealth, power, and influence in Tibet. They were noted for their charismatic zeal both as religious teachers and political rulers. Stephen Batchelor explains, "Twice they aspired for supreme leadership of Tibet, and twice they were thwarted, in both cases by a lama from another tradition with powerful Mongolian backing. The first was when the Sakya Lama Phagpa achieved control of the country under Kublai Khan, the second when the 5th Dalai Lama of the reformed Gelukpa order was enthroned by Gushri Khan in 1642."[71]

The history of the struggle for political mastery of Tibet is a complicated affair involving the Mongol empire and interlacing the various Tibetan religious orders. There was often intrigue and violence resulting in death, destruction, and long-lasting resentments. This contest for political control, in spite of China's domination, is still a part of the contemporary landscape, just as are the old bitternesses and intrigues. In order to make some sense of the current "schemings," factional squalls that currently rake even the Texas coast, a quick look at the root causes is of particular importance.

In 1240 C.E., Mongol chieftain Godan, of the Yuan dynasty, invaded Tibet and summoned the most eminent religious leader in the Land of Snows at that time, a Sakya lama, to surrender his country to Mongol control. Ironically, the Mongolian prince was so taken by the lama that he himself converted to Buddhism. A special relationship developed, personally and politically. Godan offered to protect Tibet from foreign threats, providing military force to back the prerogatives of the Sakya lama, who was expected to provide for the religious needs of his patron. Thus the patron-priest relationship was established. The actual administration of Tibet was left to the Sakya's viceroys. This pattern of relationship continued through several generations of lamas and khans, including that of Kublai.[72] This original submission to Godan Khan is being used presently as the authority by which China has absorbed Tibet.[73]

Of vital importance here is the fact that a choice was made to create a religious authority, rather than a lay political hierarchy, not so surprising since the monks had a monopoly on learning and the monasteries already had some form of communication network. A larger interest could exist with some degree of continuity of control, since the religious orders could transcend local interests where the nobility had no such choice. This arrangement would have profound effects even in the twenty-first century.[74] "Thus Tibet became subject to a single political leadership for the first time since the 9th century, at the same time avoiding direct Mongol conquest and this leadership was that of a religious hierarchy. Here, then, is the origin of that theocratic or, more properly, hierocratic rule, which was to become so characteristic of Tibet and which continued down to 1959."[75]

The ascent to power of the Sakyas did not bode well for the other Buddhist orders and challenged the premise of a natural and continuous congeniality among the four Tibetan schools. Resentment developed among other religious leaders, who began cultivating relationships with rival Mongolian chieftains. Making use of the rivalries among the Mongol clans, the bitterness that existed in Tibet because of the single national ruler resulted in endless internecine warfare between opposing religious factions. Between 1267 and 1290 C.E., the Sakyas and Brikhung, a member of the Karma Kagyu system, waged intermittent war, each with the assistance of their Mongol supporters.

In these and like struggles there was no room for Tibetan patriotism or thoughts of nationhood. It was now a matter of powerful monastic orders in close association with landed aristocratic interests seeking their own predominance by whatever available means and without any seeming feeling for their fellow-countrymen and co-religionists. The influence of the nobles was far from over, but it could hardly again be effective without cooperation with the leading religious figures. The "church" had already established its monopoly in the sphere of learning and culture, and was now well on its way to gaining political supremacy, although to the greater tragedy of the country it still remained undecided which great prelate would be supreme. It was a period of bitter, bloody deeds and unscrupulous intrigue, in which men of religion played the leading parts and monks fought in the battles, for fighting seemed already to have become the responsibility of one class of monastic inmates.[76]

Kublai Khan had a thirst for religion and invited representatives of every possible system to his court. Even representatives of Christendom were present to argue their theological case. The second Karmapa, Karma Pakshi, an adept in Tantric practice and a renowned siddha, nonetheless won the day. He became the teacher of the great khan, a position that was held by all the succeeding Karmapas until the tenth, Choying Dorje (1604–74).

When Karma Pakshi originally reached the khan's court, he was highly honored and celebrated. Nonetheless, Sakya reli-

India to Tibet: The Founding of the Karma Kagyu Lineage   73

gious-political representatives who were still firmly in control of Tibet and the khan's theological interests fiercely resented the new competition and threatened their counterpart. Despite repeated requests from Kublai that he remain, Karma Pakshi simply started back to Tibet. On the way, he founded many monasteries, converted thousands to Buddhism, and bestowed many teachings and initiations upon followers. He stopped the wind and snow in the dead of a Mongolian winter, drove away a plague of destructive pests by throwing a single handful of dirt at them, and stopped a war at the Sino-Tibetan border. The khan wanted him back. He sent thirty thousand troops to convince him by force that he should return.

> When [the soldiers] confronted Karmapa they were immediately paralyzed by his two-finger *Mudra*, but feeling compassion for them he restored their movements and freely allowed them to seize him. They wrapped him in a cloth and tied him up, but his body was like a rainbow, with no substance, and they found the task impossible. Then they forced him to drink poison, but far from having any effect, blinding rays of light began to stream from his body instead and the soldiers were very afraid. They took him to a high mountain and pushed him off, but he glided down, and landed on a lake and traveled across the surface like a duck. Unsuccessfully they tried to burn him, throwing him with two of his disciples into a blazing fire. Streams of water came out of their bodies and soon put out the flames. The Emperor Kublai Khan heard of the events and ordered that Karmapa should be locked up without any provisions. For a period of seven days people could observe heavenly beings providing him with food and drink. The Emperor relented and became his disciple. For some time he remained in the great palace and was highly honored.[77]

By the fourteenth century, Sakyapa's power waned with that of the Mongol dynasty in China. In 1368 the last Mongol emperor of the Yuan dynasty was driven out by a Chinese nationalist rival, and the Mongols were succeeded by the native Ming dynasty. Mongol dominance of Tibet came to an end. There was no rush to reach agreements with the Chinese.[79]

It must be noted that the fifth Karmapa, Dzen Shegpa (1384–1415 C.E.), was invited by Emperor Tai Ming Chen to his court in Nanking in 1407. The emperor witnessed many miracles and was so moved that he presented Karmapa with seven hundred measures of silver and bestowed upon him the title "Precious Religious King, Great Loving One of the West, Mighty Buddha of Peace." But of much greater significance, he told Karmapa that there were simply too many sects of Buddhism in Tibet and that there should be only one, that being the Karma Kagyu. Tai Ming Chen offered to simply make this happen by force. The Karma Kagyu were being offered the keys to the kingdom. They could immediately replace the Sakyapa as the rulers of Tibet.

    Karmapa explained to him that this was not his desire, nor could it be beneficial to humanity, since mankind requires varying methods of teaching and that in reality all sects are but one great family of Buddhism. Despite pressures from his Ministers the Emperor Ming Chen understood the advice of Karmapa had given him and withdrew his forces from the borders of Tibet, even though they were in a great position of strength and could easily have overrun the country. The emperor took teachings and initiations from Karmapa, eventually becoming a great Bodhisattva himself.[79]

    So the Karma Kagyu could have assumed political dominance of an empire as other sects did, but instead, on religious grounds, they chose to resist the temptation. Another order of the New School, the Gelugpa, would not resist, a fact that would eventually result in a great deal of pain for the Kagyupa, still in evidence today.

    Involved in this story of hostility and often open conflict is an object of infinite mystical significance for the Karma Kagyu Order. When Dusum Khyenpa, the first Karmapa and founder of the Kagyupa sect, attained Enlightenment, it is said that a host of dakinis not only gave him the knowledge of the "Three Times" but also celebrated the event by presenting him with a black crown woven from their hair. According to the teaching, the crown has been present, though invisible, above the heads of every Karmapa from that time on.[80]

    Stephen Batchelor tells the story this way:

    The first vision of the Karmapa wearing such a crown

was beheld in the full moon early on the morning of 15 June 1339 by Toghan Temur, the last Mongol Emperor of China, as he looked out of his palace in Peking the day after the death of his teacher, the 3rd Kamapa. He summoned a craftsman to carve an image in the likeness of the vision. Many years later, in 1407, after the Mongol rulers had been replaced by the Chinese Ming dynasty, the Emperor Yung-lo invited the 5th Karmapa to his court. During a ceremony the Emperor saw a crown woven from the hairs of one hundred thousand *dakinis,* hovering above the Karmapa's head. He ordered a physical replica to be made. It is this crown that has been in possession of the Karmapas ever since.[81]

Another story about this most important piece of Kagyupa regalia is that this Black Dorje Hat (vajra mukut) or black crown actually had its origin in the most ancient of times when it was presented to the Bodhisattva Avalokiteshwara or Chenrize by other Enlightened Ones. To this day, the Karmapas are referred to as the Black Hat Lamas of Tibet. It is said that this hat has the power of conferring Realization-on-sight to all living beings that behold it.[82]

It is believed that this most precious relic now rests in Karmapa's Rumtek Monastery in the Himalayan kingdom of Sikkim. It just may be that a subtle war is being fought for its possession. But this isn't the only subtle warfare being waged between the same adversaries at this time. The internecine conflict, often culturally based, has a long history, and the players, it seems, always remain the same.[83]

One day a family brought a young boy to Rolpe Dorje, the fourth Karmapa (1340–83 C.E.), for instruction and primary ordination. The year was 1361 C.E. Karmapa predicted that the child would become a great spiritual leader. The youth was Lobzang Trakpa, who later was the founder of the Gelugpa (System of Virtue) school of Tibetan Buddhism. Following over a hundred years of rule by lay noble clans, it was this religious school that emerged as victor in the struggle for political control of Tibet.[84]

In 1578 C.E., Sonam Gyatso (1543–88), the head lama of the Gelugpa sect, the Yellow Hats, was invited by Altan Khan to his capital, Mongolia. When the lama and the khan met, the Mongol chief conferred the title of Dalai Lama, or "Ocean of Wisdom," upon the Tibetan. In return, the khan received the title "King of

Dharma, Divine Purity." Thus was reestablished the patron-priest relationship, in spite of the fact that the Mongolians no longer controlled either China or Tibet. This meeting marked the transition of the Gelug from merely an order of Tibetan Buddhism to a ruling theocracy.

The khan showered the Gelug Order with gifts and riches. Many Mongols were converted to its system. And when the great-grandson of Altan Khan was discovered to be the reincarnation of the last Dalai Lama (What luck!), ties were permanently consummated between the powerful khans and the Gelugpa lamas.[85]

This new Dalai Lama was brought to Tibet in 1601 when he was twelve years old, and with extravagant processions and elaborate ceremony, he was installed in the local Gelugpa monastery. Such attention angered the other Buddhists in Lhasa, including the Karmapa representatives. Letters sent to the Dalai Lama by the Karmapa were interpreted by the Gelugpas as insulting, to which they replied in kind, and great antagonism developed between the two orders, an antagonism that still exists in some quarters today.

During the reign of the "Great Fifth" Dalai Lama, a large Mongol army entered Tibet with the stated intention of protecting the Gelugpas. By 1640 the Gelugpas, through the intervention of the Mongols, were victorious against all rivals. Gushri Khan attacked the Karmapa's camp in Khams, in the east, slaughtering many. Survivors fled throughout the country. The Gyalwa Karmapa was forced to flee Tibet to the Yennan region. This Dalai Lama attacked many of the Kagyupa monasteries.[87]

The king of Jyang arose in the Karmapa's defense and miraculously succeeded in destroying the Mongol army that had moved into his region of the world.

> Pleased with this success the King convened a meeting with the ministers and Generals and a decision was made to send forces to attack the Mongol armies in Tibet itself. A vow was made that if they were successful in their mission they would establish Karmapa as the Supreme Ruler. Three hundred thousand soldiers were prepared, but suddenly Karmapa himself appeared before the King and forbade any such action, saying that they should certainly not undertake warlike activities, as it was contrary to the Buddhist Dharma.[87]

India to Tibet: The Founding of the Karma Kagyu Lineage 77

Again a Karmapa elected to live the Dharma and bypassed a sure and easy road to political sovereignty in the Land of Snows.

John Powers points out that even though the fifth Dalai Lama was heavy-handed with the Karmapas, his treatment of other orders was often very generous. By 1642, Ngawang Losang Gyatso had consolidated military and political power and became the first Dalai Lama to rule a unified Tibet.[88]

Just for the record, the seat of the Karmapa lamas of the Karma Kagyu lineage came into existence with the birth of Dusum Khyenpa in 1110 C.E., as prophesied by Gautama Buddha, and that of the Dalai Lama of the Gelugpa Order, by decree of Altan Khan, a mere human, some 468 years later, in 1578.

The sixteenth Karmapa, Rangjung Rigpe Dorje, accompanied the Dalai Lama and other Tibetan dignitaries to Peking for a conference with the Chinese in 1957. Only Karmapa, it seems, came away convinced that the scourge of the north was determined to annihilate everything that had ever been called Tibet. He left the Land of Snows long before any of the other leaders, taking with him many of the treasures and texts that had been kept in the Tsurphu Monastery for the last seven hundred years. His main monastery was established in Sikkim. It was there that plans were first made for bringing the Dharma to the West.

Thus began the movement of the Karma Kagyu order from Tibet to the West, to Europe, to the United States, and then Texas.[90]

Mahasiddhi Padmasambhava's Iron Horse was on the wing. Four lamas, three from Tibet, and one from the East via Denmark, had Dharma bookings that would in time embrace the destinies of many hundreds of pilgrims in the Lone Star State.

Chapter 3

Tibet to Texas: The West Inherits the Jewels of a Diaspora

Rangjung Rigpe Dorje, the sixteenth Karmapa (1924–81), was the first of the Tibetan religious leaders to act upon the realization that his country would soon be lost to the Chinese. Even before his 1957 visit to Beijing, in anticipation of the impending fate of this country, Gyalwa Karmapa had established close ties with supporters in both Bhutan and Sikkim. In his flight from Tibet, Karmapa was met at the Indian border by representatives of the king of Sikkim, Chogyal Tashi Namgyal, and asked to resettle in his Himalayan kingdom, a province of India, where the Kagyu lineage had been active since the time of the ninth Karmapa.[1] During this early transition period, plans were already being formulated for the spread of Karma Kagyu Buddhism to the West: "There was one thought uppermost in Karmapa's mind, that though in exile, he should not rest but must take full responsibility for rekindling and revitalizing the torch of the Dharma, with the material and spiritual co-operation of the many Buddhists throughout the world."[2]

The Kagyus' seed monastery, its new national home, Rumtek Monastery, was built on a hillside across from Sikkim's capital of Gangtok. The Gelugpa order and the Dalai Lama's government in exile eventually settled in Dharmasala, directly north of Delhi in the state of Kashmir.[3]

The Indian government of Jawaharlal Nehru, sensitive to the Buddhist plight and realizing the importance of the role to be played by the young tulkus in creating some kind of stability for the devastated Tibetan civilization, established a Young Lamas' Home School in New Delhi. Over forty tulkus would be educated in this system, representing all four of the contemporary Tibetan schools of Buddhism: Nyingma, Sakya, Gelugpa, and Kagyu.

An Englishwoman, Freda Bedi, an official on the Indian Social Welfare Board, was chosen by the Dalai Lama as the school's headmaster. Mrs. Bedi, married to a prominent Sikh activist, had spent over thirty years in India and had participated in the struggle against the British for independence. Eventually this extraordinary lady would take her vows as a nun in the Kagyu order. As secretary of Karmapa, now Gelungma Kachok Palmo, or Sister Palmo, she would accompany His Holiness and his entourage on a tour of the United States. More importantly, she would have conspicuous influence and effect on the first of the four Kagyu teachers who would eventually establish sanghas in Texas.[4]

Chogyam Trungpa Rinpoche

Born in a cattle shed, in a tiny community on a high plateau of northeastern Tibet, a treeless country without even bushes, Chogyam Trungpa Rinpoche, the first lama to bring Karma Kagyu Buddhism to Texas, was recognized at the age of eighteen months as the eleventh Trungpa Tulku by Karmapa. He was enthroned as head of the Surmang monasteries in the Kham Province of eastern Tibet.[5] The family name, Mukpo, in time was changed to the position's formal Buddhist title:

> During the New Year festival on the day of the full moon, in the Earth Hare year according to the Tibetan calendar [February 1939] I was born in the cattle byre; the birth came easily. On that day a rainbow was seen in the village, a pail supposed to contain water was unaccountably found full of milk, while several of my mother's relations dreamt that a lama was visiting their tents. Soon afterwards, a lama from Trashi Lhaphug Monastery came to Geje; as he was giving his blessing to people, he saw me, who at that time was a few months old; he put his hand over my head to give me a special blessing, saying that he

wanted me for his monastery and that I must be kept very clean and and always be carefully looked after.[6]

A few months later, Gyalwa Karmapa had a vision in which it was revealed that the reincarnation of the tenth Trungpa Tulku had been born in a village within five days' journey northward from Surmang:

> [The village's] name sounds like two words, Ge and De; there is a family there with two children; the son is the reincarnation. It all sounds rather vague; however, the secretary and the monks of the Dudtsi-til Monastery at Surmang were preparing to go in search of the new Abbott when a second sealed letter was received at the monastery. Rolpa-dorje, the regent abbot of Dudsti-til, called a meeting, opened the letter and read it to the assembled monks. It said that Gyalwa Karmapa had had a second and much clearer vision: "The door of the family's dwelling faces south; they own a big red dog. The father's name is Yeshe-dargye and the mother's Chung and Tzo; the son who is nearly a year old is Trungpa Tulku."[7]

Trungpa took his novice precepts when he reached the age of eight, then immediately entered into retreat for one month. He began his Ngondro, the preliminary practices for the Vajrayana teachings of the Mahamudra, when eleven, and conducted his first empowerment at fourteen. After intensive training in meditation and philosophy, he received ordination as a monk in 1958 at the age of eighteen. The Rinpoche's guru was Jamgon Kongtrul, a lama who had been instructed by the previous Trungpa Tulku. These two tulkus would remain closely associated even throughout the remainder of their lives.

The Chinese Communists invaded the following year. So begins the beautifully courageous, unbelievably prolific, wildly passionate, mystical, often eristic, and enigmatic epoch dance of Chogyam Trungpa Rinpoche across the stage of the world.

After leading a group of three hundred refugees out of Communist-controlled Tibet, traveling by night and eating boiled leather to stave off starvation, Trungpa found sanctuary in India in the home of Freda Bedi in Kalimpong. John Driver, an Oxford graduate, became Rinpoche's English tutor and was the first to suggest that Chogyam Trungpa consider teaching in the West. The Dalai Lama appointed Rinpoche as spiritual advisor to the Young Lamas in New Delhi.

Four years later, in 1963, after the closing of the Tulku schools, through the efforts of John Driver, Freda Bedi, and the Tibet Society of the United Kingdom, Trungpa received a scholarship to Oxford University and set out for England with another lama of his generation, Akong Tulku. It is significant to note that it was Karmapa who sent these representatives of the Kagyu lineage to England. Soon after, Gyalwa Karmapa would direct other lamas to found centers in Great Britain and monasteries across France. His Holiness's plan for the West was on track.[8]

Jamgon Kongtrul Tulku, Trungpa Tulku, and Akong Tulku would for the most part remain close associates, especially in the political arena, in the search for Gyalwa Karmapa's successor.

Trungpa Rinpoche's curriculum at Oxford included the study of comparative religion, philosophy, and the fine arts, and a disciplined effort to polish his English skills, with John Driver still his language instructor. And according to Rick Fields in *How the Swans Came to the Lake,* the young Tibetan man-about-town, in his romp in Oxford and London, did not miss much.

During those university days, the senior bhikkhu of the English Sangha Vihara suggested to Trungpa that he and Akong assume responsibility for a retreat center, Johnstone House, in Dumfriesshire, Scotland. Judging that Westerners did have the capacity for the contemplative life, the Tibetans took over the center and renamed it Samye Ling Meditative Center, after the first Tibetan monastery, founded by Padmasambhava in the eighth century. This establishment in 1967 represented the first Tibetan Buddhist center in the West. In addition, Trungpa became a resident of Scotland and the first Tibetan ever to become a British subject.[9]

Chogyam Trungpa's brilliance as a scholar and poet soon drew masses of devoted followers not only in England, but also from all over Europe as well as America. In spite of what the Rinpoche considered an activity of rather small scale, with students who seemed to be missing the "point," the center thrived, but not without some problems. Stephen Batchelor tells the tale:

[Trungpa's] gifts as a teacher were only matched by his ability to attract controversy. Many of the students emerged from the anarchic restlessness of the 1960s, their interest in Buddhism fueled by a rejection of society and a yearning for new values glimpsed in a haze of psychedelic intuitions. Trungpa embraced this counter-culture with a degree of openness that alienated his more conventionally minded students. In 1969 he returned his monastic vows and Samye Ling developed a reputation in the local community for wild parties, free sex and the use of drugs. Late one night Trungpa crashed his car into the window of a practical joke shop. He was rushed to Newcastle General Hospital, to emerge many weeks later partially but incurably paralyzed.[10]

Then again, in the Rinpoche's defense, Batchelor indicates that this Tibetan teacher was the first Eastern lama to break the academic mold and use a recognizable colloquial language with a poet's gift for metaphor. Westerners could understand, if they were willing to deeply examine themselves and their own culture. Batchelor explains, "He was the first Asian Buddhist teacher to plunge into the existential plight of a Western culture and to articulate a way out of that dilemma in the language of those undergoing it."[11]

But then Rinpoche managed to compound the controversy surrounding his newly adopted lifestyle. Already defrocked, he stunned the entire community by marrying Diana Pybus, a young, aristocratic Englishwoman and devoted Buddhist. The marriage, his second, generated an intense conflict for the center, with tension and paranoia plaguing its members. He consulted the *I Ching,* and the famed oracle responded with advice to cross the great water. So instead of waging an insular campaign with opponents, Trungpa severed his ties with Samye Ling. Leaving his first child, a son of Tibetan descent, in England for the meantime, the couple flew to Toronto, Canada. They would wait there until United States visas were ready and then cross the border to Barnet, Vermont, where a group of his students from Samye Ling, Americans, had bought a 434-acre farm that was being refitted as a meditation center. The place had been named, again upon advice of the *I Ching,* Tail of the Tiger. It was May 1970.[12]

A series of lectures from Samye Ling had been published

in book form, *Meditation in Action,* as had an early biography, *Born in Tibet.* As a result, he was offered a teaching position at the University of Colorado. After a journey across the U.S., Trungpa settled in Boulder and began the foundation work for what would become his imposing and powerful Tibetan Buddhist world organization.[13]

It was a grassroots system from the very beginning. First there was a rented house for meetings, Anitya Bhavan ("House of Impermanence") and then a city center for Buddhist activities, a formal meditation facility named Karma Dzong, meaning "the Buddha-activity fortress." Soon 360 acres were bought west of Fort Collins, Colorado, and the Rocky Mountain Dharma Center came into being. Sitting, or meditations, became much more disciplined, and month-long retreat cabins were constructed at both the Rocky Mountain Center and at Tail of the Tiger.

Cutting through Spiritual Materialism was published in 1973. In the wake of its popularity, Trungpa began to enjoy national notoriety. People began sitting and studying together at urban meditation centers that sprang up all across America and in Canada. Rinpoche called these centers Dharmadhatu, which translates as "Space of Dharma." In 1973 the entire international network of centers was consolidated into a single system referred to as Vajradhatu, with its organizational offices and coordination center in Boulder, Colorado, charged with the task of overseeing and unifying the "present and future." By 1974 the Naropa Institute, a liberal arts college in Boulder, had been established and accredited. Trungpa Rinpoche also created the Nalanda Foundation, a nonsectarian educational foundation that included a psychotherapeutic care facility, the Maitri Institute, which was developed on a ninety-acre plot in Connecticut. Another retreat center, Dorje Khyung Dzong, had been established in a remote area of southern Colorado, a giant ranch near Crestone, and the first Vajradhatu Seminary study retreat for advanced students had convened in Jackson Hole, Wyoming. In addition, there was a preschool system in place, a credit union, a very active theatre group, and of course, Tail of the Tiger. It would still be two years before Rinpoche would make the decision to divide his entire curriculum methodology into two separate systems. One was the traditional Buddhist path, the other a nonreligious, secular approach to Enlightenment, through the understanding of self and human nature, which would be called Shambhala. This Sacred Path of the Warrior drew its inspiration from the mythical kingdom of Shambhala, a system Trungpa implemented, which embraces and develops the simple and universal human quality of basic goodness. In the meantime, everything was now in place for the big event. Karmapa was coming to the New World.[14] Rick Fields writes of preparations for the Karmapa's visit:

> When the word reached Boulder that Rangjung Rigpe Dorje, His Holiness the Sixteenth Karmapa, the head of the Karma Kagyu order, was coming to America, the students of Trungpa Rinpoche saw their teacher change almost overnight. This man who had divested himself not only of his robes, but seemingly of anything that was even remotely Tibetan, who smoked, drank, spoke their language and hung out with them was now carefully inspecting swatches of the finest brocade; instructing them how to starch white curtains with rice water; assembling dinner services from the best crystal, china and silver . . . driving himself to exhaustion . . . going without sleep for days on end, personally overseeing the smallest details, at times taking vacuum cleaner, needle and thread, and iron in hand. Nothing was spared, including himself.[15]

The way had been cleared by one of Karmapa's Tantric masters, the seventy-year-old Kalu Rinpoche. Kalu's first visit to Europe, Canada, and America came in 1971, in what was actually an appraisal tour, an inspection of the work being accomplished by those lamas who were the first to be sent out from Rumtek. In North America, Vancouver, Canada, became Kalu Rinpoche's main seat and center of activities. Kalu set up Karmapa's main Central European seat in Dordogne, France, which is just north of the Pyrenees. This lama was a true power in the Karma Kagyu lineage. When this Rinpoche spoke, everyone listened. Of Chogyam Trungpa, the venerable Kalu said:

> Trungpa Rinpoche was already teaching here and the characteristic style he had found it necessary to adopt was to present Buddhism from the point of view of Americans. Instead of teaching in the traditional manner, he found many skillful ways of presenting the teachings in the light of worldly fields of knowledge, so those unacquainted with

Buddhism could adapt their thinking to the Buddhist view. In this way he was gradually able to introduce the teachings to a large number of people.

This was a splendid undertaking, made possible by his own personal qualities, his superb command of English, and the fact that he was to reside regularly in the United States.[16]

Kalu Rinpoche obviously approved. It was time for His Holiness to come and see for himself, and to consolidate Kagyu Tibetan Buddhism in the West. He left Rumtek in 1974 with a party of twelve that included Sister Palmo, Freda Bedi.[17]

The sixteenth Karmapa arrived in New York City on September 18, 1974, was ceremoniously welcomed by Trungpa, then was taken to Bodi Field, the home of Mr. and Mrs. C. T. Shen, on Long Island. Mr. Shen had come from Hong Kong in 1946 and built an extraordinarily successful steamship freight company that operated on the Great Lakes. He and his wife Nancy were perhaps the most important supporters of Buddhism in America and great friends and benefactors of Karmapa. The Shens would become big players in the Karma Kagyu system in the United States.[18]

Karmapa, while in New York, performed empowerments and teachings continually, including a Black Crown Ceremony. For Trungpa Rinpoche, this visit served as a landmark confirming that the Dharma had actually taken root in America and that he had played a significant part in the transition from Tibet. Trungpa Rinpoche stated, "His Holiness issued a proclamation confirming the existence of Buddhism in America and the fulfillment of my role as a Vajra Master, further empowering me as Vajracarya, a spiritual master of the highest level."[19]

From New York, the entourage traveled to Vermont, where His Holiness changed the Tiger's name to Karme Cho-kyi-ling, "Dharma Place of the Karma Kagyu," succinctly called Karme Choling. A tour of the United States followed, during which thousands were able to receive his blessing. Texas was not one of the stops.[20]

One fundamental need was to establish a single Karma Kagyu administrative center and traditional monastery for the United States. The Shens offered property, financial support, and administrative assistance. In 1975, emissaries of Karmapa stayed with the Shens for several months, organizing the foundation for the Kagyu's main administration system and the development of a monastery facility. New York City would be the temporary center of activities. Karmapa's system was supposed to be the central nervous system for all Karma Kagyu organizations, but in reality, the entire Kagyu apparatus stood in awe and in the shadow of Chogyam Trungpa Rinpoche's formidable Vajradhatu.[21]

Khenpo Karthar Rinpoche

It was at this time that Mr. Shen arranged for plane tickets and sponsorship for the entry into the United States of the venerable Khenpo Karthar Rinpoche, Karmapa's choice as abbot and resident teacher for his North American headquarters. In time, Khenpo Karthar Rinpoche would be the second Karma Kagyu lama to establish the "Whispered Lineage" brand of Tibetan Buddhism in the Lone Star State.

Temporarily settling in New York City, in two years, the Karma Triyana Dharmachakra, Karmapa Rangjung Rigpe Dorje's main seat in the United States, came into being on a mountain above Woodstock, New York, utilizing Mead's, an old summer hotel, as its primary facility.[22]

This Kagyu national nerve center itself is referred to as the KTD (Karma Triyana Dharachakra), while across the United States the satellite centers are called KTC (Karma Thegsum Choling) centers.

His Holiness the Sixteenth Gyalwa Karmapa paid four visits to the United States, his last being in 1981, when he passed away in a hospital in Zion, Illinois, on November 5, at the age of fifty-eight.

Khenpo Karthar was born in the eastern Tibetan province of Kham in 1924, the fourth child in a self-sufficient nomadic family. Rinpoche was taught to read and write by his parents, and at twelve he was sent to the Thrangu Monastery, where he studied rituals and prayers for six years. Khenpo Kathar met the sixteenth Karmapa when eighteen years old and at twenty received his ordination from the previous Tai Situ Rinpoche in Tibet's Palpung Monastery, the seat of the Situ incarnates. Tai Situ, then, is considered Khenpo Karthar's root guru. Again a formidable closeness was forged between two tulkus and would grow into a powerful political alliance.

Tibet to Texas: The West Inherits the Jewels of a Diaspora 87

Following the Kagyu system, there soon followed a one-year solitary retreat and later the traditional three-year, three-month, and three-day retreat. During these three years of seclusion and intensive meditation, Rinpoche saw only his master, one retreat attendant, and nine colleagues also in retreat at the Thrangu Monastery. Even though it was Rinpoche's wish to spend the rest of his life in meditation, this was not how it worked out at all. Following another single-year retreat, Khenpo Karthar was placed in a special school for advanced studies in Buddhist metaphysics, psychology, philosophy, and logic.[23]

Thus, at thirty, having completed his training, Rinpoche entered the world, traveling throughout Tibet and teaching small groups about the nature of the Dharma. But everything changed when the Chinese came. It was 1959.

As for so many Tibetan monks, escape was perilous: surviving without food, eating snow to deal with dehydration, fleeing through a swamp with Chinese soldiers visibly in pursuit. The ordeal lasted two and a half months. After help was received from Karmapa at Tsurphu, the Bhutanese border was reached, but the government would allow entry for no one. A month was spent at the blockaded border, during which time the lama witnessed more than a thousand deaths by starvation. Through the efforts of the Dalai Lama, sanctuary was at last granted in India, and life began again.

More than fifteen hundred monks gathered in the Indian city of Buxa, with the purpose of organizing a Tibetan community and preserving the Dharma. Khenpo Rinpoche remained in Buxa for eight years, working as a teacher. In 1967 he was sent to Rumtek, Karmapa's monastery in Sikkim, for a two-year stint as an instructor of monks, after which there were a number of assignments in both India and Bhutan, each usually a single year in duration. Returning to Rumtek in 1975 for a short period, Rinpoche was again sent to a monastery in Bhutan for a year, then again called back to Karmapa's seat. This time, everything would change, permanently. The new job would be fundamentally different from anything that had gone before. Gyalwa Karmapa was sending Khenpo Karthar Rinpoche to the United States to be his representative in America, with the title of Choje Lama, superior Dharma master. In February of 1976, Rinpoche was on an airplane bound for New York City to begin a new life.[24]

Transplated from a farming village, Rabshi, in Kham to the

Big Apple, Khenpo Karthar was stranger in a strange land, but not for long. There would be many who wanted to listen to what this Tibetan lama had to say. From the North American Karma Kagyu center in Woodstock, New York, the Venerable Khenpo Karthar and his Vajrayana teachings would affect the lives of many Americans and in time even find their way into the very heart of Texas. Then again, another Tibetan, a lama with equally exemplary reputation but of a new generation, would soon find himself facing west.

Jamgon Kongtrul Rinpoche

When Karma Lodro Chokyi Senge was a year and a half old, he was recognized by Karmapa as the third incarnation of Jamgon Kongtrul Rinpoche, offered titles and robes, and enthroned by His Holiness at Rumtek Monastery. From that time on, he was inseparable from Gyalwang Karmapa, who supervised his education from the very beginning. Rinpoche was part of Karmapa's entourage on his final tour of the United States in 1980. After Karmapa's death in 1981, Jamgon Kongtrul continued his work for the Karma Kagyu lineage by inspiring and founding study groups, retreat centers, and social projects such as schools for underprivileged children in India, housing for elderly Tibetans, and medical centers for Tibetans still displaced. There were sponsorship programs for children and monks, preservation work for monasteries, retreat centers, and even a restoration program for Tibetan art. A network of foundations in North America as well as Europe and Asia was established to support each project. In honor of the sixteenth Karmapa, Rangjung Rigpe Dorje, Jamgon Kongtrul named the system the Rigpe Dorje Foundation. It was founded in 1986. There are only two Rigpe Dorje centers in North America, one in Montreal and the other in San Antonio, Texas. Jamgon Kongtrul, then, is the third Tibetan lama to establish the Karma Kagyu order in the Lone Star State.

The first Jamgon Kongtrul Rinpoche, Jamgon Kongtrul Lodro Thaye, was born in 1813 in eastern Tibet. Lodro Thaye's fame lay in his participation in the nonsectarian Buddhist system known as the Rime ("unbiased or nonsectarian") movement. This scholarly renaissance integrated texts from both the ancient and new schools. It incorporated teachings from those hidden treasures or terma, texts from the "oral" or Kagyu lineage, as well as teachings of Tantric or pure vision. These were brought together into a treatise or opus called the Five Treasuries of Knowledge.[25] The second Jamgon Kongtrul, Khyentse Oser, was born in 1902 and passed away in 1952, a master of the Mahamudra and an extraordinary teacher of the Five Treasuries. The founder of the Rigpe Dorje Foundation, the third Jamgon Kongtrul, Karma Lodro Chokyi Senge, has been described as "A perfect guide of unequalled kindness, whose aspirations, activity, and accomplishments for the precious Dharma and sentient beings in general, and the Kagyu lineage in particular have been a wondrous light in these dark times."[26]

On April 26, 1992, Jamgon Kongtrul Rinpoche, one of Karmapa's closest disciples, was killed in a car crash in Sikkim on the highway between Kalimpong and Siliguri while trying to avoid hitting a group of birds that had suddenly appeared in the roadway. It must be mentioned that Jamgon Kongtrul was one of the four regents responsible for identifying the seventeenth incarnation of the Karmapa, a task that at the time had become uncommonly complicated. Jamgon Kongtrul's unfortunate and premature departure would certainly mean a great deal to the unity and future of the Karma Kagyu lineage.[27]

Labrang is the Tibetan word for an association of disciples who are devoted to carrying out the activities of a Rinpoche. The Labrang is also considered the custodian of all the sacred articles, which are held in safekeeping until everything can be given to the next reincarnation. With the guidance of Dzongchen Ponlop and Khenpo Tsultrim Gyamtso Rinpoche, the Labrang has continued the annual Treasury of Knowledge program of study in the Alamo City.

The announcement was made in October 1997 of the recognition of the fourth incarnation of Jamgon Kongtrul. The child had been born in 1995 in Nepal and currently resides in the Pullahari Monastery, which overlooks the Katmandu valley. Needless to say, the San Antonio sangha anxiously awaits this Rinpoche's first visit.[28]

Lama Ole Nydahl

The fourth lama to institute the Karma Kagyu system in Texas is not of Tibetan descent, in this incarnation anyway, but rather Danish. Tracking Ole Nydahl and his wife Hannah's journey from rebellious, "druggie" libertines to disciples of the sixteenth Karmapa and founders of Karma Kagyu centers worldwide, and the eventual creation of Diamond Way Buddhism, is a daunting task. First one must trace the couple's transition from one lifestyle to another. Then there must be some description of the effort required in obtaining the teachings themselves. But most importantly and most challenging is the responsibility of describing adequately the struggle in dealing with the exigency of interpreting intelligently the deep wisdom of Vajrayana Buddhism for the self-indulgent West, and the building of a durable bridge between races, cultures, and individual human differences. Going west is one thing, but going to the East, becoming something else, and then returning with an alien message and asking for acceptance by both worlds is a much different and more difficult task.

Ole Nydahl was fortunate to have been born into a loving family that provided well both materially and emotionally. Since his father was a college professor, there was no lack of intellectual stimulation. Still, Ole was restless and wild. After military service in 1961, he attended college, engaged in professional fistfighting, and completed a doctoral dissertation on Aldous Huxley. Using pot and LSD led to dealing drugs for friends. He had adventures on the Continent, in Africa, and in the Middle East, and, most fortunately, found Hannah. They had built tree houses together as children. After meeting again at college in Copenhagen, together they tested the extreme edge of life. They witnessed the loss of many friends to that way of life, so they steadied themselves and married in 1968. Hannah was twenty-two and Ole twenty-seven. Today Ole advises, "Don't do drugs! Nothing good comes of them. The damage that does not appear at once, comes later and is difficult to repair. In order to reach Enlightenment, we need nothing but our minds, here and now, and the right teachings."[29]

While on holiday, on a flight from Bombay to Indonesia in 1967, something powerful happened. Luminous cloud formations poured over the Himalayas, making the heart remember. Hannah and Ole, watching the clouds, decided to honeymoon in Nepal. They had incidentally purchased, as a travel book, *Tibetan Yoga and the Secret Doctrines,* which happened to be steeped in Kagyu insight. These arcane secrets, author Evans-Wentz wrote, must be plumbed: "Indeed it is the root-doctrine of all the principal faiths of our common humanity that there is innate in man the Light, that the light shines in the Darkness, and that the Light, in virtue of methods which we call yogic, eventually overwhelms the Darkness, as that there remains naught save the Light."[30]

The newly married Danish couple were given silver bracelets in Katmandu by Buddha Laximi, a Tibetan refugee of Karma Kagyu persuasion, and once back home, the bracelets were responsible for some miraculous, inexplicable healings and inspired a return trip to the Nepalese capital. Hannah and Ole returned to the woman Buddha Laximi and thus were led indirectly to Lopon Tsechu Rinpoche, witnessed the Kagyupa's miraculous dissolution into a mere transparency, and ultimately received the Karma Kagyu lama's blessing. Lopon Tsechu became Ole and Hannah's first teacher. The Rinpoche said that he would see the pair again in one year. Ole's first meditations were practiced in a Copenhagen jail's hospital, and after letters by the couple to their teacher and a five-day meditation by Rinpoche, they received an unexpected invitation to accompany friends on a third adventure to the East.

It was December of 1969. For the first time in thirteen years, the Karmapa had come to a place, Katmandu, where Westerners could see him. Following a Black Crown Ceremony, a friend of Buddha Laximi, Doctor Jigme, arranged for the Nydahls to have a private audience with Gyalwa Karmapa. The meeting was magical. When Karmapa placed his hands on the couple's heads, their world changed forever. A long spiritual evolution was underway. The use of any drugs whatsoever, even alcohol, was no longer acceptable. Once, Ole had made his way in the world as a boxer. That, too, was over. Hannah and Ole Nydahl had become Karmapa's first Western students and his first Western personal disciples.[31]

There was another year's stay, this time for intensive training. The foundation was laid by Kalu Rinpoche at his monastery in Sonada, Sikkim. Karmapa had directed the couple to stay and learn through long, sustained instruction.

And so it followed throughout the fall of 1971. The preliminaries were horrendous: prostrations (111,111 of them), and the complete Ngondro, involving sixteen hours of meditating a day, to burn the seeds of future karma. Following the introductory work came the formalized Bodhisattva vow initiation, the outer version to free energies for spiritual development, the secret or

Tantric involvement in order to transform the ordinary world into the pure land of a Buddha. This work was undertaken at Rumtek, under the direction of His Holiness Kunzig Shamarpa, the senior of the four highest Kagyu incarnates. This also gave Ole and Hannah the opportunity to become acquainted with Situ, Gyaltsap, and Jamgon Kongtrul rinpoches, the other three ranking tulkus. *Tulku* translates as "illusionary body." The mandala-offering practice was competed in the Bhutia Basty, a monastery dedicated to Buddhist protectors, built in Darjeeling.[32]

In the autumn of 1971, the Karmapa decided it was time to take the activities of all Buddhas to the West. Kalu Rinpoche was being sent to America. He would be the first to bring the Vajrayana teachings in their undiluted form to North America. And to his two Danish disciples Karmapa said, "You go home."

Ole and Hannah, confused and crushed, asked, "Home? Where's home?"

"Home to Europe, of course." And Karmapa smiled. After two years of training, the greatest challenge of Hannah and Ole's life was to begin.[33]

After greeting parents and friends in Copenhagen, the couple secluded themselves in a Swedish forest cabin and, using notes taken from the teachings of Kalu Rinpoche, wrote *Teaching on the Nature of Mind*, the first of many books to be produced for those on the Diamond Way. Emerging from the woods, the next need was money. They took jobs as teachers and janitors and worked day and night. When the coffers were full, they felt that a return to Asia was necessary.[34]

Refugee camps in southern India were visited followed by a reunion with Lopon Tsechu in Katmandu, where Hannah and Ole were taught the Milam, or dream meditation. The dream meditation produces a state of mind in which the "observer" is there, whether one is awake or asleep. In this condition, the mind learns to recognize its projections and to consciously influence them:

> One becomes very aware also that our so-called waking state is really like a dream, that the world of our normal daily consciousness is nothing but a set of projections that we share with others. As this experience roots itself in the mind, the disturbing feelings which come from our be-

lief that "things are real" dissolve by themselves and great openness, great free space, appears in the mind.[35]

As Paul Sherwood puts it,

> We can only enter silence on inwardly bended knee and recognize that in its fathomless presence we are as nothing and that is what we are in reality: no-thing, which is the silent witness who is always present but never observed even as silence is the unnoticed eternal backdrop to the show of life. We are silence, and when all is said and done, to silence we return.[36]

The Westerners stayed with Rinpoche for six weeks, and then they headed for Rumtek, meeting Karmapa outside of Gangtok. The stay in Rumtek was short but extraordinarily meaningful. In Ole's words:

> The Karmapa was letting us look over his shoulder as never before, constantly showing us things that we would not fully understand until we also became responsible for others. He arranged for us to be there when he gave advice on the running of centers and retreats, when explaining which practices he wanted done and how. Frequently, he asked what we thought, how we would do a thing like that in the West, and he always listened to our ideas but never said "yes" or "no." With certainty, our next meditation or dream would then bring the evident solution.[37]

One day, quite suddenly, Karmapa again said that it was time to go back to Europe. He gave the couple a special blessing that authorized them to found centers in his name not only in Denmark, but throughout Europe and even worldwide. Gyalwa Karmapa promised to constantly guide them and to allow his transmission and blessing to flow through their work. Ole saw himself as an emanation of a Buddhist protector-deity and defender of Tibet against Chinese aggression in previous lives. The work would continue with just a little twist. Ole and Hannah landed in Copenhagen in October of 1972.[38]

Ole and Hannah's first center was their old VW bus, then a rented basement in medieval Copenhagen, and finally, with the generous help of a follower of Karmapa, a Swedish woman named Maria, a forty-acre farm on a high moor on the border between Denmark and Sweden. In time, Ole and Hannah assisted in founding hundreds of Karma Kagyu centers throughout Western and Eastern Europe, North and South America, Mexico, Australia, and in New Zealand.[39]

There was, nonetheless, a "title" problem for Ole. Since living in celibacy was not an option, what was his formal designation to be? The choice would be of great importance, because it would confer legitimacy, and in feudal structures, ceremonial designations are often synonymous with truth. It would have been simplest to refer to Ole Nydahl as "lama," as it related to what he actually did, but this was not possible because Kalu Rinpoche believed that lamas had to live in at least official celibacy. As Ole explains,

> The problem was that there existed no Tibetan term for my activity. Tibetan Buddhism had hardly moved from the country for a thousand years, and many things we had developed were new; the guided meditations in Western languages, and empowering selected friends to give the first teachings while also relying on feedback from the group process. Never before had there been such a grass roots movement ... Shamarpa first tried the title "Kyorpon," traveling teacher, but that only covered the preserving aspect of the work. Not until one late evening, sitting with the Bhutanese queen mother in her residence in Darjeeling, did he find a title that both expressed responsibility and left room for untraditional activity. With a big smile he said: "You will be our Buddhist Master."[40]

Shamarpa's pronouncement had immense importance for the future. Ole's recognition as a teacher of Mahamudra enormously increased the power and breadth of the Kagyu lineage. Suddenly Lama Ole's students were on the "inside"; they had been accepted into the Tibetan fold. The lay and yogic work founded on Western premises had now also been officially accepted. "It was an historical moment," wrote Ole, "some days later when I held the document in my hand. Blessed with Kunzig Shamarpa's signature and Jamgon Kongtrul Rinpoche's seal, it tied us together closer than ever."[41]

Hannah Nydahl would become one of Shamarpa's translators, both in Europe and Asia. The Red Hat Lama made his first visit to Europe in 1981, and the following year he was teaching in the KTD Center in Woodstock. Hannah was often present in Shamarpa's company in India, Europe, and America. A close bond and confidence was the result. This closeness would develop into a powerful alliance when, following Rangjung Rigpai Dorje's death, the Karmapa War started.[42]

Lama Ole had lived in the United States during 1958 and 1959 as an exchange student in Connecticut. With Hannah, he returned in 1976, this time to New York City to be with Karmapa and his entourage during His Holiness's second journey to the States. During this visit, they spent quality time with Karmapa, were heard on radio broadcasts over a New York station, rescued Mr. Shen and his jeep from an impossible quagmire deep in a forest, went on a sortie to Chicago for a teaching presentation, and experienced uncomfortable relations with the Dharmadhatu guards, or Dorje Kasung, khaki-clad troopers representing the old Tibetan Garpa tradition and assigned to Karmapa. They also felt an acute discomfort with Chogyam Trungpa Rinpoche himself, a sensation that would continue to escalate. Then they returned to Europe to act as reinforcement for Kalu Rinpoche in France.

The venerable Kalu had inspected Ole's system in 1974, establishing a center of his own in Paris. Lopon Tsechu had watched Hannah and Ole build the Kagyu lineage from nothing in Central Europe and had fondly approved of the results. On his first visit to Europe, Hannah had translated for Jamgon Rinpoche, and together they had visited all of Lama Ole's centers from north to south. Another inspection had been carried out by Tenga Rinpoche. In 1990, Topga Rinpoche, whom Karmapa had appointed as general secretary of Rumtek, would come to Copenhagen, and a permanent bond would be forged with the Nydalhs. Each of these associations would have intense ramifications on political alignments in the years to come.[43]

Alone this time in 1979, Lama Ole taught for a short period at the Kagyu center in the Bronx, made a reappearance on the radio circuit, and then took off for the West Coast, Alaska, and Mexico. A year later, he and Hannah were back at Woodstock briefly before heading west. There was a scheduled speaking engagement in Colorado at the Chogyam Trungpa's Dharmadhatu headquarters, but the program was suddenly canceled with no notification for Lama Ole. No official explanation was ever offered. So it was on to California, Los Angeles, San Francisco, and then north to San Luis Obispo, and a visit with lots of Danish relatives and friends. This San Luis connection would prove significant in the train of events that would eventually lead Ole Nydahl's distinctive brand of Karma Kagyu to Texas.[44]

In 1984, Lama Ole was invited to speak in a Berkeley Dharmadhatu by a coordinator of Danish extraction. Evidently, the evening's affair was looked upon with a great deal of disapproval by the authorities in Boulder. Soon, "wanted" posters picturing Ole began to appear in Dharmadhatus across the country, with a psychological profile comparing Lama Ole with Rudra, the closest thing in Buddhism to pure evil. The Danish lama attributed the entire episode to his increased popularity in the Karma Kagyu evolution worldwide, which was interestingly interpreted as a threat by others in the Kagyu hierarchy, particularly Chogyam Trungpa.

The depth of the conflict between these two Kagyu lamas had to be much more complicated than mere jealousy, but the question was whether the hostility would prove to be bigger than Kagyu Buddhism itself. Hannah and Ole certainly employed nontraditional activities in their practices, but so did Chogyam Trungpa. The difference seems, however, to be in the application. The Tibetan's changes were in lifestyle around the fringes that gained the appellation of "Crazy Wisdom" and "Beat Buddhism." On the other hand, the Danes were actually changing the rituals to fit a new culture. For example, the Nydahls stopped all bowing before gurus and altars because they felt that it simply conflicted with a Westerner's nature and therefore slowed spiritual development. Regional languages were substituted for Tibetan in Tantric scripts, except for mantras, where the original Sanskrit was maintained. Instead of Bodhisattva "vow," the reference became Bodhisattva "Promise," in order to eliminate the authoritarian edge. Ole reacted strongly against the Asian lamas' treatment of highly educated and independent Westerners as if they were Tibetan children. His opinions ruffled more than a few feathers. Also, Ole insisted on complete disclosure in financial policies, not the feudalistic practice of freewheeling behind a veil of secrecy. The real conservatives, the old-world "good old boys," cringed at this one. Neither did the old line warm to Ole's attitude toward celibacy. To the Dane, such absoluteness only represented a convenient way to escape from the healthy give-and-take of human life.[45]

Lama Ole's goal was to make Buddhism work in the West, employing whatever progressive innovations seemed necessary, keeping Karmapa as the focal point of the order, and disallowing personality cults from contaminating the Kagyu system. There certainly existed the tendency for Tibetan lamas to visit other centers as friends and then try to win their students for themselves. There was even a tendency to stake out territories, not to protect the teaching or students, but most often, in a daze of insecurity, to maintain their own base of power. In Europe, for example, zones of power eventually crystallized. England, Scotland, and Brussels still are controlled by Akong Tulku, while Barcelona belonged to Situ and Thrangu rinpoches. France, Antwerp, and Madrid belonged to Kalu Rinpoche until his death in 1984 at the age of eighty-four. From the Rhine to Vladivostok is Diamond Way territory. These partitions spring from a cultural source—surely it was the way things were always done in Tibet—but more specifically, the inherent difficulties were essentially a backdrop of the fires of the old feudalistic cauldron, and hierarchical systems simply do not function in the democratic West. Lama Ole explains:

> Whenever employed, they attract too many bloodless yes-sayers. Expecting guidance in the simplest matters, they become jealous of each other's closeness to the teacher. In contrast, everyone is empowered through the open model that I call "meritocracy." Having a say through one's devoted contribution, and in the field that one masters, brings both development and cooperation. A central structure only works where true Rinpoches are unimpeachable in their position and delegate the opportunities for growth. Khenpo Karthar does this skillfully in America. He is a shining light among the Tibetans there, non-political and open in spite of the tight administration around him.[46]

Lama Ole does not want his students to commit to anything. He wants to make them independent, not simply cogs in an organizational machine. Freedom, even to make mistakes, is the key to this lama's operation. His argument is that the tightness of authoritarianism does not fit the modern Kagyu yogi mold. Anything that even remotely smells "zombie-like," stiff, or church-ish will inevitably lead to real organizational problems. Students should always show a fine personal discrimination when selecting their path to something as profound as Realization:

> There is no doubt that that the traditional lamas sent [to the West] were too narrow and hierarchical in their thinking. They lacked trust in Westerners, actually their benefactors. Being insecure about our skills, they did not welcome the lamas and gain from what was offered. There was too little respect for the maturity that a rounded life brings, and no attempt to make the highest ideals more accessible. Though Karmapa often said that a half-good teacher was better than none, and that one would learn while teaching as long as one kept the bond to him, the sacred cow which blocks the acceptance of many a gifted teacher, even today, was Kalu Rinpoche's insistence on a three-year group retreat with strict celibacy. This rarely attracts the people we need: strong and outgoing types who can inspire others with their joy. If this retreat had been offered as one possibility among other retreats and naturally having something to offer, things could have been much easier. Then cooperation would have been possible between charismatic lay teachers and those with the traditional education, benefiting all.[47]

Lama Ole's mission, it seems, is to create a lay and yogic organization built on friendship rather than hierarchy, held together by a common trust in the Karmapa, a true grassroots system capable of bringing Buddhism into the twenty-first century as a living transmission. Stephen Batchelor does level the charge that "Nydahl's approach nonetheless has fundamentalist and sectarian overtones."[48] The trouble with zealous sectarianism is that the player must always have one foot firmly planted in the relative world, which can so easily obscure perception from the spiritual realm.

Trungpa Rinpoche's goal was to keep Karma Kagyu Buddhism pure as he envisioned purity to be. His system was much more authoritarian, much more tightly managed, with individually monitored step increments in planned spiritual development for his students. The system would get one there.

One simply had to trust the Rinpoche. Trungpa's true genius lay in the psychological and philosophical penetration of the human soul and its condition, and his genius of communicating his feelings through the writing process. The same could certainly be said of his personal charm when speaking to groups or with individuals. Rinpoche's son wrote of his father:

> His unique gift was that he was able to synthesize the ancient wisdom of Buddhism and transmit it to the West in a clear and concise way that was both meaningful and refreshing—so much so that a new generation of Western practitioners were born.
> Knowing the tremendous hardships and challenges that confronted Chogyam Trungpa, and how he was able to overcome them through his courage, humor, and his faith in the spiritual disciplines of Tibet, I have always found this book [*Born in Tibet*] inspiring.
> Often people would ask him how he was able to adapt to so many diverse cultures, and how he was able to deal with the tremendous hardships of his life. Always his answer would be that it was due to the rigorous traditional training and education that he received in Tibet while young. It might appear to the reader that the Tibet of Chogyam Trungpa's youth was medieval; it seems so distant from today's modern world, and so harsh. Ironically, however, it was this very training, with its simplicity and realness, that gave him the foundation that enabled him to relate with this modern world.[49]

Obviously, the perceptual distance in just how the teachings of the Karma Kagyu should be presented in the West between Chogyam Trungpa Rinpoche and Lama Ole Nydahl lay worlds apart. With Karmapa's death, the "forces that be" in the Karma Kagyu lineage begin to line up in several forms, including those who did and those did not approve of the practices of Lama Ole Nydahl. Or was the whole problem rooted in the simple fact that Ole was not Tibetan?

Hannah and Ole caught up with Karmapa that year in Boulder. He gave the Danes some instructions that would be significantly revealing. First, Lama Ole should support the four lineage holders in every way possible; second, Hannah and Ole should come to Rumtek next year on the first day of the eleventh month with friends; and last, the Danish lama would meet Trungpa Tulku only in Karmapa's presence. All three requests foreboded ill. As it turned out, the eleventh-month date represented the prelude of Karmapa's cremation services following his death in the United States in 1981.[50]

Lama Ole documents in *Riding the Tiger* that during the period of Karmapa's farewell at Rumtek, an incident of some significance occurred. A document was circulated which, if alidated by enough signatures, would have moved the world Karma Kagyu headquarters from Rumtek to Boulder, Colorado, until the next Karmapa was found. Nydahl considered this as nothing more than a play of power politics and objected vociferously. He wanted, in his words, to "Keep the lineage clean." The move withered on the vine, but tensions within the order tightened considerably. In fact, soon after, a letter passed through the world-wide Kagyu system charging Lama Ole with unacceptable conduct with some female students. Nydahl responded by explaining that "It was a turf war. Because of the alcoholic style of Trungpa and his organization we didn't allow them into Europe. That was the real reason for the letter."[52]

Trungpa Rinpoche died on April 4, 1986 (Batchelor, Fields, and Snelling all point to 1987), in an intensive-care unit near his monastic center and newly anointed seat of the international headquarters of the Vajradhatu Buddhist Church in Halifax, Nova Scotia. He was only forty-eight years old. The last seventeen years had been spent in North America. It is astounding how much this Rinpoche accomplished in such a short period of time. Buddhism, in various forms, had been taught in the West for some time, but it was not until Trungpa Rinpoche's direct connection with human beings, through their own language and customs, that the Dharma became real, understandable, and approachable.[53] The Vajra Regent Osel Tendzin writes:

> When Trungpa Rinpoche first presented the buddhadharma in the West, especially in North America, it was as if a bolt illuminated a dark sky.
>
> It will become more apparent in the years to come what a great effect his life will have on all of us. Even at this writing, so soon after his death, the feeling of his short stay with us is penetrating and uncompromising. Those of

us who carry on this tradition are compelled to do so because he showed us how to meet reality face to face, which he presented as the discipline and the path of Enlightened warriorship.... Every moment is, as he would say, living in the challenge, and therefore at every moment we all renew our commitment to living.[54]

But then there was Rinpoche's enigmatic shadow side. Stephen Batchelor first acknowledges that Trungpa found an intelligent and eager audience in the United States that was more than willing to help him realize his vision of establishing the Kagyu tradition within the matrix of American society, drawing upon ancient traditions while responding creatively to contemporary issues.[55] But Professor Batchelor goes on to say:

> This shining achievement was accompanied, however, by an ever-lengthening shadow, the seeds of which were already visible in Scotland. Trungpa developed a reputation for heavy drinking and sexual promiscuity. As his organization grew in power, he formed the Dorje Kasung, initially a volunteer service organization that grew into a bodyguard and finally a khaki-uniformed quasi-military corps. Trungpa's circle assumed eccentric regal trappings through his adaptation of the mythology of the Kalachakra Tantra, a complex Buddhist doctrine with millenarian overtones centered around the quasi-legendary realm of Shambhala. He became known as the "Vidyadhara" ("Knowledge Holder," a title given to him by the Karmapa); his American successor Thomas Rich as the "Vajra Regent Osel Tenzin," and his residence as the "Kapala Court"—replete with courtiers and courtesans.[56]

Thomas Rich would die three years later from HIV, a disaster for both his unsuspecting partners and the entire Vajradhatu community. Rinpoche's organization is now headed by Sawang Osel Rangdrol Mukpo, Chogyam Trungpa's Tibetan son. His formal title is Sakyong ("earth protector") Mipham Rinpoche, as well as the Sawang of Shambhala. Enthronement was held May 14, 1995, in Nova Scotia. In his inaugural address, the Sakyong indicated that there would be no major changes in the goals and administration of the Vajradhatu system.

The legacy and the work that my father did is in itself a complete journey. I've inherited something as he had inherited something. And all of you are inheriting something; all of you, I would say, have inherited along with me. One reason I feel that I am able to do this is because many of you have already been my friends and Advisors and have helped me and you are dharma brothers and sisters, fellow warriors of Shambhala.[57]

In a formal edict presented that evening, the first proclamation issued from the Lion Throne of Shambhala by the Sakyong Mipham Jampal Trinley Dradul Rinpoche, a reference was made to the "Ancient Ones," indicating an historically close association between the Karma Kagyu and Nyingma orders. This reference contains subtle political implications:

The Sakyong Mipham Rinpoche and these disciples and warriors are of one heart in vast vision of the Mukpo lineage. The future of the Mukpo lineage and of the Kingdom of Shambhala depend on the pervasion of this path throughout the world at this time. Thus the practice and propagation of the Shambhala, Kagyu, and Nyingma lineages is the pure expanse of mutual samaya and loyalty.[58]

Whereas the Diamond Way system has recognized Thaye Dorje as the seventeenth Karmapa, the Sakyong's Vajradhatu-Shambhala recognizes another, Ugyen Trinley. Followers of the Nyingma lineage, as well as virtually every other lineage, support the latter, often referred to by his opposition as the Chinese candidate. In essence, then, Lama Ole Nydahl and his supporters find themselves out there all alone in the Karmapa War. This extremely complicated and sensitive story will be approached in chapter 5. But first, Lama Ole must get his Diamond Way to Texas.

There were tours of the States in 1989, 1990, and 1991, the year that the San Francisco group first got started. Austrian Roland Peters, the owner of a very successful line of boutique shops and a long-time friend of both Hannah and Ole, had started meditations at a private house in the city. The system was distinctively that of Lama Ole Nydahl and distinctively European in style. Everyone there was a student of Ole. Jesper Jorgensen, another Dane and Lama Ole's future chief representative in North America, rented, along with Roland, a house at another location, and this became the first formal center in San Francisco. It should be mentioned that Carol Aronoff, now a teacher of the Dharma, sponsored the Marin group in the city. This was a predecessor of what would become the Diamond Way centers. When the need arose for greater distance from neighbors, as well as greater space for activities, a new home was purchased in 1991. This would become the Diamond Way Headquarters for Ole Nydahl's Karma Kagyu Buddhist operation in the United States. This Buddhist facility marked the beginning of Kagyu centers that were exclusively under the aegis of Lama Ole Nydahl. Today the KCLSF system is under the direction of Lama Ole, with the spiritual guidance of Kunzig Shamar Rinpoche, and the Diamond Way's candidate, His Holiness the Seventeenth Karmapa Thaye Dorje.[59]

During that 1991 tour, there was another jaunt up to San Luis Obispo to see relatives. This time, however, a cousin, Dudley Boysen Parrish, arranged for Lama Ole to deliver a major lecture. The gathering represented one of the largest collections of people ever to hear a Kagyu presentation in North America. Cousin Dudley chose a Unitarian church for his gathering. Another cousin, Marilyn (Parrish) Kinsey, Dudley's sister from Houston, Texas, attended. Within four months, Cousin Marilyn would arrange for the use of a Unity church facility for Lama Ole's initial Texas lecture in Friendswood, Texas. From this inaugural presentation, the first Diamond Way sangha would be established in Texas, in the clubhouse of the Bay Wind II, a condo complex in Clear Lake City, not far from the National Aeronautics and Space Administration agency.[60]

No discussion of Diamond Way Buddhism would be complete without including the intellectual and business contributions made by fellow Dane Caty Hartung, one of Lama Ole's closest advisors and companion. Her insights and input are essential and significant in the organization's development.

In review, first there was Chogyam Trungpa's Shambhala system, which initially set up shop in Austin in 1974. Khenpo Karthar's KTD organization from Woodstock then formally found a home in Dallas in 1990, even though a couple had begun meetings in nearby Duncanville four years before. Jamgon Kongtrul's Rip Dorje Foundation was chartered the same year, 1990, in the Alamo City. Finally, in 1992, Ole Nydahl's unique Diamond Way Buddhism entered the Lone Star State in Clear Lake.

How did this movement actually happen, and who were the human beings that made it work? This is their story, a lesson in dedication, introspection, and intellectual endurance; a story of independence and unyielding courage.

Chapter 4

A Grassroots History of Karma Kagyu Buddhism in Texas: The Texas Sanghas

The Karma Kagyu lineage currently has four subsects in the Lone Star State, and all of these are located in five cities. In Austin there is both a Shambhala International and a Diamond Way organization. Dallas has a KTC center and a Shambhala sangha. There are four Diamond Way centers in Houston, one recently established on the University of Houston campus, and a retreat center for which land has been purchased only in the last six months. There is also a Shambhala center in the Heights area of the Bayou City. San Antonio has two sanghas, one Shambhala center, and the single Rigpe Dorje system in the state. Within the Texas A&M system in College Station, there is a quasi–Diamond Way organization. This unusual circumstance will be explained later in the text. Since completion of research, a five-member KTD study group has been organized in Midland, Texas, by Dennis Stratton, 4606 Crockett Street, Midland, Texas 79703. In the state, then, there are twelve Kagyu centers currently in operation.

The first Kagyu sect to make its appearance in Texas was that of Chogyam Trungpa Rinpoche's Shambhala International, in Austin. This story will be told through Mr. Lawrence Wells.

Shambhala International
Austin Center
1702 South Fifth Street, Austin, Texas 78704
Lawrence Wells

Mr. Wells serves as an example of the penetrating and ranging intellect of those who are being drawn to Karma Kagyu Buddhism in Texas. He is employed by the United States Attorney's Office in Austin.

Lawrence grew up a Methodist, in Tyler, but with age he began asking philosophical-religious questions that could not get "themselves" answered. In his college years at the University of Texas, he entered an atheistic phase and then its antithesis, a continuation of the spiritual search. In time, in Austin, he got involved with a yoga group that had a legitimate teacher from New York, with whom he studied for about a year. The guru was killed in an airplane crash. As a result of the loss, those yoga associates began looking for something to fill the void. The name Chogyam Trungpa Rinpoche kept coming up. In a copy of *East-West Journal,* Lawrence found an article written by Trungpa that affected him profoundly. He wanted to know more. The group discovered shortly thereafter that Rinpoche was scheduled to speak in San Antonio at Trinity University. Some in the yoga group, which included Netam Greenleaf, Tom Harris, Mr. Wells, and a few others, made the trip.

Lawrence and his friends were totally unimpressed initially, because Trungpa did not present himself as a typical Tibetan lama. He was dressed in a beautifully tailored western suit, he was smoking, and he had a drink in one hand and a beautiful blonde on the other. The substance of his lecture, however, was fantastic. Mr. Wells remembers, "I realized that a lot of that ... He was just trying to show us that, you know, you start where you are. There is no such thing as, This is a good place to be in or this is not a good way to be. The 'holy trip,' you know. He was plugging holes in that right off the bat. This was in 1974."[1]

Trungpa was invited by the yoga group to visit Austin, and he came twice, speaking once at the university, and then in a hotel downtown. A strong bond developed quickly, and the group asked him in 1975 if he would help initiate and oversee a meditation group. That was it. There was nothing fancy about it, no books, no philosophy, just simple Buddhist meditation.

The previous yoga assembly, now a meditation group, first met in a house on Baylor Street. During the next four years, the address changed twice. In 1979, property was purchased from a local Pentecostal church, creating at last a permanent home at 1702 South Fifth Street, for the first Karma Kagyu center in Austin and in the entire state. Immediately, Mr. Wells and members planted on the gently sloping lawn near the main entranceway a small tree that is purported to be a descendent of the Bo (Wisdom) tree (*ficus religiosa*—Indian fig, a relative of the banyan) under which Gautama Siddhartha experienced Enlightenment.[2]

Teachers were sent from Boulder to Austin, usually senior students, to help with meditation practices. Sangha members were brought along ever so slowly, with exact purpose. Wells explains,

> Through the years [Trungpa] added a few things and things expanded as he told us a little bit more. We had no idea what we were getting into. That is why he brought us along so slowly. The fact is that it is so much deeper, so much more complex and more everything than you can imagine, both philosophically and practice-wise, everything. I mean, I'm not talking about a cult thing. Nobody is required to do much of anything. There was just so much more to practicing Buddhism than anyone imagined.[3]

The group was first taught the Hinayana or Theravada system of Shamatha ("dwelling in tranquility") meditation that leads to Vipassana, or insight, meditation. Trungpa Rinpoche, it seems, insisted on building a firm foundation long before the Tantras were even mentioned. In Trungpa's system, the usual grounding period between the basic meditations and visualizations is two years. At one time, it was simply a requirement. One is expected to mediate at least thirty hours a month, for about an hour each day. When the proper amount of meditation hours have been logged, a member is qualified to attend a seminary, which leads to the Vajrayana practices. To continue development, one is expected to attend a month-long meditation retreat, a Datu (Dharmadhatu—space of mind) to qualify for the visualization preliminaries, or Ngondro. The Datus are held at the Rocky Mountain Shambhala Center near Ft. Collins, Colorado.

> I just got back yesterday with my little girl. They were doing a family camp there ... They have the "Rites of Passage," which is a week-long thing. They have plenty of time to play, but they have classes that teach things like flower arranging, calligraphy, kito, which is Zen archery.

It's all mixed in. At the end of that, they have a two-hour ceremony of the "Rites of Passage" for the children. It's a beautiful ceremony. We wanted her to do that. It would be great if the Christian tradition had something like this.⁴

After a Datu is completed, one can request permission to start Vajrayana. If approved, transmission is granted to begin the Ngondro, the beginning of the Tantra. One keeps in mind that even when the advanced meditations are being practiced, Shamatha is still and always will be present. According to Trungpa, it is the fundamental container, and one is expected to practice Shamatha until "one no longer has a butt."

Lawrence Wells took his vows in 1976. Taking the Bodhisattva Vow is also the entry into the Mahayana practice, through which the student becomes acquainted with the philosophical meaning of "emptiness." Mr. Wells explained that the meaning of emptiness can be found in the reality that "things" have, and have never had any intrinsic nature of their own.

> You must understand what is meant by "empty." It doesn't mean that things are empty. It means that things have no intrinsic nature. Everything is impermanent, which is one of the four parts of existence.... Everything that is created will not last no matter what it is, even atomic particles. They will even disappear, will go away. Listen now, I have some problem with that turning into some sort of theism or God worship, worshiping an individual, or some cult sort of stuff. You have to realize that everything is basically empty. You also must understand the function of the guru that transmits the teachings. He is not to be worshiped as a god. But to do that you have to go through a lot of things that may look to an outsider like some sort of very deep religious Catholic ritual.⁵

The Shambhala system, according to Mr. Wells, is rather eclectic and has close ties with many of the other orders and sects, and with individuals within those organizations. Chogyam Trungpa was not only a Kagyu tulku, but also a tulku of the Nyingma tradition. He introduced many Nyingma teachings into Shambhala. When Karmapa was establishing the KTD system in Woodstock, Trungpa was intimately involved. Khenpo Karthar, abbott of KTD, has taught in the Austin

Shambhala center several times. KTD monks often attend Datu at the Rocky Mountain Dharma Center. When Khenpo Karthar Rinpoche traveled to Dallas to found the KTC center there, Lawrence met him and assisted. Trungpa's son, the Sakyong, the spiritual leader of Shambhala International, was born in Bodh Gaya as the reincarnation of Nipahm Rinpoche, one of the most famous Tibetan lamas ever to live. Nipahm Rinpoche was Nyingma. At the advanced meditation levels, the Nyingma practice is virtually the same as the Kagyu. The Dalai Lama, a Gelugpa, has recognized the same Karmapa candidate, Ugyen Trinley, as the KTD. So has Shambhala International, the Rigpe Dorje Foundation, and the Nyingma organization. It is obvious, then, that Shambhala International and the other Tibetan traditions interact actively and currently have an excellent working relationship that seems to be genuinely close and personal. The same cannot be said for Ole Nydahl and his Diamond Way. About Lama Ole, Mr. Wells commented, "I really can't say much personally, only that he is a controversial person. Mr. Nydahl is considered a lama and a teacher, but at one point something happened at one of the KTC centers and he is no longer welcome, or at the Shambhala centers. He has never been down here."[6]

Mr. Wells explained that Trungpa Rinpoche wanted to make sure that Buddhism was established as an orthodox, straight-line Buddhism, like that with which he grew up with in Tibet, but with a bigger vision.

> After Oxford, he spent two years over here before he ever taught a word, just learning about America and Western culture. Tibet was gone. This was a new country and he became immersed in it. I mean, he went to discos, talk shows, you name it. He could talk with you just as though [he was] raised in the Bronx. So he became real familiar with American culture. He realized that America was not Tibet, that we do not have a feudal system over here, that it is very important that people have the ability, the chance to enter a spiritual path if they want to. So he wrestled with it for a long time. Finally he decided to introduce the Shambhala teachings . . . for people who might not be interested in the "isms" of Christianity, Judaism, or even Buddhism, but just want a spiritual life. The principles obviously had to be the same and the meditation practices had to be about the same, but they are different

paths. It's like two railroad tracks going together. Most of us do both. But a lot of people only do Shambhala . . . He wanted people to realize that you didn't have to be a Tibetan yogi, to sit in a cave, to attain some sort of realization or have a spiritual life.[7]

Trungpa Rinpoche felt, Lawrence acknowledged, that it was inappropriate to try to make Americans into Tibetans. As a result, Shambhala International, from its conception, translated much of the Tibetan into English. Admittedly, some Tibetan teachers still insist upon the traditional route, with the exception of the mantras, which are usually written and recited in Sanskrit. Still, the practices themselves are orthodox as far as the Tibetan Buddhism and the Vajrayana are concerned. Shambhala has an active and prolific translation committee.

Trungpa once said that we are not really Buddhist, but your children will be. You are white Christians. Tradition is so ingrained in us. It just doesn't go away like that. That theistic stuff, that's tradition, that there is a God that can do this. And maybe there is. Our point of view is that you discover this through meditation and if you do that's fine. It's up to you.[8]

Shambhala has also been bold enough to face the issue of women in a male-dominant society. According to Mr. Wells, at least 50 percent of the leadership positions in Vajradhatu are held by women.

If fact, before Trungpa died, there was a group of women he empowered to have complete control over everything. He gave them the power even to fire the regent if they wanted to. So things are changing. This has been a big issue in the world of Buddhism. Anne Klein of the Nyingma organization in Houston, Dawn Mountain, has written a great deal about Buddhism and feminism. She is head of the Department of Religion at Rice University.[9]

The sixteenth Karmapa was in Boulder in 1976, and Trungpa Rinpoche's organization underwrote the expenses. A busload from Austin went to Colorado for the weekend. Mr. Wells was among the gang, even though he had not at the time completed his seminar training. While wandering around in the Boulder Mall, just killing time before the Black Crown Ceremony, he noticed an old monk sitting alone at a picnic table drinking a Coke. The man motioned for Lawrence to come over. The monk smiled and shook his hand. He could not speak English. There were other monks around, shopping and looking in windows.

> A couple of them came over and one asked His Holiness if he and I would like to go shopping with them. There was a huge entourage. It was incredible. I was so stupid. I didn't know what was going on. I didn't know who he was until that night when they brought him up on his throne. I didn't know who he was! It was incredible! I knew that he was someone special, but I just didn't know what. So I was lucky. We are devoted to Karmapa and the Kagyu lineage and Trungpa.[10]

The prediction is that it will be a very long time, perhaps five hundred years, before Americans reach the stage where Enlightenment is possible for those who have taken the plunge. Aggression and materialism, it seems, are the great cultural impediments to Realization. Buddhism in America seems to attract the more intellectual, professional types, and a smattering of artists such as painters, dancers, and musicians. It might be easier and quicker to become Enlightened if one becomes a monk or a nun, but Rinpoche said that it would be better for the sake of the world if Western practitioners work through lay communities.

As far as the Austin center is concerned, it is in a great location but needs desperately to be expanded. The neighborhood is good for the center, and the intention is for the sangha to be good for the neighborhood.[11]

Shambhala International
San Antonio Center
6233 Evers Road, Suite 100
San Antonio, Texas 78238
Elsa Gonzalez

> I had some sense as a child that there was something vast, a sort of vastness that wasn't touched on by the things

that you deal with in everyday life. You know, I would get these glimpses of something just enormously large going on. And then I would say as I got older, that got very, very, very narrowed down into me. That sort of sense of a larger universe got narrowed into ... being absorbed with one's own life and one's own relationships and dimensions. But I found a lot of this extremely dissatisfying and couldn't understand why I kept looking for solutions. . . .[12]

Elsa Gonzalez has spent her entire life trying to unravel the meaning of that "vastness" and in the end believes that the discovery is to be found in understanding the nature of one's own mind. After trying many different systems, she has chosen the Karma Kagyu tradition as her pathway to Realization. She is a special-education teacher in San Antonio public schools.

Ms. Gonzalez lived in San Antonio until she was eighteen, then moved to Mexico City and later to Wisconsin. It was the sixties, and experimentation was in. There seemed to be a swing between political and spiritual poles for finding solutions to the prevailing questions of the day. "I would get very frustrated because it seemed to me that the people involved in the political movements sometimes mirrored in their own actions what the rest of the world was doing, the world that we were supposedly helping."[13]

At times, Ms. Gonzalez immersed herself in the Theosophical Society, and then there was the Academy of Universal Truth. In 1970, feeling that Washington state was "the place" for spiritual development, she hitchhiked out to Seattle. An intense period of reading began—Gurdjieff and Ospenskey, things with an eastern, mystical tilt. Discovering that she felt a tendency toward racism and anti-feminism, she returned to the political solution and moved back to the Midwest.

Through the Theosophical Society there, she met John and they married. Both were searching for similar ends and at the time were interested in Krishnamurti. It was John who ran across Chogyam Trungpa's *Cutting through Spiritual Materialism,* which affected Elsa profoundly. The human mind seemed to be the key. There was a Trungpa center in Seattle. Ms. Gonzalez moved west again and this time stayed for fifteen years.

Experimentation continued in Seattle, but this time it was between two competing Tibetan systems, the Dharmadhatu of Trungpa Rinpoche, and that of a more traditional Sakya center that worked exclusively in the Tibetan language. The Sakya system was very colorful and melodious, and quickly involved its students in the Vajrayana visualization practice, and there was a real lama right there in the flesh. The Dharmadhatu was led by a western woman, and the approach, Ms. Gonzalez believed, was slow and painfully boring. She opted for the Sakyas. Within three years, however, unrest came again. Women were not being treated the same as men. They were not even being treated as real students. The solution, she decided, was to find a female Sakya teacher. One was located in New York State. She and John made the move.

It did not work out. John worked construction, and Elsa found employment on an egg farm to pay for the mistake. The problem seemed to lie with personal problems of the teacher, who seemed to think that every woman in the center wanted to abscond with her husband. Regarding the teacher, Ms. Gonzalez said, "You know, I'll have to say that she was a very remarkable person, but I was bumping into a lot of cultural stuff and I didn't know how to break through that and actually get to the pith of the teachings."[14]

The couple returned to Seattle. All of their belongings had to be left behind because they had was no money and no car. The discouragement and frustration were total. Their marriage ended. But still there was the sense of that original "vastness." There was something about the Dharma that just would not let go.

Ms. Gonzalez returned to Trungpa Rinpoche's books, meetings at the Seattle Dharmadhatu, and thence a woman's conference in Boulder, where she met the American Buddhist nun Pema Chodron.

> What she said was actually really pivotal in my path, completely. She told me that even if [they] were to prove beyond a shadow of a doubt that Trungpa was a complete charlatan, I would always be grateful to him for what he showed about my own mind. And there was something about her saying that, that made me realize that I had been looking outward for a journey, you know, basing it on how this teacher was teaching it . . . I had forgotten or totally missed the point, which was working on my own mind. It might seem ridiculous that this point can be missed. Quite frankly, I see practitioners missing that point all of the time. Getting sidetracked, you know, mis-

taking the exterior for the path. And forgetting that the path is just about constantly working with one's own mind no matter what's going on. That changed things for me. From that point on, I continued with my path.[15]

In 1976 Elsa made the trip to Tail of the Tiger in Vermont for a month-long retreat and in 1984 completed the three-month seminary in Colorado. First Mahayana and then Vajrayana vehicles were introduced and studied. The fundamental Shamatha meditation, of course, never ceased, nor did the Vipassana practice.

Her immediate intention was to eventually move to Gampo Abbey in Nova Scotia and train to be a nun, but Ms. Gonzalez's parents in Texas were getting old and needed attention—and she was pregnant. There was a Dharmadhatu in Austin. That was close enough. In 1984 Elsa Gonzalez was back home in the city of her birth, San Antonio, practicing Trungpa Rinpoche's Karma Kagyu Buddhism alone.

The isolation was temporary. She received a call from a woman named Linda Ladonna, who was also a Vajradhatu practitioner. She was married to a flamenco dancer from San Antonio. He was also a Buddhist, but of a different school. The three started a little study group they called Sangha del Corazón, which met at Ms. Gonzalez's home on Sundays. Soon a study group developed, even though it was certainly an eclectic collection of souls, including New Age, Buddhist Peace Fellowship, Thich Nhat Hanh Zen, and Japanese Nichiren practitioners. The numbers began to grow. The meeting spot was moved to a local New Age school in the city. It was 1987, the year that Trungpa Rinpoche died and the problems for Unsel Tinsen (Tom Rich) became public. It was also the year that Jan Puckett, eventually the founder of San Antonio's Rigpe Dorje Center, joined Mrs. Gonzalez's organization.

Ms. Puckett had been teaching herself Zen meditation but after spending time with Sangha del Corazón decided that Vajrayana was the way to go, even though all options were still open. Others were also seeing options. Some Corazón members wanted to specialize, including Ms. Gonzalez. It was time to separate from the more generic organization. In 1988, the Buddhist Study Group came into existence. This time it was strictly Vajrayana, and they met at Ms. Puckett's home.

Suddenly, the picture shifted all over again. Ms. Gonzalez,

her son Joaquin, and Ms. Puckett flew out to Los Angeles to meet the famous Kagyu tulku Jamgon Kongtrul Rinpoche, founder of the Rigpe Dorje Foundation. This meeting, because of the heart-centered connection Ms. Puckett instantly felt for Jamgon Kongtrul, would begin a series of events that would eventually end in her separation from the Buddhist Study Group as well as singular involvement in the Shambhala system. Ms. Gonzalez's interest was still with Trungpa's Dharmadhatu organization.

In spite of their different leanings and teachers, Ms. Gonzalez and Ms. Puckett held joint meetings, utilizing a friend's extra office space on Mossrock Street. The differences between the two practices, however, soon proved to be too great. Even though the number of participants was growing, another metamorphosis was inevitable. It happened quickly.

Elsa received calls from veteran Trungpa disciples Steve Winn, Allen Cross, and Dorea Guterias. Together, along with Joaquin, who was thirteen years old now and had completed his own dhatu, they founded the Shambhala International Center in San Antonio. The space itself was a tiny mother-in-law cottage behind Dorea's house on Linwood Street. The groups would not be mixed again. This was exclusively Vajraydatu. Dorea's number was put in the phone book, public classes were offered, and people began to come.

The cottage would hold only five people and their cushions, so a move was made to a rented railway boxcar in the downtown area of the city. Problems there proved overwhelming. There was no air-conditioning, there were fire ants, and a nearby bar played very loud music. In spite of the difficulties, Ms. Gonzalez felt that this inhospitable boxcar should be designated as the first Shambhala Center in the city. The positive thing about the downtown location was the easy access for everyone from any part of town. As a result, more people had access to the Dharma.

The final move was made to the suite on Evers Road in 1994:

> I am a meditation instructor and a teacher ... I ended up with a teaching role by default. There was no one else to do it. I had no intention of taking that role. Remember, I was going to be a nun in Gampo Abbey in Nova Scotia, but ended up going in a different direction. I did not want

to teach, but there was no one else to do it. So now, that is sort of the whole story. The fantastic thing to me is what's going on in the center these days. We are proceeding. People are getting their meditation instructions and training. Classes are being taught. This is exciting. It's like watching a lineage at work.[16]

The inspiration is obviously Tibetan and Karma Kagyu, but the work is "getting itself done" by the Texas hands. It is the grassroots system in its greatest simplicity and purity, and the roots continue to spread.

Shambhala International
Houston Shambhala Center
1003 Studewood, Suite 102
Houston, Texas, 77008
Celeste Budwit

Celeste Budwit grew up in Houston, attended Waltrip High School, the University of Houston, and the University of Texas in Austin, where she majored in psychology with a business management minor.

During those formative years in the Bayou City, a boyfriend introduced Ms. Budwit to the tapes and books of Chogyam Trungpa. The friend's interest seemed to be only philosophical and intellectual, with little concern for actually pursuing the practice. Ms. Budwit, however, was affected profoundly.

In Austin, she was quick to check out the Shambhala Center, which was very active, but decided to remain on the periphery. All of the responsibility accompanying her university work was quite enough to fill a day.

In 1989, she was anticipating a move to San Antonio. From a flyer in the Austin center, she found out that a little Shambhala group was just getting started down south. She made a phone call, and Elsa Gonzalez answered. "I met Elsa Gonzalez, received meditation instruction, and that was it! I have been on the path, whatever that means, at any particular moment, ever since. Suddenly it clicked. Suddenly it all made sense. It was very personal. I took refuge late in 1993."[17]

Family obligations—her mother's illness—drew Ms. Budwit back to Houston in 1994. Her mother's death, she explains, was "an enormous teaching, a direct and undeniable teaching."[18]

In time Ms. Budwit, like Ms. Gonzalez, made her way to Gampo Abbey in Canada. She took her doctorate at the Naropa Institute in February of 1995. Students are required to have been a part of Trungpa Rinpoche's system for at least two years. The curriculum is an intensive study of the traditional Kagyu view of the Dharma. "It was a winter retreat, beautiful. A doctoral is considered very important on this particular path. One month of sitting. Sit, sit, sit most of the day, and eat—that's it. You eat yogi style so that you don't even leave the shrine room for meals. It is a rich program."[19]

According to Ms. Budwit, there had been a Trungpa group of some sort in Houston as early as the 1970s, but it had vanished by the 1980s. When she got back to the city in 1994, there were three or four people sitting, but the effort was completely undisciplined. In essence, the group meditation was nothing more than a social gathering. It was very discouraging, but things soon changed. She invited people to her home. There she could insist on the fundamental requirement for spiritual development: sitting. But using your own home always means some risk.

> It is not a neutral space. You have to be polite and you have to be social. You have to like the persons who are visiting. There are all sorts of connotations when going into someone's house. Security is also a thing. I couldn't publicize much, because I was living alone at the time. I didn't want to invite all of Houston to my house. I never quite wanted to invite all of Houston to knock on my front door.[20]

Shambhala Day, honored on the Tibetan New Year roughly at the end of February, was celebrated in her family home, in 1996. But the problem of danger in the private home was still real. Another facility was an absolute necessity. An experiment in a Korean Zendo, the Zen Academy on Bunker Hill Road, did not work out very well because of restrictions of being in a shared space, different rules for different cultures, and of course language. "A lot of their Korean population did not speak very good English; we never did build a very good bridge. We didn't do a very good job of making friends of our host. They kept to themselves, and we kept to ourselves. Eventually it all fell apart."[21]

The Houston Shambhala Center moved to the Studewood address, its present location in the Heights, in 1998. The center offers its members access to both paths. The Shambhala system involves a series of weekend programs called "levels." The weekend itself is referred to as "Heart of Warriorship." Ms. Budwit explains that there are five such levels. First is learning to appreciate the "Art of Being Human," where the student learns to experience the world as sacred, viewing this existence from the perspective of basic human goodness. The second level involves the recognition of habitual patterns as well as discovering the nature of fearlessness. This training is called "Birth of the Warrior." Developing personal confidence in one's daily life ("Warrior in the World") and allowing, through intuition, the individual to communicate with the world ("Awakened Heart"), the third and fourth phases of development. The final level, referred to as "Open Sky," teaches one to trust who "you" are and to genuinely care for others. The weekends always begin on Friday with a public talk and go until late Sunday. The system includes both sitting and walking meditations. There are group discussions and individual interviews with a meditation instructor. Of the Three Gates under the Shambhala umbrella, Vajradhatu, Shambhala training and Nalanda, the Houston Shambhala Center offers access to the first two. Ms. Budwit explains:

> The Nalanda Gate includes calligraphy, Chado (tea ceremony), dance, drama, horsemanship, ikebana (flower arranging), Kyduo (archery), Mudra (space awareness), poetry, and the visual arts. These are considered paths. These kinds of activities are usually offered only at the bigger centers. You have to have the facilities, materials, and lots of teaching experience. You can't teach without that experience.[22]

Meditations in the Houston center are always taught by a "live" person, not by tape or read from print. The idea is for there to be a human-to-human experience, for the meditations to be grounded in personal experience. The MI, or meditation instructor, is required to maintain a sitting practice of at least twenty hours per month.

On the Shambhala training path, you are out in the world, not in the sense of engaged Buddhism, but you don't deny your family, you don't deny your livelihood. You are a good citizen like Marpa the Householder. You actually fully inhabit your life as it is. So the two paths are complementary. In both paths there is a very specific, progressive approach. In Buddhism you start with the discovery of suffering, with sitting on your butt, on a cushion for long periods of time and work with your own mind. You work with yourself. You take refuge, which only means that you are acknowledging your own loneliness. You are a refugee. You are only looking at your own life as it is. You live alone. You die alone. That's your life. You are really inhabiting that. It's the ground of the Buddhist Path.[23]

Shambhala International
The Dallas Shambhala Study Group
Joan Klein

When Ms. Klein was sixteen, she read Hermann Hesse's *Siddhartha*. With deepening interest, she studied Eastern religions at Syracuse University in New York. In 1974 she met Chogyam Trungpa and personally studied with him. She completed her university work at Berkeley in California and became a social worker. She moved to Texas in 1993 because she had become seriously ill from extreme sensitivity to chemicals, and Dallas had the only environmental-illness treatment center in the United States.

Once in Dallas, Ms. Klein discovered the KTC organization and instantly made friends. Whenever possible, she would travel to Tail of the Tiger in Vermont and study with the meditation master Khenpo Tsultrim.

In August of 1997, Joan asked permission of the Sakyong, Sawang Osel, to start a study group in Dallas. He gave his consent. The Dallas Shambhala Study Group was then founded in September of 1997 and held its meetings in the Unity Church in Dallas.[24]

Karma Triyana Dharmachakra (KTD)
Dallas Karma Thegsum Choling (KTC) [Satellite Center]
312 South Winnetka
Dallas, Texas, 75208
Beth Condrey Kennan

There is still a sense inside myself, like a default into old habits. It's like I was still a devout Southern Baptist. I think there is always a tendency toward theism where you externalize the perfection, their God or Jesus, or anything. How can our minds align with our backgrounds and our prejudices? There are ways that can lead one out of the fog.[25]

Beth Kennan began her probing of the spiritual world in the late 1980s. She attended a meeting in the home of Jo Wharton, a Thursday-night meditation group that focused on woman's empowerment through the Goddess Movement. The gatherings were generally eclectic in nature. The range of personalities usually present was enough to open the door to various philosophies, perceptions, and pathways for exploration. In time, Beth found the courage to make a choice and walk right through those doors into another world.

Happenstance, she explains, finally drew her to Buddhism. One night she dreamed that she was taking part in a ceremony with a little man in robes and was given a new name. Soon after, while attending a refuge given by Khenpo Karthar Rinpoche, she got into a line with others to get the Rinpoche's blessing. She was amazed when her new name was called. It was the same as she had dreamed a few nights before.

> While I was certainly open to precognition, it was certainly stunning and took me aback. Other things happened, too, which enabled me to see the potentiality of these people and the philosophy they expressed. How did they do that? They did it through Buddhism. So I really began to study in earnest. I began doing everything I possibly could to understand more of the Buddhist teachings and to just be around them.[26]

In 1992 Ms. Kennan accepted as her principal teacher Lama Dudjom Dorje, a Karma Kagyu lama who had come to Dallas from Santa Cruz, California, as a visiting instructor. She made the trek to Nepal the following year out of intense curiosity about Tibetan culture. In 1994, she was enlisted as a secretary and traveled with Buddhist monks throughout the continent of Australia. She remembers, "There were days when I wasn't in contact with Westerners at all. It was very important in helping me understand the monastic culture, the Tibetan culture and everything else. I taught English to the little monks there. It was a fascinating experience."[27]

Like Celeste Budwit, Beth Kennan is quick to stress that in Buddhism, because one is on one's own and must sit and reflect, in time everything will change—how one feels about something, even the personality. Holding on to anything is useless.

> I think what happens is that there is a refinement of the dross into perhaps the Buddha family qualities that one exhibits. You become more purely that piece of your pattern, of that eternal pattern that's reflected in Buddhist psychology. We just become more refined. That's why we are so "eaten up" with it. It's like we know that there is that perfection and we can feel it.[28]

The story of the creation of the Dallas Karma Thegsum Choling had its beginning before Beth Kennan joined Ms. Wharton's meditation group on Thursday evenings in Dallas. There were other players.

Two students of Khenpo Karthar Rinpoche, Kay and Jerry Adams, had formed a KTC center in Columbus, Ohio. In September of 1983 the couple moved to Duncanville, Texas, and were soon giving talks in their newly carpeted garage. Soon, a move was made to the Alpha Biotic Center, where Mr. Adams lectured one night a week. The first to attend were Jo Wharton and Terri Wallace. The Biotic Center proved to be a wonderful venue for all kinds of alternative groups and their views. Khenpo Karthar visited Texas in 1988, and a large assembly involving a teaching on "Death and Dying," as well as a Chenrerzig Empowerment, was held in the Duncanville garage. In 1989, the center was moved to Jo Wharton's home in Plano. Another move was eventually made, this time to a nearby shopping center, the Office Park, also called the "Keystone Courts." But everything changed in January of 1990 when Khenpo Karthar Rinpoche, accompanied by Bardor Tulku, paid his yearly visit. As Ms. Kennan puts it, Rinpoche told the gathering that it was time to have a proper center. He gave them some money to get started and said, "Go do it! Go find it!"[29] "And so for the next six months that is just what we did. We looked and looked and looked. Maps, going, sectioning, and home tours and getting our money together, and meeting, and meeting, and meeting."[30]

The place was found in the Oak Cliff section of town, on

South Winnetka Street, a beautiful old Winnetka Heights historic home with over four thousand square feet, built in 1908. Administrating the financial arrangements proved to be a nightmare, but it was eventually organized with no single titleholder. The ownership was collective. There were three members then, Ms. Kennan, her boyfriend Bruce Rowe, who is now the director, and Dr. Bill Swanson. The three paid the first three years' rent in advance so that the remittance would also represent the initial down payment. It worked! And so did the sangha members. Renovations were begun immediately and are still in progress after five years.

The Dallas center uses visualization in their practice relentlessly. Beth does everything in Tibetan:

> I wouldn't think of changing that, because you've already got the track laid down... There is also a track with all of those people who have reached Enlightenment or Realization doing exactly these syllables and exactly this cadence and exactly this thing. This means that you have to do a little more, work a little harder, but if one isn't really interested then that person is not going anywhere anyway. Understanding the Tibetan language and realizing the preciousness of the meaning of what is being said is not an onerous task. The difficulty of it all in fact serves a purpose. The people who do the stuff in English, well that's fine for them. It just slows the process.[31]

Throughout the KTD system, teachers can make use of any of the satellite centers. Lamas can also teach in any of the other Kagyu lineage organizations, when invited by local organizers and representatives. The Karma Kagyu lamas have been given some degree of independence in seeking locations and assignments. If a particular center wants or needs either a temporary or resident (live-in) lama, then a request is circulated. Any lama can correspond, make the necessary arrangements, and make the move. He may prove successful, and he may not. Nevertheless, the national center in Woodstock, New York, will invariably sanction the assignment. This is how Lama Dudjom Dorje found his way to the old house on Winnetka. Lama Dudjum will split his time between Dallas and Santa Cruz. There is no doubt, Beth Kennan believes, that this teacher, her root lama, will prove to be the greatest of successes.

You know, ideas from Tibetan Buddhism are already permeating the new age. The best parts of it are continually going to influence the archetypal consciousness of the country. As they are introduced and disseminated ... Everyone knows of the efficacy of happiness created by meditation. It's not just another flavor. It will integrate itself into the whole ... There will be a large influence on the Southern Baptist. Like it or not, Bible-beaters, they will be influenced by the Buddhist ideas. They can be compassionate. Tibetan Buddhism is fabulously rich. The Diaspora and the fall of Tibet was a bonanza for us. We will be eternally grateful![32]

Karma Triyana Dharmachakra
Dallas Karma Thegsum Choling
Lama Dudjom Dorje

In an interview, Lama Dudjom, resident lama of the Dallas KTC Center, made the following evaluation concerning the contact of Buddhism with the western mind.

I think it is accelerating. It is moving fast, but inside the mind of the disciples ... How are they benefiting and how are they receiving the transmission? This is something that will be watched from now on. Perhaps in a hundred years we will know more about it. Buddhism is increasing because the teachings are based on the psychology of the mind. It's related to science and is a very practical tool.[33]

Lama Dudjom agrees that both cultures have made accomodations; both have changed to some degree. For instance, in the chanting, the accents from country to country always vary. The old culture in the background is also very influential, in that there can be a great deal of resistance to change, or an easy transition. On the other hand, there are Buddhist themes and disciplines where nothing has changed at all. The transmissions and meditations presented in Tibetan Buddhism are always fundamentally the same. Otherwise, the Tibetan feels, no one would ever achieve Enlightenment. The essence of Enlightenment is the same in any country regardless of the culture. As far as chanting in English goes, Lama Dudjom commented:

> English readers chant and meditate in English. I haven't seen many people who have achieved Idealization yet. Perhaps in time, maybe in a hundred years. Maybe some practitioners will achieve a higher Realization in reading just the English translation. If that happens, maybe we can say that language doesn't matter because what is being contacted is all that matters. But in Tibet, there is a long history of Enlightenment. They use that language and it seems to avoid mistakes.[34]

The lama has obviously enjoyed his years in the United States. He took classes at the community college in Santa Cruz and learned how to "swim" in the culture. And how does Lama Dudjom Dorje feel that he has been treated by his new culture?

> Americans treat me like anyone else. I hope so. Different parts of the country are different. There is racism. Some people might think that I am a little bit strange, but others might think that this is very good. I haven't seen any problems. In fact, it seems that the people are enjoying meeting me. So I hope that I will stay for a very long time, or forever.
>
> For people, not only in Texas, but for all in general on the planet Earth, we have to share the space. We breathe the same air, and we walk on the same road and path, and we share the food and water. It's very good to be compassionate, to have patience with each other and to try to love each other. We need to increase love and compassion to each other by using patience and respect.[35]

The Rigpe Dorje Foundation
San Antonio Rigpe Dorje Center
Post Office Box 690995
San Antonio, Texas 78269
Jan Puckett

Surrounded by a sea of Buddhists, but having minimal personal contact with their institution, Jan Puckett was born and raised Christian in Japan. It was much later, in the United

States, when the bug bit, the reading started, and a spiritual search was underway. There seemed to be some influence from her childhood, however vague, because the sitting came automatically, as if demanded by some inner force. That was in 1986. The following year, Ms. Puckett, like Celeste Budwit, made contact with Elsa Gonzalez, who was still a part of the Sangha del Corazón group that met at the New Age School in San Antonio. Ms. Puckett joined this small organization, and after some soul searching, she discovered that it was Vajrayana, not Zen, that really interested her the most. Ms. Gonzalez, with her Vajradhatu connections, introduced her to the world of the Rocky Mountain Dharma Center. Hearing that a famous Kagyu Rinpoche was practicing there, Ms. Puckett traveled alone to Red Feather Lake, Colorado, looking for her teacher. The lama in residence was Tai Situ Rinpoche, the second foremost disciple of the sixteenth Karmapa. She absorbed a great deal from his presentations and took her refuge vow: "I had never met anybody so smart in my life, intuitively or intellectually. He was extraordinary. There was this big mind, but he wasn't my teacher, I knew that. But I connected with the lineage through him, the Karma Kagyu Lineage."[36]

Jan thought again that Zen Buddhism might be her real path, and she began the process of teaching herself the discipline. She also trained in the Shambhala system, but Trungpa's system was not traditional enough for her. She liked more ritual, and the methodology seemed too confining. The Buddhist path would be her way, but the exact direction was still being sought. She was looking for more. It was Ms. Gonzalez again who was responsible for helping her discover her destined path.

In the fall of 1988, Ms. Gonzalez suggested that Ms. Puckett accompany her and her son to California. Jamgon Kongtrul Rinpoche was going to be teaching in Los Angeles. Ms. Puckett recalls, "I fell in love with Jamgon Kongtrul. It was a heart connection. He was teaching from a text called the Treasury of Knowledge, which was written in the late 1800s by the first Jamgon Rinpoche. He told me not to worry, to continue to sit. When I came back, it was pretty clear that he was going to be my teacher."[37]

Jan continued to sit with the mixed Buddhist group, but on her own she developed a daily meditation practice, always sitting for at least two hours. In 1990 a gradual separation from the others began. Those inclined toward Jamgon Kongtrul began to gather in Jan's house, but soon an apartment was rented for more space. There was a trip to the Rigpe Dorje Center in Toronto, Canada, and in 1991, lamas and other Kagyu teachers began to arrive in the Alamo City. But a small problem intervened. The landlord raised the rent.

Fellow seeker Connie White, a massage therapist in the city, volunteered some of her office space for the cause. The massage table had to be moved when they met, but it worked. The traditional Buddhist shrine room was visible to public view, but few seemed to care. Ms. White said, "A couple of born-again Christians got a little bit miffed, but I didn't care because I figured that that was their problem."[38]

When an adjoining business moved, the sangha acquired the additional space, and the Rigpe Dorje organization was properly housed. There was to be one more move. A small adobe building, the perfect place, was discovered near Boerne Stage Road. With no hesitation, Ms. Puckett jumped at the opportunity, and in August of 1999 it became the present San Antonio Rigpe Dorje Center and is formally referred to as Richen Drak.

The foundation has its North American headquarters in Los Angeles. It is basically a charitable organization. There is a coordinator in New York, a westerner. There is also a coordinator in Kathmandu. Communication, it seems, is quite easy. The main monastery, Pullahari, is in Nepal. It is now the residence of the fourth Jamgon Kongtrul Rinpoche.

"We are fairly independent," Ms. Puckett explained. "We are not officially associated with Woodstock. We do get a lot of teachers who are affiliated with other centers because of our connection, you know, the Karma Kagyu Lineage ... Because Jamgon is a very high lama, other lamas have been helping take care of us. When we call and say that we are having our Treasury of Knowledge retreat, they are always willing to come and help. We have been very fortunate."[39] The Treasury of Knowledge retreats are usually held at the Omega Center in Boerne, Texas, once a year. Space is rented, and the Dzogchen, Ponlop Rinpoche, brings his infinite wisdom. Once a year may not sound like the frequency one would like in order for the most effective development to be possible. But according to Ms. Puckett, "If you make a connection with a real teacher, they don't have to come so often. They give you enough to work on.

You are always ready to see them, but you always have plenty of work to do. We are still too small for a live-in teacher."[40]

Rigpe Dorje Foundation
San Antonio
Connie White

Connie White was raised Catholic in Massachusetts and was kept in boarding school until she was eighteen. Her father's three sisters were nuns and her uncle was a priest. One of her cousins was a secretary to the Pope in Vatican City and was also the president of a Catholic university. All of Ms. White's sisters are Catholic, and one is a secretary for a parish priest.

Nevertheless, when Connie married, she chose a man who had no religious background, nor any interest in religion at all. Eventually she left this husband behind, went out to Tucson, and studied the art of healing through therapeutic massage. She also became accomplished in the skill of Jungsin Jutzu, a Japanese form of healing.

Connie was brought to San Antonio by a man of Moslem persuasion because he wanted her to be his therapist. Office space was rented, and as fate would have it, an acupuncturist occupied the suite above. Mr. Wong Ho and his wife also taught Buddhist meditation in the style of Thich Nhat Hanh. The entire enterprise interested Ms. White, so one evening she joined the Hos at their home for meditation instruction. Jan Puckett happened to be there that same night, and Ms. White's involvement with Jamgon Kongtrul Rinpoche's Rigpe Dorje Foundation began. It was 1991.

With a friend, Lisa, Ms. Puckett and Ms. White made the Toronto trip to meet Jamgon Rinpoche. Ms. White was profoundly impressed: "I decided then and there that I wanted this lama to be my teacher for the rest of my life. It was totally life-changing for me."[41]

At this point, it may be growing obvious to the reader that more women than men are involved in Texas Karma Kagyu Buddhism. Also noteworthy is the liberal interplay of members and teachers among the Kagyu subsets. For example, Mr. Wells of the Austin Shambhala assisted the KTC in Dallas and worked with Woodstock and Jan Puckett's Rigpe Dorje Center in San Antonio. The exchange seems to be lively and appreciated by all of the subsets except one. It seems that Ole Nydahl's Diamond Way Buddhism is invariably left out of the loop. The Woodstock lamas rarely if ever visit and teach in his centers. Yet the Diamond Way is vivid, vital, dynamic, powerful, and growing rapidly worldwide.

Diamond Way Buddhism
The Clear Lake Center (inactive)
The Baywind II Clubhouse
Marilyn Kinsey

Marilyn Parrish Kinsey and Lama Ole Nydahl share the same great-grandparents, which also means that Nydahl's father and Ms. Kinsey's mother were second cousins. The families have always been very close and have exchanged visits between Copenhagen, Denmark, and San Luis Obispo, California, more than once. During the 1970s, another cousin sent Ms. Kinsey a copy of one of Mr. Nydahl's unpublished papers on Buddhism. She read it, labeled it "interesting," and filed it away. This was her introduction to the Dharma. After attending one of Lama Ole's lectures in Los Angeles in 1979, she offered her cousin a guided tour of the City of Angels. Instead of the grand tour, he asked only to be taken to a secondhand clothing shop to fulfill his commitment of wearing only used items of clothing. Even so, Ms. Kinsey discovered the world of Karma Kagyu Buddhism.

In 1979, Ms. Kinsey's husband, an aerospace engineer, was a transfer to Texas, to the Space Center at the National Aeronautics and Space Administration in League City. The couple divorced in 1990.

Her mother was elderly, so a great deal of time was spent back home on the West Coast in San Luis Obispo. From time to time, Lama Ole would appear, and Cousin Marilyn would never miss a lecture. They were always fun, and the spiritual content was always absorbing.

Back in Houston, Ms. Kinsey became involved in the Unity Church for Love and Light in Friendswood, a New Age positive-thought movement. The minister, Carolyn Wenzel, a friend, Wally Dolmert, and Ms. Kinsey often walked in the mornings together, talking, sharing views, and solving the greatest mysteries of the universe. She also did some serious reading:

I was actively seeking spiritual direction and had read some books on the correlation between Quantum Theory and Buddhism, *The Dancing Wu Li Masters* and *The Tao of Physics*. These works had aroused my interest in Buddhism at this time as a unified body of evidence tested over millenia. I saw that Buddhism agreed with the most basic truths of all religions, predating most of them and even further, correlated with more modern, Western-based, scientifically acknowledged principles defining our universe.[42]

Ms. Kinsey expressed the view, however, that the New Age philosophy or approach does not seem to have a core practice, that there are too many unsubstantiated and disjointed ideas that usually lead nowhere. There is nothing to hold on to. "I am like Ole, a hard-headed Dane, and want to temper any flashes of insight, however brilliant, with down-to-earth common sense and practicality."[43]

After numerous San Luis visits and Ole lectures, Ms. Kinsey wondered, Why not in Houston? In March 1992, she asked Ole to speak in Texas, and he was delighted and eager. Arrangements were made by his Polish assistant, Tomek Lehnert. Mr. Lehnert was later to author the striking and controversial book *Rogues in Robes,* about the Karmapa War.

Ms. Kinsey approached her friend Carolyn Wenzel with the idea of an Ole appearance, and the minister enthusiastically agreed. On April 1, 1992, Lama Ole Nydahl presented his lecture, "Teachings on the Nature of Mind," Kalu Rinpoche's commentaries, in Friendswood's Unity Church. A week later, Marilyn arranged to use the clubhouse of the Baywind II condo complex in Clear Lake, Texas, as a mediation center. Diamond Way Buddhism had entered Texas. Membership at the center was initially rather modest, consisting of three or four regulars at most, and one of them, Samuel Rosa Ruiz, became quite famous for his amazing narcolepsy during meetings.

Lama Ole returned to Friendswood in October of the same year, 1992, teaching this time on death and rebirth. Jesper Jorgensen, the Diamond Way North American coordinator from the San Francisco headquarters, paid a visit and assisted. The numbers began to grow at the League City center. There was a need for greater space.

Ms. Kinsey, a tour guide worldwide by profession, has continued to be a real force in the Diamond Way movement in Texas. Marilyn was and is responsible for the initiative which will ultimately result in the establishment of what will be the Texas Retreat Center for Diamond Way Buddhism in the Lone Star State.[44]

Diamond Way

Clear Lake Center
Pattie Hollestein

Pattie Holestein was one of the originals in the Baywind II Clubhouse. When Marilyn was off on one her tours, Ms. Hollestein was sometimes the only practicing member.

I had been working with a group for about a year, an Edgar Cayce Search for God Study Group. It was strange to sit with a group and meditate and chant. We did dream analysis. We read and prayed. It was a Christian organization, but it was a different kind of Christianity, kind of New Age. I would find myself sitting with this group and would almost have to stifle a laugh, because I was a consultant for the Arthur Andersen Group as well as for a doctor. And here we were, all sitting on the floor focusing on our belly buttons and chanting. It was an odd group, but it led me to Unity Church in Friendswood. I quit the Search for God group and started going to Unity. It was a friend from Angleton that I saw maybe twice a year who suggested that I should give the Unity Church a shot. Carolyn Wenzel made it possible for us to begin. Unity gave us a place to flourish.[45]

A week before Lama Ole was to speak in Friendswood, a workshop was held at Unity, with the purpose of its attendants making contact with both their male and female aspects through the process of drawing. The format included asking a question of the images and exchanging gifts with one's gender aspects. "I had a very, very incredible experience in both of these meditations," Ms. Hollestein said. "It was a shaking experience, very intense, and profound. It brought me to tears. Even now I'm effected by the memory of it. I don't know if this was to lead to anything else or not."[46]

During this art meditation, Pattie drew an image of a man. He donned a red hat. She asked the question, "What is our connection?" The answer received was, "You are of my lineage. We go forth together." At the time of the Unity workshop, Ms. Hollestein knew nothing about Karmapa and little about Buddhism. Even her introduction to Lama Ole was still several days in the future. Nevertheless, the gifts she offered were a book, a box, and a pillow. The gift given in return, from the drawn image of the male aspect, was a blue light. The drawing depicting her female aspect, it turned out, was the spitting image of Hannah Nydahl. The strangeness of it all was revealed several weeks later when Jesper Jorgensen presented a film at the Clear Lake Center. Karmapa had come calling. The book was the Dharma, the pillow was for meditation, and the purpose of the box remains unknown. Blue light is the energy that connects the heart centers in the sixteenth Karmapa's Guru Yoga Meditation.

A week after this workshop, Lama Ole made his initial presentation in Friendswood. Ms. Hollestein was present. (She had noticed a flyer on a lamp pole.) It was a magical night. The world seemed suddenly to fall into place. She was on the Diamond Way. Eventually, it would cost her a husband, a profession, a home, her accumulations, and all of the advantages that often accompany financial sovereignty. Needless to say, she and her two children are survivors.

Letters to her lama always resulted in responses. As far as Pattie Hollestein was concerned, this was the real thing. In 1992, she flew out to San Francisco for a Phowa, a class in conscious dying. This is a practice in which students exercise sending their consciousness out through a portal in the top of their head, prefiguring the process that will be undergone when the physical body expires. The idea is to practice the phenomenon of dying so that when the actual event takes place, one will not get lost. Participants practice recognizing the particular "moments," usually color sequences, at which Enlightenment is possible. Pattie was one of the early practitioners to move into a live-in Diamond Way center. She has completed over 30,000 prostrations and 6,000 or so Dorje Sempa Meditations, paying for it all by cleaning homes and offices and delivering pizzas. And what has Buddhism done for her in return?

> The big difference is that now I don't see everything as a threat. I know that things are temporary. Things that

would have put me in the hospital with some kind of chronic long-term illness years ago, now I just go, "Okay, okay." My client quit. My client can't afford me anymore, okay. I'm smiling while knowing that something new is coming and wonder what it will be! And what is it that is actually happening? The fact is, Buddha is entering the world through you![47]

One thing that Ms. Hollestein adamantly objects to at the centers is the personality that insists on "taking over." She feels that such people inevitably stifle the entire group. Those people who are not contributing regularly are not doing so, she believes, because they simply have not been encouraged to:

We are a very much a "fly by the seat of our pants, sit down, and no one is in charge" type of group. It is like the totalitarianism that is inherent in feudalism. And there is another version of this concept. We in the West have been trained not to believe that somebody is a god, or some mystical, magical being, just because he is wearing robes and sitting above high on some dais. Americans know better than to believe in that person's personal perfection. It is part of the East-West conflict that is developing as the Dharma takes its place in the United States. We can't let the ritual get in the way of the practice.[48]

When asked about the possibility of Enlightenment, Ms. Hollestein related the following story:

There have been times when I was meditating where I felt like I was not solid. I have a friend that plays cello. One time I took him to practice and stayed to listen. While sitting in the band hall, naturally I was saying my mantras and kind of working with my beads inconspicuously. I had this feeling come over me. It was like I wasn't solid. It was like you could put your hand right through me. It was like I was plugged into everything. It was freaky! And it did scare me. I was afraid that if I didn't control it . . . my atoms would just go out and there would be my son by himself. This has happened more than once. You just have to control it.[49]

Ms. Hollestein now lives in Oklahoma and is a university student again.

Diamond Way
Friendswood Center (Inactive)
Tore Fossum

In October of 1992, Tore Fossum made the astounding offer of his spacious Friendswood home as a meditation center. The move was made before he had time to change his mind.

Tore had met Marilyn Kinsey through the Unity Church. He was there for Lama Ole's first lecture in April and had made the California trip with Pattie Hollestein and Ms. Kinsey for the November Ngondro teachings. When Ole's Diamond Way entourage returned to Friendswood that October, the entire group stayed in his home, and then again the following year. Mr. Fossum's business required a great deal of traveling, often in Europe. Merging his business responsibilities with his interest in Ole Nydahl's European activities proved to be no problem. So Tore toured with the group across Germany and Poland in 1993 and was a Texas representative in Spain in 1994.

The Diamond Way was not Tore Fossum's first encounter with esoteric philosophies of the East. He had previously tasted a little Zen, a bit of Hinduism, and even some Buddhism of the Gelugpa school, which had not "spoken to him" at all. But Lama Ole's approach caught his imagination and provided a definite direction for his spiritual pursuits. Mr. Fossum said, "Ole has the capacity, the facility of taking the teachings from this Tibetan environment, milieu, and putting them into terms that are useful for a Westerner much more than anyone else I've met."[50]

Tore is Norwegian. With both men Scandinavian and the languages so similar, communication was always easy.

Tore's home became an active center in May 1993 and was the second live-in Diamond Way sangha in the United States, the first in Texas. Practitioners rented their rooms, because there were bills that had to be paid. Michael Savage was the first to move in, while Leigh Bowa and her son were the last to leave when the center closed in 1997. In all, perhaps eight different people made the center their home.

A Tibetan man, Lama Caffasan, lived there in 1995–96. Tore allowed the lama to perform maintenance work as well as do some renovations in order to compensate for his rent. In time, the Tibetan lama got his green card and became the manager of a local restaurant.

In any communal living arrangement, togetherness can often result in some degree of disharmony. In this case, it seems that the introduction of a form of commercialism into the center caused a great deal of upheaval. Some live-ins, in order to deal with their impecuniousness, got involved with a multi-level marketing program selling blue-green algae. The original dealer would always get a cut of the next sale. The object of the whole exercise was innocent and honorable enough, that is, to support the teachers and make life possible for the students. The fallout, however, proved to be too much. In time, instead of the Dharma being the center of conversation, it was blue-green algae. Members tried to hard-sell their fellow practitioners. One woman living there was actually making $90,000 a year from the arrangement. The warm fellowship that once pervaded the home soured. Some, like Mike Savage and Mary Anne Fields, simply found somewhere else to live.[51] Carol Boethel relates this story about the algae god:

> It was a fly in everyone's ointment. I felt like, what's going on here, Buddhism or blue-green algae? Discussions of the sales would go on before and after meditations. Everyone who lived in the sangha was eating it, bathing in it, and forcing it on anyone who walked through the front door. It was all totally inappropriate and stalled the evolution of the Diamond Way in Texas.[52]

Kagyu teachers would come from time to time, and there were many delicious potlucks and gatherings around Ole's visits. Lopon Tsechu Rinpoche, Ole and Hannah's first teacher in Nepal, stayed there in May of 1996. According to Tore Fossum: "It was an honor of the highest order to have someone so respected stay in the center. He carries the same stature as someone like the Dalai Lama. Having someone of such eminence present caused a stir in the entire Texas Kagyu community."[53]

It also caused quite a stir in the Friendswood neighborhood. During the week, the lamas would take their walks, in order to keep themselves in some descent physical repair, as well as to see a little bit of Texas up close. The complaints, addressed through the neighborhood homeowners association, came pouring in, and they were about more than the strolling Tibetans. Neighbors complained about a pile of compost in the back yard, a rope dangling across the roof, and a brush pile nearby. They complained about the cars, the fact that public meetings were being held, and the possibility that more than two persons not related were living in a single-family dwelling. Friendswood wanted to shut the center down.

There is no doubting the fact that when Tore was away on business, the place tended to get a bit unkempt, but to the Norwegian, all of the turmoil was about something else entirely. Mr. Fossum explains, "These are the fundamentalist Christians who don't want any competition. So they attacked us. It was religiously motivated, but they never admitted it. Offering this place as a Diamond Way Center was a great blessing for me. It was the very best thing that I could do with my home. I would do it all again in a heartbeat."[54]

All the same, Tore needed to sell the house. This had been on the agenda for a long time. His business demanded it because he needed to make a move to Santa Fe. The fate of the Friendswood Center looked rather grim. But many people had met and mingled at the center. Sanghas in Austin, College Station, and on the campus of the University of Houston would eventually form from friendships that originated in that Diamond Way sangha. From that same source, another center would be created in downtown Houston under the umbrella of the First Unitarian Universalist Church and through the efforts of Donna Russell and Carol Boethel.

Diamond Way Buddhism
Unitarian Universalist Church Center (Inactive)
5200 Fannin Street
Houston, Texas
Donna Russell

By the age of twelve, Donna Russell had figured out what it was that the Lutheran Church was supposed to believe, and she made the judgment, "Oh, well, I don't believe in that!" From H. G. Wells' treatment of Zoraster, she gained the insight that there are those who are perfectly willing to simply make up religious stories and pass such nonsense off as the "truth." It was author Edward Gibbons who taught her that many of the Christian beliefs were no more than rationalizations for political expediency and means for ascendancy to power.

> I've always been intent on not being taken in, you know, not to be tricked and be fooled by believing something that is not true as best as I can tell. There has always been the fear that I am going to be captured by some outrageous ideology while at the same time believing that I am not worthy of its attention. It is a voice rattling away in my head all of the time. I could never believe in a God that is watching everybody, the policeman-in-the-sky type. By the seventies I had started looking for something else. I started reading intensely.[55]

The novel *Ishmael,* a work concerned with wrong decisions made by the human race and their consequences, had a powerful impact. There was an unsatisfying search through the world of shamanism and the Mediterranean worship of the Kore. But in 1992 she found *The Tibetan Book of the Living and Dying,* written by Sogyal Rinpoche of the Nyingma tradition. "I read the book and I got well. And I realized that I had always been a Buddhist."[56]

Wishing that she was in California, where Buddhism is easy to find, Ms. Russell began to search the Houston area for kindred souls. There was the Jade Buddha Temple, a type of Zen, a Chinese Pure Land tradition based in Taiwan, but the cultural gap proved to be too much of a stretch. And there was the Zen genre at the Unitarian church, but she felt no attraction to it. She went to a Gelugpa lama, but the language barrier was impossible. One evening, however, while in the Aquarian Age Bookshelf bookstore on Chaucer Street in the village, Ms. Russell noticed a flyer announcing a lecture on Tibetan Buddhism by Jesper Jorgensen out in Friendswood. (Pattie Hollestein had left the flyer in that bookstore.) The lecture was to be October 6, 1992. Donna attended and was disappointed. She did not think that she exactly fit. This was not the group that she was looking for. These people were too loose, too easygoing, simply not serious enough for her intellectual taste. But she hung around, resisting an illogical, unaccountable attachment to the group all weekend. Even after long, argumentative discussions with Jesper, in the end, she was hooked. She was stuck like a fly on flypaper. She signed up for a Phowa that would soon be held in Miami.

Everything about this Phowa proved difficult, from transportation horrors to swampy camp accommodations, to crowds of strangers, chants in a language she could not understand, and pain in her back that would not go away. But by the end, something in her had changed.

> I went home and people told me that I seemed different. I had no idea how. And then, maybe three weeks later, one day I was looking out of my window and I realized how quiet it was. And I started thinking about what it was that was so quiet. Suddenly I realized that it was that little voice in the back of my mind that used to say, "You're not good enough." And "You know you can't do it!" It had left. It was all gone. I still worry about these things, but now I wouldn't know a depression if it walked into the room.[57]

Once, Ms. Russell had just participated in a Chenrezig empowerment ceremony and was sitting quietly with her eyes closed, saying her "Om Mani Peme Hung" mantra and not getting it at all. Suddenly,

> There was this voice right behind me, in my head or somewhere, and it says, "Everybody is Chenrezig." It was like you were right behind me, shouting at me. It startled me. I opened my eyes, and everybody was Chenrezig. The room was brilliant white. Everybody was shining white. They are all lined up, singing "Om Mani Peme Hung," getting their blessing from Chenrezig. They are all Chenrezig. I remember seeing Tore there. He was in a Light Body. So there is Tore and around him is the white light shell of Chenrezig. It was amazing.[58]

Ms. Russell believes strongly that the Buddha wanted colleagues, not worshipers, and she views the place of the lama in much the same light.

> I realized at one point that the lama is just a tool. It's kind of like he is a hammer and nails with which I am going to build my own approach to my mind. And I use him. The only way that I can use him is to be devoted to

him, so I am devoted. It is not because of him, but because of myself, because it is useful to me. This works fine with Ole. He's non-hierarchical. He's not about power and money. His system is pure and clean. I think this is pretty rare. He is authentic. He is a real one. It is pretty amazing that of all the millions and billions of people in the world, that here in Texas you run into someone like Ole. It is really amazing.[59]

Ms. Russell has worked mainly as a schoolteacher. During this period, however, she was employed as a nanny. The professional obligations fit well enough with her involvement in the Diamond Way organization.

Ms. Russell and Carol Boethel's downtown meditation group met on Tuesday nights. Ms. Russell accepted the responsibility for conducting most of the lectures, because Ms. Boethel was inundated by her personal scholarly pursuits at the graduate level. At times a dozen persons would attend, sometimes fifteen to twenty. But the space, Ms. Russell recalls, was very bare and sterile. There was no altar and there were very few pictures. And even though the Unitarian church is extremely tolerant, it seems that there was a sense of competition there between the various groups that used the church facilities. Also, Ms. Russell had become extremely dissatisfied with her role as a professional nanny. She quit her job and moved into Tore's Friendswood Center in the fall of 1996.

A downtown regular, Bob Dazey, picked up the responsibility of teaching the Dharma. Ms. Boethel also geared up her reserve of courage and began presenting some of the teachings. All went well until the summer of 1997. Unexpectedly, the church decided to close its doors on Tuesday nights. The sangha was suddenly dislocated. The selection of another weekday evening seemed to satisfy no one. Attendance declined abruptly and precipitously. It was truly a difficult season for Carol Boethel.[60]

Diamond Way Buddhism
First Unitarian Universalist Church Center (inactive)
Carol Boethel

Carol's first experience with the spiritual was nothing like an event or a single dramatic experience, but rather a simple feeling over time. She was raised as a Catholic in San Antonio. During the summer that she was taking catechism, she discovered an isolated grotto on the church's property. Instead of running and jumping rope with the other children, she would invariably find herself there, in the garden, doing something much like meditating. The peacefulness of this meditative air lingers to this day.

As a teenager, Ms. Boethel wanted to become a nun. Her parents objected, and by the end of high school, this urge vanished. "I didn't know what I wanted to do when I grew up. I still don't. Isn't that pitiful!"[61] After two years of college, she dropped out. She married, and by 1975 she had her first child.

Despite her youthful dream of becoming a nun, Catholicism never suited Ms. Boethel very well, and when her daughter as a teenager declared her atheism, all allegiances were abandoned. At this point, she tried something new, the First Unitarian Church. As a result, she met Donna Russell. Ms. Russell then introduced her to Buddhism through the Friendswood Diamond Way Center. She started doing the practices, the meditations, on a regular basis.

> Some things began to change. I felt more confidence. It's interesting. Confidence slowly began to manifest itself. Some people have really dramatic experiences that cause dramatic changes, but I can't say that I've experienced it that way. The things that have gone on with me in relation to this have just kind of been gradual. I feel much more relaxed about everything now.[62]

Ms. Boethel feels that her main interest is in the practice of Buddhism, not the history or philosophical trappings. She likes to keep the meditations simple while identifying with Buddha himself. It is the depth in the practice itself, what is changing within the greatest recesses of the mind, that captures her imagination.[63]

A 1995 Christmas party at Mike Savage and Mary Anne Fields' home proved pivotal. Mr. Savage at one time had lived in the Friendswood Center, where he met Mr. Boethel and Ms. Russell. Both young women were still members of the Unity Church in Houston, taking classes in meditation mechanics but frequently driving down to Friendswood for their Buddhist practices. It was at this party that the decision was made to form a downtown sangha. By February of 1996, meetings were underway. Donna and Carol tried to assure everyone that this was not an exercise in power and usurpation, but only a way to make things a little easier for those who lived in town. Some people grumbled anyway. But all went well—very well—for over a year.

In the fall of 1997 however, a decline began for the entire greater Houston Diamond Way system. It started with the loss of Donna as the well-organized administrator and teacher, followed by the Tuesday-night closing and the collapse of the downtown sangha. Then there was an assault upon the Friendswood center by the local community homeowners and Tore's imminent move to Santa Fe, which would involve the sale of his home. Meanwhile, Lama Ole was due to lecture in Houston in November. It was a very busy time. The impermanence of the phenomenal world was never so evident for Houston's members of the Diamond Way. Others would soon step in and save the day. One of these heroes was Bonnie Cooper.

Carol Boethel has completed her master's degree and is working in the social services field in Houston. Concentration in the practices of Kagyu Buddhism is still her joy, major focus, and forte.

Diamond Way Buddhism
League City Center
1611 Dakota Street
League City, Texas 77573
Bonnie Cooper

In 1994, Lama Ole was to speak on "The Buddhist View of Relationships." The forum was being held at the Friendswood Unity Church, of which Bonnie Cooper was a member. "Lots of women," she said, "want to hear about relationships. It was a hot topic and the Buddhist twist was intriguing."[64]

She attended and returned every year thereafter when the Danish lama made his Houston trip. It was Lopon Tsechu, however, who was responsible for Ms. Cooper's eventual decision to submerge herself into the Dharma. Accompanied by Lama Ole in 1996, Tsechu Rinpoche gave an empowerment of the Buddha Amitabha in the downtown church. Bonnie was blown away. "For the next two weeks I was incredibly, blissfully happy. Everything was funny. It was the most amazing, incredible feeling I've ever had in my life. It was very clear to me that I wanted more of that. That's when I decided to start practicing and meditating regularly."[65]

It was the following year that Tore received a sobering letter from the homeowner's association. The long-anticipated move was finally made. Bonnie stepped in. She was living in the upstairs garret of an Aikido studio in League City. The building itself was spacious. It would make a perfect place for sangha meetings. All of the arrangements were made, and the planned transition from Friendswood to the Clear Lake area transpired without the slightest hitch. The Houston area was now back to a single sangha, the League City Center.

Ms. Cooper refers to the establishment as a "virtual center," because it appears as a martial arts facility most of the time, but on Sundays a Vajrayana Buddhist shrine and a meditation center suddenly materialize. The only permanent evidence of Buddhism is a space that serves as a bookstore stall and lending library. The Sunday format usually includes the Green Tara Meditation, a discussion session, and the Three Lights Meditation. Then attendees enjoy tea, snacks, and talk. Eight to twelve is the usual number of participants, unless an outside speaker is scheduled, and then the numbers most often triple, depending on advertising.

> I grew up with an angry God, a God who had his foot on your throat all the time just waiting for you to screw up. I quickly figured out that was not going to work for me. I needed a different point of view. All of that guilt was simply too much, especially in the Catholic Church. The Episcopal Church was healthy for me and made the transition to Buddhism a very small step.[66]

Bonnie has moved to the house immediately next door, and the League City Center still thrives.

Diamond Way Buddhism

The Houston Center
4245 Jack Street
Houston, Texas 77006
Michael Savage and Mary Anne Fields

What are the odds of two unmarried people both being

employees within the National Aeronautics and Space Administration complex, both having backgrounds in the game of rugby, and both being fledgling Vajrayana Buddhists? Mike Savage and Mary Ane Fields were a match made in Titsula Heaven. He was living in the Friendswood Center. She picked up a Clear Creek newsletter one morning and noticed a flyer that concerned itself with metaphysical happenings in the area. There was an announcement advertising a lecture by Bob Sacks that evening in Friendswood. Ms. Fields and Mr. Savage have been together ever since.

In 1996, Mike made the "algae decision," and the couple moved into a house in Dickinson. They lived there for a year and a half, practicing in their home, and at the Friendswood center when Lama Ole made it to Houston.

In 1996 they moved downtown. Mr. Savage made a trip that year to Katmandu, Nepal, to witness the dedication of Lopon Tsechu's monastery there. Mr. Savage had served as Rinpoche's personal attendant during the lama's visit to Texas, and a special closeness developed between the two men.

In September 1997, when the First Church Diamond Way Center closed its doors, there were still those who wanted to continue to practice but did not want to make that long drive out to League City. The couple had only recently purchased a large condominium at the intersection of Richmond and Jack streets, right in the middle of downtown. Everything fit. The sangha simply moved from the church to Mike and Mary Anne's, and the Houston Diamond Way Center was born:

> The goal for this center is to make it a practicing center. I don't feel comfortable exchanging a lot of philosophy or Buddhist knowledge. I feel most comfortable teaching people how to meditate rather than sitting, reading a text, and discussing what it means. I don't feel comfortable giving people my interpretation of a Buddhist text.[67]

Mr. Savage is an environmental engineer with the Lockheed Corporation. In addition, and in the spirit of the Bodhisattva realm, he is also a licensed massage technician and professional hypnotist. Years earlier, when trapped in a "constricting" assignment with a mining company in Jewett, Texas, high blood pressure via stress became a real problem for him. Meditation was his solution.

In a desperate drive to leave East Texas behind, Mr. Savage spent grueling months commuting to Sam Houston State University in Huntsville to finish the required hours for a newly offered degree in the environmental sciences. He was hired by Houston's Laurel Corporation (Lockheed), which got him out of the wilderness.

Mr. Savage became what he refers to as a "spiritual dilettante." Houston has a diverse metaphysical community, and Mr. Savage played the field. He tried New Age groups, with their meditation systems, horoscopes, breathing systems, and rebirthing techniques. He took the "Course of Miracles," which works with Christ consciousness. He also tried Ram Das Hindu practices, and one evening something extraordinary happened when he was completing a meditation upon the Buddha. "I had what could be called a religious experience. I felt the Buddha in the room with me where I was sitting. It was totally real. I was hooked at that point. I was hooked."[68]

Like Mary Anne, Mike eventually found the Unity Church in nearby Friendswood. In time, Lama Ole made one of his annual appearances. When receiving a blessing following the lecture, the lama placed the gaul which had been given to him by Karmapa on top of Mr. Savage's head.

> I felt this cool energy course down what I know now to be my central energy channel. Back then I thought the central energy channel, the Kundalini that the Hindus work with, was the vertebrae. As it got to my heart, I felt this intense pain. It stopped then, and basically what was happening was my heart chakra was opening up from being closed from a failed relationship. I'm a very physical person, and this sensation and the bliss state that I went into there made me throw rocks at any dregs [from] the past. I mean, I was "totally blissed out." It was one of the best feelings that I have ever experienced in my life. I was completely hooked. I knew that I had met someone who could teach me something. If this man could do this to me, he had something to teach me.[69]

Ms. Fields and Mr. Savage explained that in Vajrayana Buddhism, one puts on the mask, that is, visualizes one's self as a Buddha, until the mask can no longer be taken off. They emphasized that the time required for such an interconnection is usually much shorter than one would ever expect. According to Mr. Savage,

> Buddhism is colorless; it's very adaptable. Buddhism will change to meet social issues. The tenets and precepts will never change, but the method of practice will. This is its strength. Buddhism is not a religion. It is a methodology for an individual to realize his or her own potential. Ole's genius is taking out what is cultural and leaving in the Buddhism. One must be careful not to throw out the baby with the bath water.[70]

As far as the strategy goes for expanding the Karma Kagyu Lineage and the Diamond Way system in Texas, Mr. Savage explained:

> Karma Kagyu is a grassroots tradition. Yes, there are monasteries, but it is the yogi tradition of Tibet. Tibet's greatest yogi, Milarepa, was Karma Kagyu. It's good to have a sangha, but in reality Vajrayana is one-on-one. It's not highly structured. It is not hierarchical. It moves around. We will never have an imposing edifice where it will be set for sixty years. It's gonna be spread through the households of America. It is a lay movement. Western Buddhism, American Buddhism will never be of a monastic order.... This is the strength of Buddhism.[71]

The center on Jack Street meets once a week on Sunday evenings. There are twelve regulars, and around twenty to thirty who come occasionally. When Lama Ole is in town, one can usually count on one hundred to five hundred people in the audience. The Houston Diamond Way Center is vital, happy, well organized, and productive, and it is turning out to be the communication and information nerve center for the entire state.

Many people from every age category passed through Tore's home in Friendswood. Among those were a young woman, Beth Harrison, and two young men, Dylan Carter and Justin Coody. These three, along with others, were eventually responsible for founding the Diamond Way Sangha at the University of Texas in Austin.

Diamond Way Buddhism
Austin Center
1701 Piedmont Avenue
Austin, Texas 78757
Dylan Carter and Justin Coody

Dylan Carter was reared by a very open-minded, metaphysically oriented mother who attended a nondenominational church, the Unity Church in Friendswood. Through Unity, Dylan and his brother met Tore Fossum, Pattie Hollestein, and eventually everyone else. One afternoon, the phone rang in Mr. Carter's home, and it was Jesper Jorgensen calling people on Tore's list of "people who might be interested" to invite them to a lecture by Lama Ole. Ms. Carter and the whole family attended. And Dylan Carter's reaction?

> I looked at [Ole] and said "Okay, This guy knows something I don't know." I felt that Lama Ole was amazing and that even if he was wrong, even if Buddhism makes no sense, even if people disagree with the philosophy, I would still like to experience life the way this lama does.... The first time I saw him, I knew that something was there.[72]

That evening, he bought Ole's *Teachings on the Nature of Mind* and read it cover to cover before morning. He was sixteen at the time, a sophomore at Clear Creek High School. Critical thinking was his forte. Everything had to be checked out, tested, and measured thoroughly before even a particle was acceptable as true. Buddhism would have to withstand the same tough scrutiny.

It was during that sophomore year that Mr. Carter and Justin Coody met. They had the same English class. Mr. Coody had read his first book on Buddhism at the age of ten. He admitted that he did not understand a great deal, yet his interest was intense. He recalled:

> I was with a parent or friend one day and we went into a bookstore. I looked around until I found the section on Eastern thought and saw a book with a picture of Buddha on it. I just reached up and grabbed it. There was something about that book that made me want to have it with me more than anything in the world. From then on, I've always felt the same. At first it was nothing that I talked to

anybody about. I didn't tell anyone that I was studying Buddhism, much less that I it all made perfect sense to me. I told no one that I was trying, even at that age, to live up to the ideals that Buddhism tries to offer. It was something that I naturally connected with. I continued to read and think.[73]

The pair would go to the Friendswood Center whenever a "big" teacher came through. By this time, Justin's girlfriend, Beth Harrison, one of the three original Austin Sangha members, was also a part of the group. And there was another friend from Clear Creek High, Mark Hayes. One evening, the four piled into Mr. Carter's car and drove down to the First Unitarian Church to hear Lama Ole speak. This was the occasion when Lopon Tsechu was part of the entourage. After the formal presentation, something extraordinary happened. The four were invited back to the Friendswood Center, where they spent all night in conversation with Ole, Hannah, Lopon Tsechu Rinpoche, and Jesper. It was unforgettable. Mr. Coody said, "That night we got to ask questions about the lecture we had just heard, or about anything. As the conversation moved along, we realized that we were discovering something, something very honest and authentic to share with the world. From then on, I've spent a lot of time studying Kagyu Buddhism itself."[74] After graduation, he went to the University of Texas in San Antonio. Mr. Carter, Mark Hayes, and Mr. Harrison attended UT-Austin.

When in Texas, Jesper Jorgenson would usually visit Mr. Coody in the Alamo City. Even though a Diamond Way center never developed there, the younger man's interest in and commitment to Buddhism never waned:

I stayed in contact with Ole through Jesper, and I continued to meditate. I read a stack of books on Buddhism and Hinduism, philosophy, like logic and psychology. At first for me, there was a new proposition, so I had to challenge it, justify it, and investigate it. As that process continued internally through formal sitting during the day and during my activities in life, I realized that I changed so much moment to moment. There was so much fluctuation biologically, psychologically, and environmentally, that the things that I would attribute to being a solid "being" were really unjustified. My body was constantly changing—my emotions, my physical body. Nothing is independent. I realized that there is no independent nature. And ultimately all of this is possible because of the nature of emptiness. That point came to life. When I understood the nature of emptiness, I was able to realize who I am. At that point I also realized how much freedom there is, freedom to create your life, and the world, for that matter. There are no substantial barriers.[75]

In time, Justin Coody would see Buddha Gaya, the site of Sakyamuni's Enlightenment in India, and visit the monastery of the sixteenth Karmapa in Rumtek. He would also seek out Kalingpong, where Thaye Dorje, the seventeenth Karmapa as recognized by the Diamond Way, currently lives. But most astoundingly, he would formally attend the Kagyu International Buddhist Institute (KIBI), Kunzig Shamarpa's school in New Delhi.

Back in Austin, Dylan Carter began the process of organizing a Diamond Way center through the University of Texas. At first he attended a Buddhist Association meeting, but the language difference proved too disconcerting. This group was 99 percent Asian, and the presentations were invariably in one Chinese dialect or another. So he, Beth Harrison, and Mark Mayes filled out all of the papers required by the university administration, received their confirmation letter in November of 1996, and had their first formal meeting before Thanksgiving. Eventually, the university offered free space in the Texas Union. There was advertising via flyers and publicity through the university's *Daily Texan* newspaper, and the sangha was off and running. Donna Russell gave the Austin Sangha a complete set of Ole tapes. These were used as working source material, along with meditation booklets contributed by Jesper Jorgenson. More often than not, twenty-five people or more would come to the meetings, and for special speakers, it would be standing room only. The Diamond Way was in business in Austin.

Before I die I would like to see that every town in the United States has a Karma Kagyu Center so that every American can hear Lama Ole speak. This is my ultimate aspiration. Ole has often said however that only 10 percent of the world's population are even open to the teachings, and that even a smaller portion of these would ever actually practice. He feels that 95 percent of the world's people are perfectly content with the way things are for themselves and are destined to remain forever oblivious. The Karma Kagyu Lineage is certainly growing, but on the world scale, it's still fairly small.[76]

Preparations have already been made for the inevitable loss, via graduation, of the three founders. The library will remain in place, all materials have been duplicated, and two have already volunteered for leadership roles, Corey Ferguson and Sergio Ayala.

Diamond Way Buddhism
Austin Center
Sergio Ayala

I came to the Kagyu centers through my brother Robert. He had met Ole at a lecture in Phoenix, Arizona. Being impressed, he phoned me in Austin, Texas. He sent along two books of Ole's and mentioned that there was a Diamond Way student group at the University of Texas. The next year in early summer I participated in co-founding a Diamond Way Center, which opened more possibilities for the community. During the last two years, I have had the opportunity to live with our San Francisco group for a while and experience the Diamond Way.[77]

There is no doubting the fact that the Austin sangha for Buddhism of the Diamond Way is in experienced and capable hands.

Diamond Way Buddhism
Texas A&M University Buddhist Association
College Station, Texas
Nathaniel Rich

Inundated totally by Catholicism during his childhood in Fort Worth, Nathaniel Rich, even at the age of five, found himself attending mass with his grandmother every day before school, reading theology in the fourth grade, corresponding with monks, and envisioning himself as a priest in a contemplative order. During his eighth-grade year, he spent a week in seminary. "I use to have these spiritual stirrings," he said. "I was always convinced that there was more than I saw, more than what I heard and what I touched. I use to call it God. I've been spiritual all of my life."[78]

Things changed abruptly, however, when Nathaniel reached high school. Sheltered in tiny, parochial settings his entire life, he found himself confronted with "bigness," strangeness, and an open curriculum for the first time.

In the world of literature, Mr. Rich discovered the "beat" poets, Allen Ginsberg and Jack Kerouac. His first exposure to Buddhism was through the Dharma Bums. He also delved into the philosophies of Plato, Aristotle, Nietzsche, Hegel, and Kant. Through friends, Nathaniel was introduced to the Gnostics and the Baha'i faith. The former he rejected for its dualism, but the Baha'is made considerable impact, especially one outstanding Baha'i practitioner.

> I think what really made me start questioning the faith that I was brought up with was the fact that here was someone who was, in my mind, the kindest, most virtuous, most spiritual person I'd ever met and he didn't even believe in Jesus. So I realistically for the first time started questioning everything that I had been taught to believe. I guess I was trying to get past the dichotomy concept, this evil-good, light-dark, God-Satan dualism. I was also rebelling against the whole idea of Theism, of having to conceive of the "ultimate" as a person. The anthropomorphic simply makes no sense to me, not anymore.[79]

And then there was a minor recreational detour through the world of drugs, marijuana, and mushrooms. Ironically, the experiences there seemed, according to Mr. Rich, to verify the Buddhist notion of the nonreality of things. He also concluded that it was, and is, very un-Buddhist to do drugs.

The first authentic book about Buddhism that Nathaniel Rich read was John Powers' *An Introduction to Tibetan Buddhism*. He found it unappealing. He filed it away but for some inexplicable reason kept coming back to it. Shortly after high school graduation, Nathaniel picked up a copy of *Awakening the Buddha Within* by Lama Surya Das, an American. The effect on him was profound.

> I can remember reading this book in my back yard in the evening. It was May. I was, like, only twenty pages into the book and I don't even remember what I had read, but I closed the book, put it down, and knew that I was a Buddhist. I put it down and I knew. Instantly, everything made perfect sense to me. After all of the searching, the reading, the questioning, suddenly it all fell together. I spent the rest of the summer reading nothing but Buddhism.[80]

In late August of 1997, Mr. Rich was a freshman again, this time at Texas A&M University in College Station, majoring in philosophy with a history minor. He soon found that there was a Buddhist Association on campus made up of anyone who considered themselves to connected to Buddhism in any way whatsoever. Most members were Asian. He felt that he needed to meet with people who could relate more directly with his own experience. One day while browsing through Web sites on Buddhism, he happened upon the title "Diamond Way Buddhism." Following the link to the main site, then to the centers, Nathaniel discovered that there was a group at the University of Texas at Austin. He sent an E-mail message to someone named Dylan Carter. Mr. Carter answered the next day. Mr. Rich made a trip to Austin when Lama Ole lectured, and unexpectly followed him to Houston the same weekend to hear more.

> I had never been that happy in my life, for no reason, absolutely no reason. Just being in the room with this guy [Lama Ole], being surrounded by people, like-minded people. It was very powerful. I can remember saying goodbye. Ole said something about not worrying, that we'd been together many lifetimes. College Station was a pretty depressing place after a weekend like that.[81]

In the spring of 1998, Mr. Rich got involved again with the Buddhist Association on campus, but this time he participated a great deal by lecturing on the subject of Karma Kagyu Buddhism and the Vajrayana vehicle. People appeared to be interested. Jesper Jorgensen came from the Diamond Way Center in San Francisco and gave a lecture. The excitement was growing. The question to answer was whether to form a totally new association or to remain integrated with the existing organization. The option chosen was to be nonsectarian, to remain a part of the original Buddhist Association, and to have two meetings each week, one of which would be strictly Diamond Way. The administrative procedure for establishing an organization is much more complicated at A&M than at UT. All of the red tape cried out for consolidation with the old group. There was, nonetheless, some reorganization. Nathaniel Rich was elected president of the new order. The group is doing well.

> A lot of interest has been expressed in the Diamond Way. The vice president this year, a friend of mine, is an undergraduate. It's the first time that there have been undergraduates in the association. The original organization is now inclined toward the Diamond Way system and the Vajrayana practice. We are all just scratching the surface, but things are positive, very positive these days.[82]

Realizing that Sakyamuni Buddha framed his teachings for his audience, Mr. Rich is careful to point out that he is attracted to all forms of Buddhism and is in no way a strict sectarian. All practices are welcome in the association. In reality, however, there needs to be a completely separate Diamond Way organization. Needless to say, a visit by Lama Ole would be of the greatest importance. Help from Houston and Austin would more than likely accelerate the movement toward establishing a pure Diamond Way sangha. Nonetheless, there is a time restraint. In two years he will graduate. And what then?

> Like I said, I wanted to be a priest for the longest time. That's one option that I am going to explore, living as a monk for a year after graduation. That would be the most skillful choice for me. I could also see myself teaching perhaps, teaching something that has to do with the Dharma. For me that is all that matters, living my life centered around the practice and study of the Dharma. I've always been drawn to monasticism, but how my life plays itself out, as monk or teacher, I simply can't predict right now. I have a couple of years to wrestle with that one.[83]

About the nature and meaning of the Dharma, Nathaniel Rich offers this enticing description emphasizing the depth of those who so often are encountered when profiling the Texas people who are drawn to Karma Kagyu Buddhism.

> The Dharma, more than any other religious practice that I have been involved with, really sets itself apart. Rather than just saying that you believe in something, something that is incidentally external, that is outside of yourself, the Dharma is something that is to be personally experienced and, most importantly, something that can't be separated from yourself. My whole thing, the problem I had with the Christian God, was that it was portrayed as something outside of my being. I didn't want to worship God, I wanted to be God. As long as you have an anthropomorphic being in the middle, it can't happen. The Dharma is totalistic. It works with every aspect of your life. Buddha is the supreme position and the Dharma is the supreme medicine. It heals all of your ills. The Dharma doesn't leave anything out. All I can do is to plant positive seeds in as many mindstreams as possible. There are people out there who are ready for the teachings. All our organization can do is to make them available. Isn't it something that one does not have to go to the East anymore?[84]

The A&M center can only be classified as a quasi-Kagyu organization, because of its lack of total commitment to the Diamond Way system. Mr. Rich intends eventually to do graduate work at the University of Texas. At this time, the center will more than likely cease to exist as a Kagyu sangha.

Diamond Way Buddhism
University of Houston Center
1822 Mill Creek Road
Houston, Texas 77008
Beth Harrison

When Beth Harrison was in the third grade, her parents began to have some problems with the bureaucracy of the Presbyterian church and their attendance became intermittent at best. By seventh grade, their daughter felt the loss. She discovered that she needed some kind of religious foundation and wanted to start a spiritual journey of some kind. On her own she found a church, a Christian church that was nondenominational, liberal, and open-minded. Her parents were wonderful about the whole thing. The adventure was intellectually invigorating, but in the end, there were still unanswered questions. Those questions have since been answered through her experiences with Buddhism.

Ms. Harrison's father spent some time in Thailand during the Vietnam War era and established a fond relationship with a group of Buddhist monks in the area where he lived. In fact, every week he would take rice to their monastery. She believes that he was intrigued by the way they lived but that the experience was mostly intellectual. Nonetheless, she has received strong and unfailing family support in her development as a Buddhist. For college graduation, she was given a meditation cushion.

Ms. Harrison and her family moved to Texas in 1996 from Delaware, by way of Ohio. She enrolled in Clear Creek High School and met Justin Coody in chemistry class. The two had a lot to talk about. In fact, they began a spiritual journey together that is still unfolding. In the beginning there were rich conversations and plenty of reading. But something seemed to be missing. "I was reading a lot of stuff that sounded beautiful," she said, "but I couldn't find that something that was practical enough to integrate into my daily life. There was all of this silly, really beautiful poetry, but I couldn't make any of it useful to myself."[85]

Dylan Carter was also a Clear Creek student and another friend of Justin Coody's. One day Mr. Carter appeared in English class with an Ole Nydahl flyer he had found. The three seventeen-year-olds were off and running, and the Friendswood Center was their first stop. In Fannin, they heard their first Lama Ole lecture and received the blessing of Lopon Tsechu Rinpoche. That evening, with Mark Mayes, the youngsters had the incredible fortune of sitting in an all-night conversation with the venerable Rinpoche, Ole, Hannah, and Jesper. As a result, Ms. Harrison became a regular practitioner of the Vajrayana vehicle in Friendswood. But suddenly the high school years ended and life started all over again.

Ms. Harrison was a major player in establishing the Diamond Way in Austin during her collegiate years.

> So it started out with three of us in a dorm room, meditating. Then we decided to make it into an official school organization. We went through the steps and got a very

tiny space. It was terrible. It had hard floors with the chairs nailed down. But the sangha grew in spite of it all. The whole thing was very grassroots. With Ole's blessing, it just exploded. I think that now there are thirty or forty strong members and probably a hundred and fifty who have been in and out. They've just moved to a larger house. It was a very nice experience.[86]

Beth Harrison graduated from UT in 2000 and is now a graduate student in the field of speech pathology and audiology at the University of Houston. She spent the summer months after graduation in Boston. Not having access there to a sangha of her choice proved to be a little disconcerting. Mary Anne Fields helped her establish a Diamond Way Buddhist Center on the University of Houston campus.

I really wanted to have something when I got back from Boston. The university is really behind me and I am reaching out to the university community. So many resources are available now because of the current interest and emphasis on multiculturalism. The university is just throwing money at us. You can get anything you want and get it cheaply. Right now we are very small. I put up our Web site, but the university did not get us into their network in time this semester. So we aren't really out there yet.[87]

Beth has been able to incorporate Buddhism in her work. As a part of her graduate studies responsibilities, she logs her clinical hours by working in a day-care facility for homeless toddlers. She sees the experience as an amazing teaching that she is receiving.

It's made me realize the precious opportunities that I had in my life. To see a four-year-old whose mother has just passed away from AIDS is heartrending. If forces one to think. There is a lot of crack and domestic violence in the world. There is so much instability. These kids are amazingly resilient, but they are so far behind because they have had so much change in their lives. Just to have a constant place to go home to every night to meditate is such a gift. That's something these children don't have. It's nice to be able to work with them, to give them attention, to help nurture them. I may never drive a Lexus, but I will have made the difference in the life of a child.[88]

Like Nathaniel Rich, Ms. Harrison never believed in the idea of a monolithic god at the center of things. Since she was moving around a lot during her high school days, she spent a lot of time within herself. And when she went to Ole's lecture,

> It was like coming home. It just felt right. I think that I have always been a compassionate person. So now I'm trying to develop a greater capacity for wisdom through my practice. Ole says that you can get a heart like a watermelon and a brain like a walnut when you get too compassionate. I don't want animals to get killed. I don't want anybody to be sad. But you can't do all of that. It just doesn't work. You have to have wisdom tempered by compassion. I also need to work very hard on my attachments. Attachment is a constant problem for me still.[89]

Mr. Harrison feels that most Westerners associate Tibetan Buddhism with frightening-looking monsters with big heads, necklaces made of skulls, and fire scorching the skies, and that people are immediately put off because it just seems too weird. She points out that such images are cultural and people must be taught the psychological significance of the pictorial metaphors. "There is a precious opportunity here in Texas and I am very optimistic. I hope things work out here in Houston. I think they will."[90]

Diamond Way Buddhism
The Texas Diamond Way Buddhist Retreat Center
302 East Palm Road
Fresno, Texas 77545 (Ft. Bend County)
Marilyn Kinsey

A year ago, Marilyn Kinsey, Lama Ole's cousin, dreamed that she was in a retreat center. There were a number of people living in wooden cottages connected by a large deck. A lake stretched out behind, almost surrounding the manmade structures. There was also a beautiful house in the forefront. Inside she could see a well-furnished gompa (shrine room). Another room, obviously an office, was evident. The images were as vivid as those of a lucid dream. There was a sense that the center was in Texas and a part of the Houston Diamond Way system. Ms. Kinsey told everyone at the League City Center about her vision. The excitement was so great that Melody Templeton agreed to be the chairwoman in charge of a property search. This was in the late fall of 1998.

At the end of July 2000, Karola Schneider, a student of Lama Ole who lives in the Schwarzenberg Retreat Center in southern Germany, was lecturing in Houston. One meeting was held in an old house that was being renovated at the time by Susan Lupton and her boyfriend. Diamond Way signs had been placed outside so that those searching for the place would not stay permanently lost. The neighbors took exception to the meeting. They got up in arms and vocal about it. The meeting went forward as scheduled, but as part of the fallout, sangha members fervently expressed their wish for a permanent place, a center large enough for retreats, with live-in accommodations, lots of green space, and light and water. Karola sealed the wish with a special blessing.

When Susan went home that night, she got on the Internet and found multiple listings of properties available in the Houston area. One possibility, only twelve miles south of downtown, looked so good that the next day, Gaye Cummins, Rami Owens, and Ms. Kinsey found the place, climbed over a fence with the neighbors watching, and explored. It was remarkably similar to the center Marilyn Kinsey had envisioned in her dream the year before. It was perfect! Ms. Lupton immediately started the real estate negotiations. Everything fell into place. It is now a part of the Diamond Way system.

The site consists of twelve acres and has a lovely three-bedroom house built in 1954, which is on two acres fronting the major access road. It is surrounded by large oak, magnolia, and pecan trees. There is also a garage with a two-room apartment that has a kitchenette and a large bathroom—along with termites. There are two lakes on the back ten acres; one of them is large enough to ski on and has its own islands. It has been named Lotus Lake. The smaller but deeper lake is called Dakini Pond. The more remote area is covered with native plants and trees. The entire place was a steal at $185,000.

A nonprofit corporation out of San Francisco, a part of the Diamond Way system, will eventually own the two acres in front and all of the structures. This will be financed through rental charges, retreat fees, and donations. The back acreage is being bought collectively by Ms. Kinsey, Michael Williams, Rami Owens, Gaye Cummins, Melody Templeton, and Bonnie Cooper. The intent is to build an environmentally friendly townhouse complex near the lakes, an "intentional community" that leaves lots of space, lots of room for retreats. This will make the fourth Diamond Way center in the greater Houston area.

Michael Williams and Rami Owens have already moved into the home. One of the bedrooms has been converted into an administrative office. If Dylan Carter, now a graduate of the University of Texas, can find employment in Houston, he plans to move into the garage apartment, termites or not. The Texas Buddhist Retreat Center is already up and running. Ms. Kinsey said, "This will make a fourth sangha in Houston. I don't want it to sound like it is my center. I'm just the catalyst. We have a beautiful vision statement. Everyone is thinking of it as such a boon for all of Texas. We've all had that feeling from the very beginning."[91]

In spite of all of the goodwill, by all appearances, the sangha on Jack Street will be closing its doors. Mike Savage and Mary Anne Fields believe that the two centers are too close together to justify the existence of both. Mr. Savage has resigned his position as travel secretary and is looking forward to simply practicing. Sergio Ayala has volunteered to assume the ponderous secretarial responsibilities. The regular Monday meditations have been discontinued.

As noted earlier in the text, Tibetan lama Gampopa is noted for his fusion of the yogic path with monasticism, giving the Karma Kagyu Lineage a firm foundation on which to establish a broad and vibrant tradition. By providing an authentic home base, the creation of the Texas retreat center will also contribute a definite sense of stability, as well as provide a platform for expansion of the Diamond Way in the state.

The preceding biographical sketches represent but a fraction of the stories that account for the generation of the Tibetan Vajrayana practice in Texas. These dedicated individuals portray the human side of Buddhism, the spiritual turmoil and human evolution one endures in making one's way to the Dharma through the Karma Kagyu lineage.

Human fallibility, on the other hand, has caused discord between various Tibetan Buddhist traditions, as well as actual conflict between Karma Kagyu subsects. Presently there are two candidates vying for recognition as the legitimate seventeenth Karmapa, and there is no resolution in sight for the unhappily divided Kagyus. This internecine hostility is tearing the Karma Kagyu lineage apart worldwide. This problem, its origin and development, deserves a closer look.

Chapter 5

The Karmapa War: An Overview

Karma Dondrup and his wife Loga, nomads in Tibet's eastern province of Kham, in the small village of Barkor, wanted desperately to have another child, a son. The couple asked the great yogi Thogden Amdo Palden Rinpoche if he would intercede through special empowerments on their behalf. Rinpoche consented with the stipulation that if a boy was born, it would be given to him. Loga became pregnant and on June 26, 1985, gave birth to a son.[1]

At the time of his birth, the villagers reported hearing the sound of conch shells coming from all directions. It went on for over an hour and was followed by the sound of other musical instruments. Again the source of the sound could not be found. Flowers grew that had not been seen in the area before. Perhaps the most dramatic of the many signs were the three suns which shone in the sky, seen by all present. They were the same size and appeared in a row. Over the middle sun arched a rainbow, each end of which dissolved in the flaming suns. The phenomenon was reported throughout Eastern Tibet.[2]

When the child reached the age of four, Amdo Palden assumed parental responsibilities and took the yet-to-be-named boy to his monastery, Kalek Gompa. From birth, the boy's older sister had called him Apo Gaga, which means "happy brother."

The sixteenth Karmapa had predicted his own successor by writing a sacred letter disclosing the time and place of his next birth, as well as the parents' names. The letter was hidden within an amulet and given to Tai Situ Rinpoche in 1981 six months before Karmapa's death. The sacred letter of prediction was not discovered until 1992. Copies were sent to Drupon Dechen Rinpoche at Tsurphu Monastery, the original seat of the Karmapa lamas, in Tibet. With permission of the government, a search for the tulku was immediately conducted by Akong Rinpoche and Sherab Tarchin, representing Tai Situ and Gyaltsab rinpoches. Prior to the arrival of this entourage, the child had insisted that he be allowed to visit his parents, who were with their cattle herd in the spring pasture in the hills near Barkor. As a result, when the child Karmapa was found, the family was in the exact place as described by the sixteenth Gyalwa Karmapa in his prediction letter to the world. Greeted by thousands on a cold and misty morning of June 15, Karmapa returned at last to his monastery, the Summer Palace of Tsurphu, for enthronement as Ugyen Trinley, His Holiness the Seventeenth Karmapa.[3]

For many, this is the only acceptable version of the discovery and installation of the seventeenth Karmapa. Ugyen Trinley was tentatively given recognition as Karmapa on June 9 by His Holiness the Dalai Lama and was formally recognized on July 3, 1992. Tai Situ, when asked for proof of authenticity of his candidate by *Asiaweek* magazine, responded, "There is no such thing as proving, it is proved already. The Karmapa is the Karmapa, Buddha is Buddha, the Dalai Lama is the Dalai Lama. We are believers. That's it."[4]

There is another community of Karma Kagyus, however, who have a very different story to tell. It goes like this:

For protection from Chinese brutality, Mipham Rinpoche was hidden in the mountains by his Nyingma teacher for many of his youthful years. In 1982, after a general relaxation of restrictions on religious practices, the Rinpoche moved to Lhasa to contribute what he could toward rebuilding Buddhist institutions and practices. In time, he became the head of thirteen monasteries. During that period, his yidam indicated that if he took a consort, he would have several children who would become Bodhisattvas. He married Dechen Wangmo, a Chakrasambhara practitioner, and settled in an apartment in Lhasa near the Jokhang Temple. A son was born in 1983. At the age of two, the little boy started telling people that he was the Karmapa. One day in 1985 an old Sakya lama, Ngorpa Lagen, while strolling near the temple, noticed the child and out of courtesy nodded in greeting. The boy called out, "Don't you know that I am the Karmapa!"[5] Taking the exclamation very seriously, the lama asked for a blessing: "The boy stretched out his arm and touched the lama. According to the lama, he instantly felt something akin to the post-meditative experience of deep calm and expansiveness that prevails over all forms of gross emotions."[6]

Ngorpa Lagen told this story to Lama Sherab Rinpoche, who made it a point to visit the Mipham household. When in the presence of the child, Rinpoche started to tremble and was unable to stop. His attendant reported that he had experienced exactly the same sensation. Lama Sherab told of his encounter with the boy as well as that of Ngorpa Lagen to Kunzig Shamar Rinpoche in 1987. Just the year before, the Shamarpa had been given this account of a dream by Chobgye Tri Rinpoche, a Sakya lama.

> Shortly before the late Karmapa passed away, I had had a dream. His Holiness went around a stupa wearing his usual Dharma robes. He appeared to be sad. In my dream, I too felt sad and shed tears. Soon after my dream, Karmapa died. Then, just a few days before coming here, I had yet another dream. This time, His Holiness was clad in a yellow robe while again he walked around a stupa. The color of his vestment was radiant, and his mood was cheerful. At noon the same day, a relative who had arrived from Lhasa visited me. He brought a photograph of a young child who was well-known in the area my relative came from. People there knew that the child had on several occasions said that he was Karmapa.[7]

Based on this information, three emissaries, including Lopon Tsechu Rinpoche, were sent to Lhasa to investigate the authenticity of the claims, the family, and the possibility that this was actually the next Karmapa. During this time, a "mystery person," an anonymous, well-respected devotee of the sixteenth Karmapa, approached the senior regent. This still-unidentified person, it is said, presented Shamarpa with the astounding news that Rangjung Rigpe, the sixteenth Karmapa himself, had given him instructions for finding His Holiness's incarnation. Taking what limited information he had into account, Shamarpa then entered into a meditation retreat. Two auspicious dreams occurred, one in which he threw rice toward a Buddha and the grain turned into rain that fell on the statue. Light then started radiating in all directions from a very large butter lamp that was filled with nectar. It seemed to be a sign for action.

After a personal attempt to visit the family failed, a ritual was practiced in which two slips of paper were put in a box, with an indication that the boy was the Karmapa written on one and the opposite on the other. When the game was played, four out of four times, the scrap of paper indicating that Karmapa was the Mipham youth presented itself. The decision was made by the Sharmapa. This child was the incarnate Karmapa lama!

In January 1994, the young boy and his parents applied for permission to visit Katmandu. Unwittingly, the passports were granted. Traveling overland, the Mipham clan escaped from Tibet to Nepal and then to India. The child was taken to New Delhi, where at the Karmapa International Buddhist Institute on March 17 he was formally recognized by Sharmapa as the seventeenth Karmapa. In November 1996, the new Karmapa joined the monkhood by receiving refuge vows at the Buddha Gaya Temple. He was then given the name Thinley (Buddha activity) Thaye (limitless) Dorje (unchanging). Thaye Dorje now resides in Kalimpong, India, less than five miles from the mountain kingdom of Sikkim and the Karmapa's Monastery of Rumtek.[8]

Within Buddhist cosmology, there is room for both stories; two simultaneous emanations of a spiritual entity are entirely acceptable. It is in the realm of the relative, in the Machiavellian world of *realpolitik* that the fireworks often occur when the unorthodox becomes fact. The Karma Kagyu lineage "should" have one Karmapa, a single spiritual fountainhead, so accompanying the two candidates is a great deal of trouble. This case is now in its eighth year. Realizing how sensitive both sides are about their version of the truth, it is virtually impossible to discuss even the background of the tale without angering and alienating one group or the other. Yet if there is "first cause" for the Karmapa War, it would have to be China. A second cause would be a personal drive for religious and political power. A third, subtle cause is a continuation of the struggle for political supremacy of the Tibetan people between the Gelugpa and Kagyu orders.[9]

The Chinese Communist government has adopted an uncompromising policy of total domination of the territory that used to be Tibet. Military presence is one method of control; another is domestication of Tibet's religious hierarchy. If Beijing can determine who gets recognized as the next Dalai, Panchen, and Karmapa lamas, their control over Tibet will be sealed, since these figures are revered so deeply by the Tibetan people. Such a move is already well in process.

The tenth Panchen Lama, the Dalai Lama's traditional second-in-command, died in 1989 with no recognized reincarnation. In 1995 the Dalai Lama announced the discovery of a five-year-old as the successor. The Chinese immediately arrested the child and installed Gyaltsen Norbu, another boy of five, the son of a Communist official, as their own eleventh Panchen Lama. Since both Norbu and the present Dalai Lama are of the Gelugpa Order, in the event of Tenzin Gyatso's death, Gyaltsen Norbu has the authority to recognize the fifteenth Dalai Lama. Since from the mid-1990s the Chinese have controlled both Panchen Lamas, and therefore the succession of the Dalai Lama, their attention could from that time forward focus on gaining command of the Karmapa, the senior lama of the Karma Kagyu. And there is no doubting the fact that Beijing did just that.[10]

When the sixteenth Karmapa died in 1981, Dhamcho Yongdu, then Karmapa's general secretary, called for the creation of a committee of regents to locate the next reincarnation. It should be noted that, according to Kunzig Shamar Rinpoche, this task was traditionally the sole responsibility of the Sharmapa. Shamar Rinpoche nonetheless dutifully acquiesced, and the committee to oversee the transition was formed of the four senior Kagyupa tulkus, the senior regent Shamarpa himself, Tai Situ Rinpoche, Goshir Gyaltsap Rinpoche, and Jamgon Kongtrul Rinpoche. By tradition, a letter would soon be found containing details of the future birth, but this time, nothing appeared until 1990, and it was not made public until March 1992, when Tai Situ made the announcement. When Shamar Rinpoche examined the prediction document, however, he declared it to be a forgery. From this point, events unfolded rapidly, dramatically, and unhappily. Jamgon Kongtrul, as a neutral in the controversy, had been asked collectively by the other three regents to enter Tibet and to begin a methodical search for the authentic Karmapa following the instructions of the prediction letter. He was killed in a car wreck on April 26, 1992. Even though Jamgon Rinpoche had been given the sensitive assignment of examining the child, on April 8, a team from Tsurphu, on the orders of Tai Situ, had already found their way to the village of Barkor. On the 24th, a pick-up party was in the field. On June 9, Situ and Gyaltsab rinpoches contacted the Dalai Lama by fax and phone in Brazil, and on the 15th, the boy finally arrived in Tsurphu Monastery. The Chinese government acknowledged Ugyen Trinley as the Karmapa Tulku on June 29, and the eight-year-old was officially enthroned on September 27, 1992, in Tsurphu Monastery. Shamar Rinpoche took no part in the ceremonies. In September 1994, Karmapa was invited to Beijing to be congratulated by President Jiang Zemin and told that he was to receive six years of training in communist ideology. In 1999, Karmapa finished his training and the Joint Action of Sikkim Committee secretly met with Chinese officials in Lhasa. Three months after the committee's meeting, Ugyen Trinley departed Tsurphu Monastery for India, leaving a note saying that he was going to collect his crown.[11]

China sees Buddhism itself as the threat to its sovereignty in Tibet. Since the ultimate goal of Beijing is to have a passive Tibetan province, selecting their own top lamas is considered one of the most convenient ways to achieve this end. By all appearances, they had their game in the bag by 1994, until two extraordinary events spoiled their well-thought-out political objectives. The first of these events was the announcement by His Holiness the Fourteenth Kunzig Shamar Rinpoche of the arrival and enthronement in India of Thaye Dorje as the seventeenth Karmapa, a tulku over whom the Chinese could exercise no control whatsoever. Second was the escape from Tsurphu Monastery, and Tibet itself, of Karmapa Ugyen Trinley. Presently, Ugyen Trinley is residing in the Gyuto Monastery, just down the hill from the Dalai Lama's residence-in-exile in Dharamsala, India, north of New Delhi. His arrival surprised the Indian government and put its officials in a difficult position. The Indian officials will have to decide whether to allow or disallow the young Tibetan's entry into Sikkim and his possible enthronement in the Karmapa's seat in Rumtek. His enthronement would no doubt infuriate Beijing. A question of great importance now is which candidate will inherit control of Rumtek Monastery and the holy religious items, including the famed Black Crown, that have been stored there.[12]

Beijing's immediate recognition of Ugyen Trinley's claim as the Karmapa Lama begs the question of prior knowledge and involvement in the recognition process of this candidate. It points to the second cause of the Karmapa War, a personal drive for religious and political ascendancy.[13]

First, it would be appropriate to make a historical reference. Once, a conflict between the Nepalese and Tibetan governments concerning the circulation of counterfeit currency ended in an invasion of Tibet by the Nepalese King Bahadur Shah. China intervened on behalf of the Tibetans, who were being badly beaten, and peace was negotiated in 1792. The tenth Sharmapa, who had sought refuge in Nepal at the time, was blamed for the political and military debacle. In retaliation, the Tibetan government banned the enthronement of all future reincarnated Shamarpas. A major Kagyu monastery was also confiscated and converted to the Gelugpa order. Even though there was an official ban of the Sharmapa seat, it continued de facto as if there had been no interruption. In 1956 the sixteenth Karmapa invited Tenzin Gyatso to Tsurphu and requested that he revoke the ban. All was agreed, but the Chinese invasion again interrupted the process. In an attempt to unite the Tibetans, at Rumtek in 1963, the seat of the Sharmapa was finally formally reinstated. As a sidelight, however, the ending of this two-hundred-year banishment resulted in a feudal shift in the Karma Kagyu hierarchy. Sharmapa's reinstatement as number two behind the Karmapa knocked Tai Situ and his entourage down a rung. And as reported in *Asiaweek* commentary, "The scene was set for trouble."[14]

There is no contesting the fact that there had been extensive contact between the Chinese government and two of the regents, Tai Situ Rinpoche and Gyaltsap Rinpoche, as well as a colleague, Akong Tulku. It was Akong Tulku who saw and took advantage of China's new open-door policy begun by Deng Xiaoping in the late 1970s to repair some of the damage caused by the Cultural Revolution. He made numerous trips to China and became Tai Situ's representative to Beijing. To his credit, successful humanitarian efforts were made through his charity in Tibet. For this work, the Chinese government declared

Akong to be a "Living Buddha." By working with the government in power, no doubt the suffering in Tibet could be eased in some way. Yet one cannot help but wonder if there was a price to be paid, in the form of Beijing establishing their own Karmapa. Legal assaults were made upon the Sharmapa's office, as well as upon that of Topga Yulgyal Rinpoche, the general secretary of both Rumtek and of the Karmapa Charitable Trust, the office responsible for all financial and legal functions of the Karma Kagyu Order. The legal assaults all failed. A physical attack was initiated against Rumtek Monastery, resulting in the ousting of the monks loyal to Sharmapa and in the installation of those favoring Tai Situ's Karmapa. Another assault was attempted at the Karmapa International Buddhist Institute in New Delhi during Thaye Dorje's enthronement, but it was beaten back by monks loyal to Sharmapa, reinforced by European Kagyus of the Lama Ole Nydahl's Diamond Way. Hannah Nydahl and Tore Fossum were present during this confrontation.[15]

In the "Karmapa Papers," a 1992 publication by Michael Nesterenko, it is stated that Tai Situ Rinpoche had visited the monastery in which Ugyen Trinley was a monk as early as 1991. In a newsletter of Sherab Ling, Situ Rinpoche's monastery in India, it was printed that in September of the same year, Tai Situ stayed for a week in Beijing, where he met with Chinese officials and with Nagabo Jigme, the former governor of the Tibetan Autonomous Region. The article also states that a party had already "been with the boy" as early as February of 1992. Nesterenko, putting it all together, questions, "Had everything been carefully planned well in advance, i.e. long before Jamgon Kongtrul Rinpoche's mission to look into the matter? And if so, wouldn't it have been presented [as] a 'fait accompli?'"[16]

The evidence painfully points, for whatever reason, to collusion between Tai Situ and Beijing, with the intent of bypassing the Sharmapa in the selection and recognition process of the seventeenth Karmapa. If it is actually for the purpose of gaining personal political power, then there is another, interlocking possibility. What if the Dalai Lama dies in the near future while the Panchen Lamas are essentially inactive? If there follows no Dalai Lama at all, since China would be calling the shots, then the Karma Kagyu lineage would ascend to political dominance of the Tibetan people. After all, the Mongols did exactly the same for the Gelugpas in the thirteenth century. So the Chinese will, most likely, try to do the same in the twenty-first century for the Kagyus, through a Karmapa that is "theirs," Ugyen Trinley. The real winners would be those who were most helpful in the process to Beijing, those highest in the Kagyu hierarchy. With a discredited Sharmapa, Tai Situ Rinpoche would assume the position once held by the fourteenth Dalai Lama, a position of international acclaim worthy of a war perhaps, or at least a major motion picture.[17]

Of course, one could accept that Tai Situ Rinpoche's prediction letter was authentic from the very beginning, and that Sharmapa's need to find his own Karmapa was a fraudulent operation, and that it was the Sharmapa's personal ambition that led to the present state of affairs. One could expect this opinion, certainly, from the supporters of Tai Situ, Gyaltsab, and Akong Tulku, as well as Shambhala International, Woodstock, the Karma Thegsum Choling satellites, and the Rigpe Dorje Foundation membership. Clearly, the letter should be brought under the forensic microscope. If this does not happen, speculation is our only recourse. As Beth Condrey Kennan of the Dallas KTC Center commented, "Those who know aren't saying. Those who are saying, don't."[18] In reality, though, the Texas Karma Kagyus, regardless of the evidence, will most likely simply choose to acknowledge the Karmapa candidate that their lamas tell them to. Amy Lavine points out in *Faces of Buddhist America* that the KTD system in New York is working diligently toward establishing a home for Ugyen Trinley in their Woodstock facility.[19]

If two emanations are actually possible, then does the discord really make any difference, as long as the individual practitioner's meditations are not compromised? Yes, there are still real problems, on a higher level. The conflict could cause the paralyzation of the entire Karma Kagyu lineage. Continued hostilities would also create an opportunity for "open season" on all of Tibetan Buddhism and jeopardize the credibility and influence of the government-in-exile.

The Karmapa conflict has opened the door to Chinese involvement in Tibet's politics of reincarnation. Another problem for the Kagyu lineage is the Dalai Lama and his Gelugpa school of Tibetan Buddhism. It is significant that Ugyen Trinley is not only referred to as the "Chinese candidate," the "Commiepa" for short, but has also been labeled the "Dalai Lama's Candidate."[20]

Kunzig Shamar Rinpoche wrote in a statement to all Kagyupa members on October 14, 1999,

> In my humble opinion, the root cause of the turmoil surrounding the identification of the reincarnation of the late Karmapa ultimately can be traced back to his relentless challenge to the policy of His Holiness Dalai Lama and the Tibetan Government in Exile to unify all the different religious schools of Tibet. While agreeing with the policies for political and ethnic unification, the late Karmapa, and many other Tibetan religious leaders, however, feared that the religious policy would extinguish the rich, meaningful diversity of Tibetan spiritual life. The late Karmapa's leadership role in opposing this policy subjected the Dalai Lama to considerable pressure ... As a result, it is understandable that the Tibetan Government in Exile would want to use the recognition of the 17th Karmapa for its political benefit to avoid any possible future challenge from a strong, independent spiritual leader like the 16th Karmapa.[21]

In the 1960s, the Dalai Lama's brother, Gyalo Thondup, attempted to bring all Tibetan Buddhist sects under Gelugpa control. It was insinuated that force would be used if necessary. Exile settlements united to fight his political design. Unrest erupted within the community. *Asiaweek* reported in its October 20, 2000, issue, "In March of 1977, settlements leader Gungthang was shot several times at point-blank range. The murderer said he received 300,000 rupees from the Tibetan Government in Exile. He claimed it offered him even more to kill the 16th Karmapa."[22]

Again in 1962, the fourteenth Dalai Lama attempted to merge all four schools under his authority. The Tibetan government-in-exile issued a proclamation asserting its power to recognize the reincarnations of all four schools. The declaration went unchallenged in the media, which reinforced the misperception about the extent of the Gelugpa school's spiritual authority. Representatives of the Nyingma school, ignoring the Dalai Lama's choice for the reincarnation of Dudjom Rinpoche, the highest Nyingma lama, closed ranks and elected their own independent leadership under Penor Rinpoche in 1991. All of the disciples followed their own school's choice, ignoring the

Dalai Lama completely. No harm befell the Nyingmas. The Kagyus, because of China's influence, and approachable Rinpoches who may have truly believed that they were doing what was best for Tibet, simply fell apart. The Dalai Lama's embracing of Ugyen Trinley served to further shatter the Kagyus, thereby strengthening the domination of Tibetan Buddhism by the Gelugpas.[23]

Traditionally, the Dalai Lama has never had the power to recognize the Karmapa. With all of the powers that the office commands, he is respected and revered as the political leader of all Tibetan people. His influence as head of the government-in-exile is tremendous, and winning the Nobel Prize certainly enhanced his prestige and the range of his political supremacy. However, historically, his *spiritual* authority has never extended beyond his Gelugpa school. In fact, the Dalai Lama has no spiritual authority whatsoever over any of the Tibetan schools of Buddhism. It is the responsibility of the Karmapa and Sharmapa to protect the spiritual integrity and pure lineage of the Karma Kagyu.[24]

The first Karmapa lived in the twelfth century, over three hundred years before the Gelugpa school was ever founded and before the first Dalai Lama was recognized. Five Karmapas reincarnated before the first Dalai Lama appeared. It is, then, a historical impossibility to claim that the Dalai Lamas have always anointed the Karmapa reincarnations. In addition, the Nyingma, Sakya, Kadam, and Kagyu schools each ruled the government of Tibet at some period before the Dalai Lama's ascendancy. Hostility has been a way of life in Tibet's cultural and political arenas. In the spirit of tradition, and probably much to the chagrin of the government-in-exile, Kunzig Shamar is proving every bit as obstreperous and as tenacious to the Karma Kagyu cause as was the sixteenth Karmapa, Gyalwa Karmapa.[25]

In the spirit of harmony, Sharmapa, under great pressure from an old teacher he greatly admired, Ugyen Tulku, as well as Lopon Tsechu, accepted Tai Situ's candidate, Ugyen Trinley, as Karmapa in June of 1992. This acknowledgment was quickly rescinded. Presently, again seeking some degree of harmony, Shamarpa Rinpoche proposes that both nominees be respected. This might prevent any schism in the lineage. In this scenario, Ugyen Trinley would inherit Tsurphu Monastery, the Karmapa's traditional seat, and Thaye Dorje would be given Rumtek Monastery. This compromise has merit. As a citizen of

China, the Chinese candidate is forbidden ownership of property in India. For the Indian candidate, however, there are no such restrictions. As far as the Karmapa's property being held in the Rumtek Monastery, it is stated in the rules of the Karmapa Charitable Trust that all assets must be released to the Karmapa when he reaches the age of twenty-one. Since the trust has no authority over determining the legitimate Karmapa, the property will be given to both nominees. Ugyen Trinley will reach the appointed age in 2006, Thaye Dorje in 2004. In essence, the two young men will have to solve the problem between themselves. How each performs his duties, and the depth of their spiritual development, as expected of the seventeenth Karmapa, are, in the meantime, absolutely critical to determining who will win the minds and hearts of the followers of the Karma Kagyu lineage in Tibet, Europe, and South and North America.[26]

It would be appropriate now to stand back and look at Texas Buddhism for a moment as a part of the much larger national picture. In North America, in all reality, there are two Buddhisms. One is Asian, made up mostly of an immigrant population. The other is the Euro-American version, often referred to as Western or Anglo Buddhism, and its practitioners known as white Buddhists, or converts. There is "Buddhism in America," and there is "American Buddhism." The two systems, for the most part, are essentially isolated one from the other. One community views the other as intellectually arrogant, elite, and privileged (the Anglos), whereas the other is perceived as fundamentalist, dogmatic, and too devotional.

Asian centers certainly exist to teach the Dharma, but at the same time they exist to provide a place for social interaction, as well as to preserve and nurture a traditional way of life. Cultural heritage is definitely a barrier between Asian and Anglo practitioners, but as one would suspect, language is the most divisive element. Now that so many English translations have been made of Buddhist texts, with the encouragement of teachers such as Trungpa Rinpoche and Ole Nydahl, Westerners naturally seek out these English-speaking centers, not only for ease of communication, but also for the safety of cultural familiarity. Most Asians are also choosing to remain in their own Buddhist communities. As a result of this natural isolation, in the Anglo sanghas, the Dharma is changing into something that seems very familiar to North Americans.[27]

There are features now that can be called markedly Texan and American. American converts have created exclusively a lay community, and they are practice-oriented. Sitting, meditating, and seeking Enlightenment is what it is all about for the Anglos. Texans want to live the practice, to live the Realization presented by Gautama Buddha, but outside of monastic constraints. The lay communities have preceded the monasteries in the West. Historically, it has always the other way around.

The Western practitioners are not afraid to be inspirational, experimental, and innovative in their Buddhist path, even at the expense of doctrine and dogma, because the culture itself has always been forward-looking, with an insatiable need to inquire. Western Buddhism is egalitarian and democratic in its structure, nonhierarchical, and noninstitutional. Centers form their own boards of directors these days, and teachers are told when their stay has outlasted their welcome. There is even a tendency for the Western practitioner to have a more intimate relationship with "Emptiness" than with the guru. Just as the Protestants eliminated the role of the Catholic priest, a similar tendency is evident in Western Buddhism. Such a step would certainly diminish the power and prestige of the traditional Vajrayana hierarchy, challenging the entire structure of the guru yogi system.

Western Buddhism is gender-equal and is being shaped radically by feminist insight. Sadly enough, this democratization was accompanied by a series of scandals and incidents involving sexual misconduct by early lamas. Even the great Kalu Rinpoche found himself among the accused. These scandals led to the questioning of the hierarchical structure of the systems and the close inspection of the authoritarian aspect of the student-teacher relationship. As a result, protocols have changed, and democratic procedures have been implemented in the sanghas. The old regime, the European feudal system, was never able to plant its roots in North America, so it is not expected that the same cultural feature, in its Asian form, will fare any better. As a direct result, then, feudal elements like antinomianism have been declared unacceptable, and accountability is now expected. The amount of literature discussing women in Buddhism from the Western perspective is growing exponentially in the post-patriarchal Buddhist period. Richard

Seager is quick to point out that Buddhism's "non-theistic character means that there is no creator, father, and judge as in Judaism and Christianity, a form of anthropomorphism often identified as a source of oppressive attitudes and practices toward western women."[28]

There is a tendency in Western sanghas to be integrative rather than reclusive. Sanghas operate with families in mind and acknowledge a practitioner's professional responsibilities. So follows the inclination for some secularization. This process in some circles has evolved into the implicit or explicit abandonment of the idea of reincarnation. Another evolving concept is to view cosmic deities as metaphors, with some groups regarding rituals as only personal and collective means of expression. A development such as this is certainly unacceptable for the many traditionalists.[29]

Western psychology has embraced Buddhism, using its meditation techniques as a new methodology for easing human suffering. It is sometimes called "domesticated Buddhism." Because of the often confusing cultural baggage that has accompanied the Dharma of the East, some Westerners, Stephen Batchelor in particular, are calling for an agnostic practice, a "Buddhism without beliefs." Jon Kabat-Zinn, founder of the Center for Mindfulness, Medicine, Health Care, and Society at the University of Massachusetts Medical Care Center, has indicated that he wants a Buddhism without Buddhism, one without religious ties, that uses its meditation methods to serve mankind. Mr. Kabat-Zinn feels that one does not need to believe in anything in order to reap the benefits of meditation, because the Dharma, the practice, transcends culture and even absorbs Buddhism itself. Buddhism in this sense is a "therapy about selfishness" and the Four Noble Truths are a "therapeutic recipe." The Dharma he envisions arising in America could very well be one that is not even Buddhist.[30]

The integration of Buddhism into the fabric of Western society, this understanding of interconnectedness through non-duality, is instilling in American Buddhism a sense of optimism and even activism, as opposed to the traditional tendency toward renunciation of life and withdrawal. By taking the inner spiritual essence of the Dharma and making a practical application in the relative world, "engaged Buddhism" is resulting in a new face of Buddhism. In its deepest meaning, this activist approach to social problems means re-directing the personal quest for transcendence to a collective transformation of society. The Buddhist twist is that the external problems, whatever they are, are solved only as inner peace finds its place in the daily lives and in the hearts of those concerned. As the individual learns the secret of tranquility, the personal becomes the collective, and society changes. Meditation itself in this sense could be defined as perceiving collectively. It is "trickle-up" model—change from the inside out.[31]

With Buddhism's new inclusiveness, women as leaders are becoming universal, gays and lesbians are finding acceptance in the sanghas, and racial barriers are breaking down. But, admittedly, problems still exist. Bell Hooks, a professor of English at City College of New York, made this comment about racism in the convert sanghas:

> Implicit racism in many convert circles tends to relegate both African Americans and ethnic Asian immigrants to the margins of the community. In the United States there are many black people and people of color engaged with Buddhism who do not have visibility or voice. Surely it is often racism that allows white comrades to feel so comfortable with their "control" and "ownership" of Buddhist thought and practice in the United States. They have much to learn, then, from those people of color who embrace humility in practice and release the ego's need to be recognized.[32]

Nonetheless, with the loosening of the bonds of selfishness and the revelation of interconnectedness, Buddhist-inclined Westerners are beginning to look at the "whole" for the first time. The Buddhists see the relevance of taking proper care of the Earth, the "little speck of dust" on which the human being resides. Richard Hughes Seager refers to this aspect of twenty-first-century American Buddhism as "Dharma Gaia," Earth consciousness, a distinctively American characteristic. Alan Badiner, an ecology essayist, draws parallels between the Gaia Hypothesis and the interdependence of all beings, and he speaks of a "cosmic ecology": "The Buddhist emphasis on awareness and mindful living opens our perception to the interdependence and fragility of all life, and our indebtedness to countless beings, living and dead, past and future, near and far."[33]

This sense of wholeness through the Buddhist concept of interconnectedness, interdependence, and nonattachment is dissolving the old logic of fundamental theism and creating a new starting point for Western perception. From this viewpoint, the definiteness of opposites no longer exists. One simply cannot say that there is only right against wrong, death versus life, man versus nature, woman versus man, or them against us. In systems theory, nothing is independent. The entire universe and everything in it is a single, undivided whole, and is impermanent.[34]

Most Anglo Buddhists see these Western adaptations as necessary and correct. What remains to be seen is whether certain core values of the twenty-first century will persist—the ones described by Surya Das as America's Three Jewels, Me, Myself, and I. Mr. Das feels that unrestrained individualism, so close to the heart of every Westerner, will prove to be unalterable. Certainly a question to ponder is whether other collective national characteristics, such as unbridled consumerism and a bent toward militarism, will also prove intractable? There is also the possibility that the historically dominant North American religious traditions, Protestantism and Catholicism, will meet the challenge and be able to recapture the wandering flock. It is also entirely possible for Buddhism in the West to wither on the vine. One can imagine the cynical accusation that the Buddhists, with the loss of their homeland, simply chose the richest country in the world so they could grow "fat" perpetuating an empty, godless philosophy and continuing a way of life where they sit high upon a feudal dais and enjoy being petted and worshiped as always, by the multitudes from afar.[35]

Yet Charles Prebish, author of *Luminous Passage: The Practice and Study of Buddhism in America,* sees the unfolding of the American Buddhist practice in an entirely different light, "a future American Buddhism in which the rich and varied forms of practice spawn communities of self-reliant, energetic, spiritually healthy individuals."[36]

Robert Thurman, Professor of Indo-Tibetan studies at Columbia University, in an address at the First Buddhism in America Conference in 1997, using Zen Master Gadjin Nagao as a reference, captured what both believe to be the true importance of America in the evolution of Buddhism. Thurman pointed out there are five peaks in the history of Buddhism. The first was the time that Buddha himself taught, the second was the rise of Mahayana, third was the appearance of the Tantrayana or Vajrayana, and the fourth was a period of Buddhist renaissance in both Tibet and China. Gadjin Nagao's analysis of the fifth peak, however, was nothing less than startling, capturing the incredible and fundamental importance of the development of Buddhism and the Dharma in North America.

> There will be no fifth peak, unless it happens here in America. This is the only place where there could be a fifth peak in the history of Buddhism, a fifth great renaissance in Buddhism, and it can only be created by you. Then, if you did it, it will reverberate back in Asia where Buddhism was, where people have the forms of Buddhism. But it will not be able to originate there in Asia. It will only happen here.[37]

North Americans are now in their third generation of teachers, instructors who have been trained by Westerners in the West. Charles Prebish points out in *Luminous Passage* that no less than twenty tulkus have been reborn in America, and through the Dharma, Americans are well on their way to finding the fountainhead of their own true nature. In past ages, it took centuries for new Buddhist systems to arise from the old, but with the speed of twenty-first-century communications, the appearance of a distinctive American Buddhism will surely be apparent within decades. Jon Kabat-Zinn appears to agree:

> It may not be appropriate for the traditions, whatever they are, to perpetrate themselves here, and it may be that there's something much deeper going on that is in some way going beyond religion as we know it—perhaps a merging of religion and science, native understanding, multiculturalism, all sorts of things, and there's a new something emerging that none of us are really capable of holding in our consciousness.
> What feels to me like the possibilities of fueling a renaissance at the turn of the millennium that, in many ways, is far beyond the scope of the renaissance of Europe in the 14th to 17th centuries. Far beyond it in terms of going beyond art and architecture, and that would not just be the sacred quality of one tradition—the Catholic Church—but something that embraced all of humanity.
> If we could begin to understand and live according to

those principles—whether you want to call it Tao or the Way or the Dharma or something else—it would be amazing. It's not the name that's important, but the level of understanding which really appreciates indigenous cultures, science, religion, spirituality, and medicine, allowing for the infinite possibilities of being human.[38]

There will be an American Buddhism, and the Karma Kagyus in Texas will have played their part and played it well.

In order to provide a frame of reference for the entry of the Kagyupa in Texas, some pivotal dates for Buddhist activities in North America will be helpful. In 1842 Ralph Waldo Emerson offered in his essay "Poetry and the Imagination" this comparison of Buddhist ideals with those of the hard materialism of an industrialized West: "Better men saw heavens and earths; saw noble instruments of noble souls. We see railroads, mills, and banks, and pity the poverty of these dreaming Buddhists. There was as much creative force then as now, but it made globes and astronomic heavens, instead of broadcloth and wine glasses."[39]

Henry David Thoreau introduced the Lotus Sutra in the English-speaking world in his article "The Preaching of the Buddha" in 1844. Thoreau, Rick Fields believes, was perhaps the first American to explore the nontheistic mode of contemplation that is the distinguishing mark of Buddhism. It was through the arrival of Sir Edwin Arnold's *Light of Asia* in the United States in 1878 that Americans were given the opportunity of discovering en masse the story and the teachings of the Buddha. America's first Buddhist temple was built in San Francisco's Chinatown in 1853. Intensely influenced by the Chicago World Fair's World Parliament of Religions of 1893, a New York businessman was the first American to take his refuge vows.[40]

The first U.S. teacher of the Vajrayana vehicle, Geshe Wangyal of the Galugpa Order, joined the faculty at Columbia University in New York in 1955. In 1961, a Sakyapa, Deshung Rinpoche, became an instructor at the University of Washington at Seattle. The first Vajrayana congregation in the United States, the Tibetan Nyingma Meditation Center, was founded in Berkeley, California, in 1969. It was not until 1970 that Chogyam Trungpa Rinpoche entered the United States. All of these events certainly emphasize the late arrival of the Dharma in the Lone Star State.[41]

It would be appropriate to point out that most Texas Indians incorporated a form of Transcendentalism in their supernaturalistic mythologies and religious beliefs, assuming an a priori form of reality outside of the human sense experience. W.W. Newcomb Jr. explains in *The Indians of Texas: From Prehistoric to Modern Times:* "The Wichitas' conception of the universe was very different from ours, for everything—animate and inanimate—possessed a soul spirit ... all things contained or could contain more-than-natural attributes ... They felt that all spiritual knowledge come from revelations, and even that all knowledge of material advancement came from the supernatural powers."[42]

Frank and Sherry Glover, members of the Jade Buddha Temple in Houston today, believe that a Japanese Buddhist, Reverend Seki, visited and preached in West Texas in the 1930s. The Glovers suggest that at the time there was quite a bit of hostility toward Japanese-Americans and thus the reverend's efforts passed with little notice.[43]

The first Buddhist temple in Texas was begun in 1977 in Houston. It was a Vietnamese Theravada temple called Phat Quang Pegoda. The next temple, also Theravada, was built in Port Arthur in 1979 but moved to Orange in 1986. Houston's Thai community established a center in 1984, and Houston's first downtown temple, the Phap Luan, was constructed in 1984; it is now on South Post Oak. One will remember that it was in late 1974 that the first Karma Kagyu study group, a satellite of the Shambhala International organization, began holding its first formal meetings.[44]

In the United States, however, it is estimated that there are anywhere from 1 to 5 million Buddhists, of which 800,000 are converts. Three-fourths of all Buddhists in America are new immigrants. It is estimated that across North America there are approximately 3,000 meditation centers.[45]

The Venerable Kamburagalle Nanda, president of the Houston Buddhist Council and abbot of the Houston Buddhist Vihara, estimates that there are more than 50,000 Buddhists in Texas. There are 20,000 Vietnamese alone presently residing in the state. "They're in every corner of Texas. They come from every ethnic group. Thai, Vietnamese, Sri Lankan, Chinese, Cambodian, and Laotian. The Cambodians themselves have a mailing list of more then 10,000 people."[46] Mr. Nanda indicated that by his observation, only 2,000 of these Texas Buddhists attend meditation.

There are forty-seven Buddhist temples and meditation centers across the state, sixteen more than five years ago. Fourteen of these are in Houston, and ten are in Austin. It is estimated that there are 20,000 Texas Buddhists. There is even a Buddhist college in Texas. Beginning in 1998, the Jade Buddha Temple in Houston has offered a twelve-week course twice yearly, for laypersons interested in the Dharma. This organization presently has over 1,400 members.[47]

The numbers of the Tibetan Karma Kagyu lineage pale by comparison, but they are nonetheless significant. There are an estimated 258 Kagyupas in Texas, which is not bad, considering that there is no concentrated ethnic foundation where the membership is looking for the familiarity of a cultural base. One must consider, too, that in the spirit of Buddhism, there is never active recruiting, that contact is almost always personal, a true grassroots system.

Of the total Kagyus in the state, 136 are women and 122 men. Between the ages of zero to seventeen, the youngsters, there are only 9 practitioners. In the mid-range, ages eighteen to twenty-five, there are 89, and 160 are adults age twenty-six and older.

The Texas sanghas are 91 percent Caucasian, 8 percent Hispanic, and the remainder Asian. As best as can be determined, 35 percent of center members have a Protestant background, 33 percent a Catholic background, and 32 percent profess no religious background at all. Previous Buddhists and others round out the numbers. For those who are interested in Karma Kagyu activities and have asked for current information, the Texas centers provide mail-outs for 2,365 people across the state.[48]

But why Buddhism? In a culture that seemingly has absolutely everything the world can offer, why would anyone be even remotely interested in becoming a dispossessed, unattached, unfettered Buddhist?

Even with the whole world at one's feet, suffering is a profound reality. All one has to do to untie the knot, destroy the primal illusion, remember the luminous passage, and take the magical leap. As being is undone, mind fills the dreamer. Space unfolds and disappears. There is light; creation is all around, inside and out. There is perfect peace, perfect joy, and perfect freedom—treasures of incalculable worth. This wealth is unmatched by anything on this earth, yet it is the earth, and it is the only reason to be.

Appendix

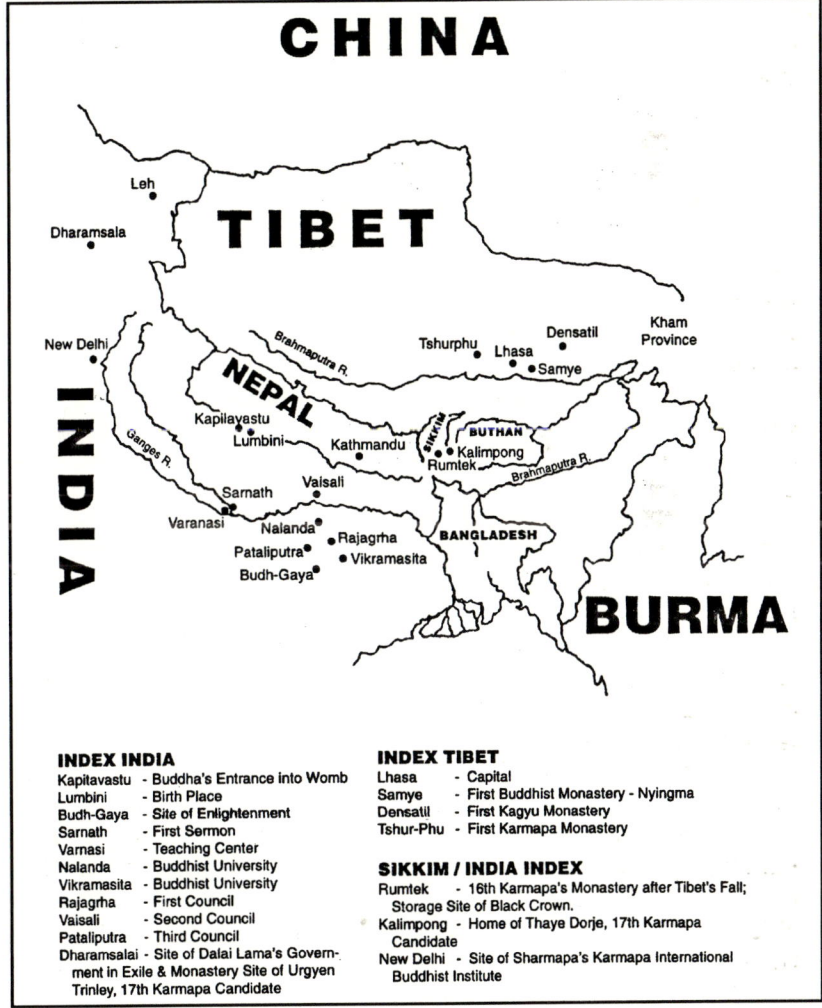

INDEX INDIA
Kapitavastu - Buddha's Entrance into Womb
Lumbini - Birth Place
Budh-Gaya - Site of Enlightenment
Sarnath - First Sermon
Varnasi - Teaching Center
Nalanda - Buddhist University
Vikramasita - Buddhist University
Rajagrha - First Council
Vaisali - Second Council
Pataliputra - Third Council
Dharamsalai - Site of Dalai Lama's Government in Exile & Monastery Site of Urgyen Trinley, 17th Karmapa Candidate

INDEX TIBET
Lhasa - Capital
Samye - First Buddhist Monastery - Nyingma
Densatil - First Kagyu Monastery
Tshur-Phu - First Karmapa Monastery

SIKKIM / INDIA INDEX
Rumtek - 16th Karmapa's Monastery after Tibet's Fall; Storage Site of Black Crown.
Kalimpong - Home of Thaye Dorje, 17th Karmapa Candidate
New Delhi - Site of Sharmapa's Karmapa International Buddhist Institute

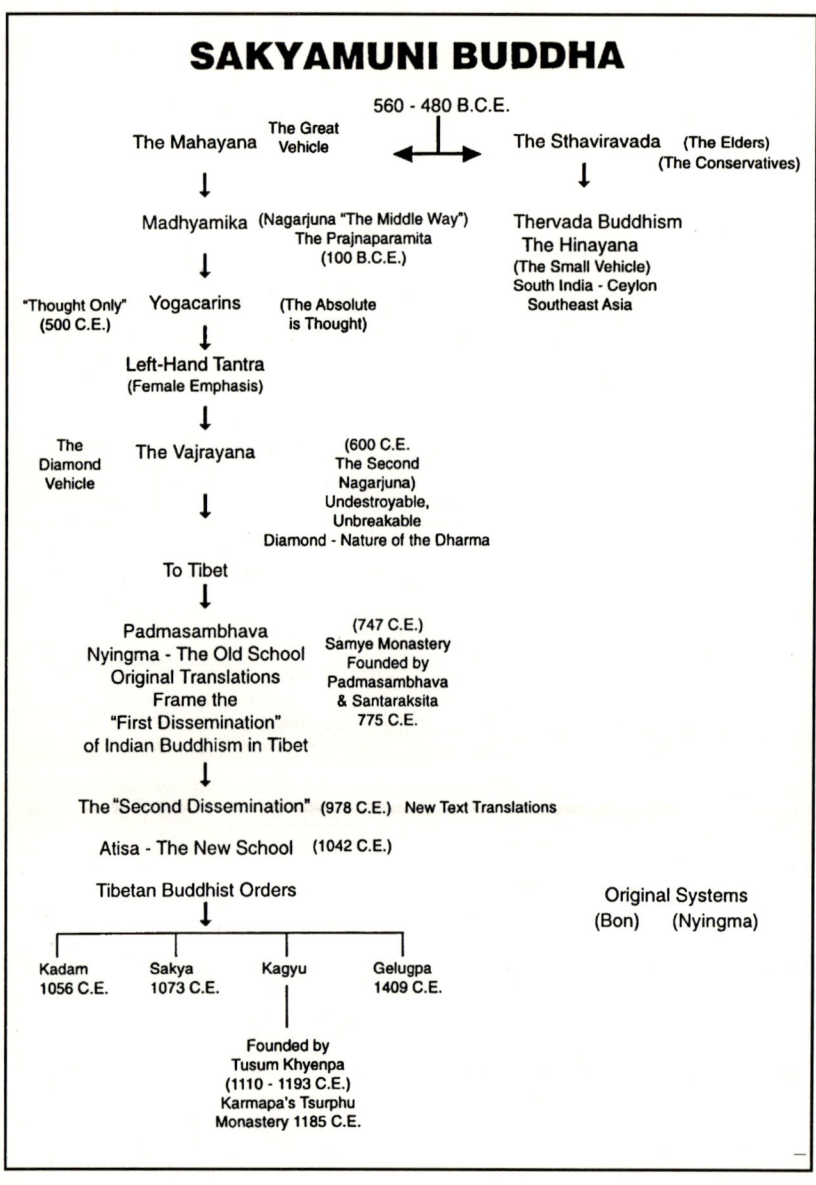

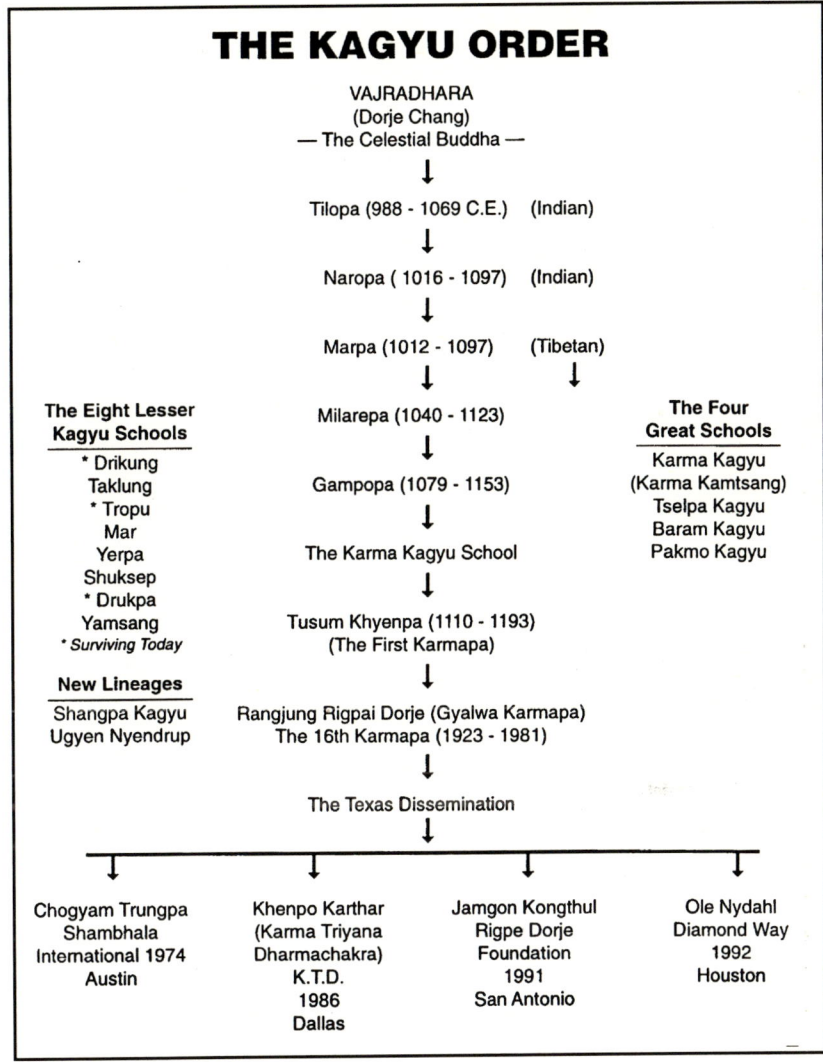

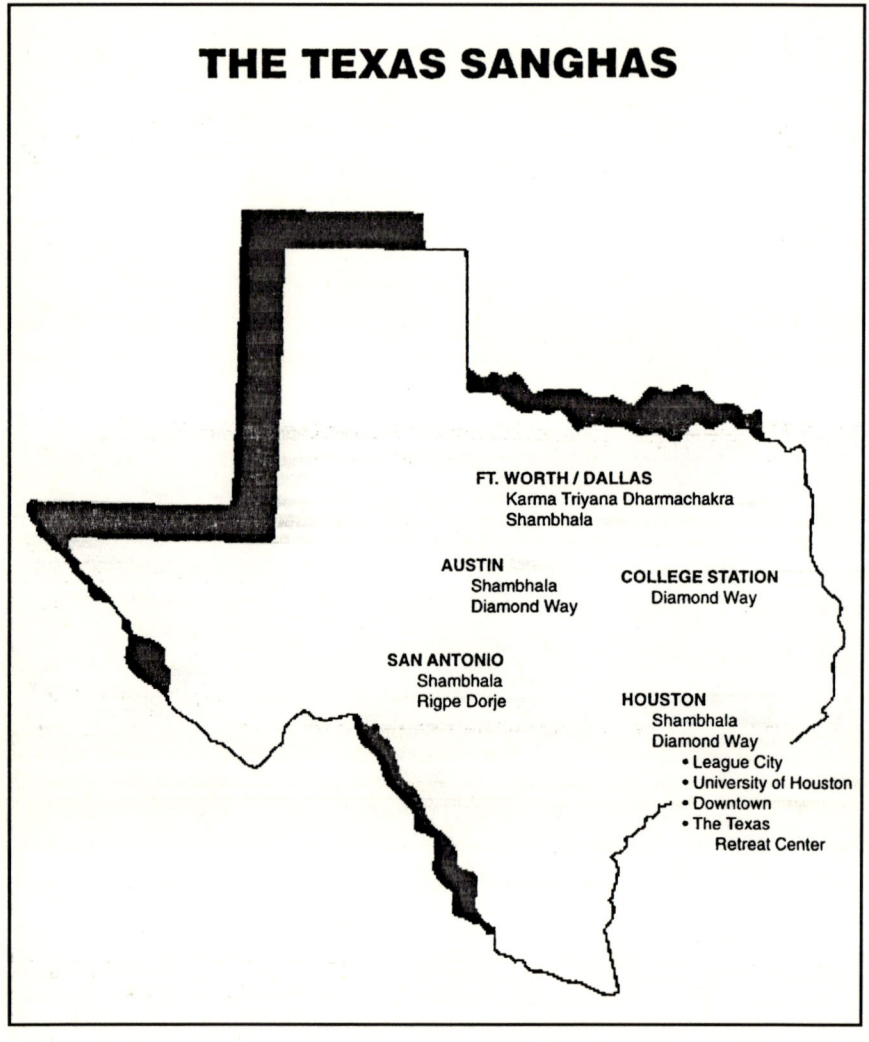

TEXAS STATISTICS

The Sanghas	Total Membership	Female	Male	Ages ● = 0-17 # = 18-25 * = 26+	Ethnicity C=Caucasian H=Hispanic AA=African Am AS=Asian	Religious Background P=Protestant C=Catholic I=Islamic H=Hindu N=None	Mail Outs
Shambhala International							
Houston	20	10	10	*20			90
Austin	84	42	42	● 7 # 35 * 42	C 96% AS 27% H 2%	P 50% C 30% N 20%	600
San Antonio	30	15	15	● 1 # 3 * 26	C 70% H 30%	P 33% C 33% N 33%	700
Dallas	6	3	3	* 6	C 100%	P 50% N 50%	65
Rigpe Dorje							
San Antonio	8	6	2	* 8	C 90% AS 10%	P 10% C 80% Buddhist 10%	300
Karma Triyana Dharmachakra							
Dallas K.T.C.	40	20	20	*36 # 4	C 75% AS 15% H 8% AA 2%	P 50% C 12% H 2% N 26%	250
The Diamond Way							
League City	15	8	7	*11 # 4	C 80% H 20%		150
Houston	10	7	3	● 1 # 8	C 98% H 2%		70
Austin	38	14	24	# 17 * 21	C 70% H 8% AS 8% Italian 16%	P 67% C 16% Buddhist 5% N 6%	43
College Station	10	2	8	#10	AS 70% C 30%	N 70% P 20% C 30%	50
University of Houston	5	3	2	#5	C 100%		10
Texas Retreat Center	10	8	2	*10	C 100%		20

Notes

Chapter 1
1. Richard Hughes Seager, *Buddhism in America* (New York: Columbia University Press, 1999), 230-247.
2. Stephen Batchelor, *The Awakening of the West: The Encounter of Buddhism and Western Culture* (Berkeley, Calif.: Parallax Press, 1992), xi.
3. Elizabeth Cook, ed., 1992, *Light of Liberation: A History of Buddhism in India,* Crystal Mirror Series volume 8 (Berkeley: Dharma Publishing), xx-xxv.
4. Edward Conze, *Buddhism: Its Essence and Development* (New Delhi: Munshirma Manodarlal Publishers Pvt. Ltd., 1997), 34.
5. Gwendolyn Bays, *The Lalitavistara Sutra: The Voice of the Buddha,* vol. 1 (Berkeley, Calif.: Dharma Publishing, 1983), xxii.
6. John Snelling, *The Buddhist Handbook: A Complete Guide to Buddhist Schools, Teaching, Practice, and History* (Rochester, New York: Inner Traditions International, 1991), 34-71.
7. Jeremy Thomas and Francis Bouygues, prod., *Little Buddha* (Burbank, Calif.: Miramax Home Entertainment, Distributed by Buena Vista Home Entertainment Video, 1993), videotape.
8. Lama Thubten Yeshe, *Introduction to Tantra: A Vision of Totality* (Somerville, Mass.: Wisdom Publications, 1987), 69.
9. Snelling, *The Buddhist Handbook,* 51.
10. John Powers, *Introduction to Tibetan Buddhism* (New York: Snow Lion Publications, 1995), 61-65.
11. Ibid., 65-69.

12. C. G. Jung, *The Archetypes and the Collective Unconscious* (New York: Princeton University Press, 1995), 3-53.
13. Lama Anagarika Govinda, *Foundations of Tibetan Mysticism* (York Beach, Maine: Samuel Weiser, Inc., 1969), 66-69.
14. Samuel Bercholz and Sherab Chodzin Kohn, eds., *Entering the Stream* (Boston: Shambhala, 1993); "Kharma and Its Fruit," Nyanaponika Thera, 128.
15. Paul Sherwood, *Falling Silent: A Seeker's Journey* (published privately by Mildred Sherwood, 1998), 228.
16. Snelling, *The Buddhist Handbook*, 41.
17. Powers, *Introduction to Tibetan Buddhism*, 54-56.
18. Ibid., 241.
19. Conze, *Buddhism: Its Essence and Development*, 99.
20. Ibid., 110.
21. Kalu Rinpoche, *Profound Buddhism: From Hinayana to Vajrayana* (San Francisco: ClearPoint Press, 1995), 16.
22. Snelling, *The Buddhist Handbook*, 77-78.
23. *Light of Liberation: 1992, A History of Buddhism in India*, Crystal Mirror Series, volume 8, part 4: Mahayana (Berkeley, Calif.: Dharma Publishing,), 297-299.
24. Bercholz and Kohn, eds., *Entering the Stream, A Short History of Buddhism*, Sherab Kohn, 47.
25. Edward Conze, *A Short History of Buddhism* (Oxford, England: Oneworld, 1980), 42.
26. Snelling, *The Buddhist Handbook*, 83.
27. Lex Hixon, *Mother of the Buddhas: Meditation on the Prajnaparamita Sutra* (Wheaton, Illinois-Chennai, India: Quest Books–Theosophical Publishing House, 1993), 9.
28. Ibid., 10
29. Snelling, *The Buddhist Handbook*, 84.
30. Radmila Moacanin, *Jung's Psychology and Tibetan Buddhism: Western and Eastern Paths to the Heart* (Boston: Wisdom Publishings, 1986), 6.
31. Conze, *Buddhism: Its Essence and Development*, 67.
32. Ibid., 136.
33. Ibid., 137.
34. Snelling, *The Buddhist Handbook*, 89.
35. Hixon, *Mother of the Buddhas*, 6-7.
36. Conze, *A Short History of Buddhism*, 48.
37. Conze, *Buddhism: Its Essence and Development*, 161.
37. Snelling, *The Buddhist Handbook*, 90.
38. Ibid., 91.
40. Will Durant and Ariel Durant. *The Age of Voltaire: A History of Civilization in Western Europe from 1715 to 1756, with Special Emphasis on the Conflict between Religion and Philosophy* (New York: Simon and Schuster, 1965), 7-8.

41. Lama Yeshe, *Introduction to Tantra: A Vision of Totality*, Jonathan Landaw, ed. (Boston: Wisdom Publications, 1987), 76-79.
42. Conze, *Buddhism: Its Essence and Development*, 166.
43. Ibid., 168.
44. Ibid., 145.
45. Ibid., 155.
46. Ibid., 173.
47. Snelling, *The Buddhist Handbook*, 94.
48. Abhayadatta, *Buddha's Lions: The Lives of the Eighty-Four Siddhas* (Berkeley, Calif.: Dharma Publications, 1979), 2-19.
49. Bercholz and Kohn, eds., *Entering the Stream*, "The Tantric Teachings," 251-252.
50. Conze, *Buddhism: Its Essence and Development*, 176-177.
51. John Snelling, *The Elements of Buddhism* (Rockport, Mass.: 1990), 25.
52. Reginald Ray, "The Temptress and the Monk," in Bercholz and Kohn, *Entering the Stream*, 259.
53. Batchelor, *Awakening of the West*, 73.
54. Abhayadatta, *Buddha's Lions*, 10.
55. Snelling, *The Elements of Buddhism*, 25.
56. *Light of Liberation: A History of Buddhism in India*, Crystal Mirror Series, volume 8, 355.
57. Lama Anagarika Govinda, *Foundations of Tibetan Mysticism*, 93.
58. Greene, *The Elegant Universe*, 111.
59. Govinda, *Foundations of Tibetan Myticism*, 93.
60. Lama Ole Nydahl, "Buddhism, The Way and the Goal," lecture in Houston, Texas, November 18, 1998 (videotape).
61. Snelling, *The Elements of Buddhism*, 24.
62. Georg Feuerstein, *Tantra: The Path of Ecstasy* (Boston: Shambhala, 1998), 224-227.
63. Kalu Rinpoche, *Secret Buddhism: Vajrayana Practices* (San Francisco: ClearPoint Press, 1995), 96-97.
64. Govinda, *Foundations of Tibetan Mysticism*, 150.
65. Nydahl, *The Tantric View of Life* (videotape).
66. Snelling, *The Buddhist Handbook*, 101.
67. Govinda, *Foundations of Tibetan Mysticism*, 159.
68. Nydahl, *The Tantric View of Life* (videotape)
69. Govinda, *Foundations of Tibetan Mysticism*, 135.
70. Snelling, *The Buddhist Handbook*, 95.
71. T. S. Eliot: *The Complete Poems and Plays: 1909–1950* (New York: Harcourt, Brace & World, Inc., 1971), 145.
72. Kalu Rinpoche, *Secret Buddhism*, 134-135.
73. Snelling, *Elements of Buddhism*, 24.
74. Govinda, *Foundations of Tibetan Mysticism*, 18.
75. Ibid., 19.
76. Ibid., 20.

77. Snelling, *Elements of Buddhism*, 24.
78. Nydahl, "Buddhism, The Way and the Goal" (videotape).
79. Yeshe, *Introduction to Tantra*, 146.
80. Miranda Shaw, "Everything You Always Wanted to Know About Tantra . . . But Were Afraid to Ask." *What Is Enlightenment?* 13, spring/summer 1998: 36.
81. Kalu Rinpoche, *Profound Buddhism*, 44.
82. Rick Fields, *How the Swans Came to the Lake: A Narrative History of Buddhism in America* (Boston and London: Shambhala, 1992), 307.
83. Ibid., 11-12.

Chapter 2
1. Crystal Mirror 4 (Berkeley, Calif.: Dharma Publishing, 1975), 77.
2. Powers, *Introduction to Tibetan Buddhism*, 21.
3. George N. Roerich, *The Blue Annals* (Delhi, India: Motilal Banarsidass Publishers, 1949), 29.
4. Powers, *Introduction to Tibetan Buddhism*, 12-126.
5. Roerich, *The Blue Annals*, 38-40.
6. Crystal Mirror 4, 80.
7. Ibid., 81.
8. Snelling, *The Buddhist Handbook*, 168-169.
9. Per Kvaerne, "Tibet: the Rise and Fall of a Monastic Tradition," 256. Heinz Bechert and Richard Gombrich, eds., *The World of Buddhism: Buddhist Monks and Nuns in Society and Culture* (New York: Facts on File Publication, 1984).
10. Powers, *Introduction to Tibetan Buddhism*, 434.
11. Ibid., 443.
12. Crystal Mirror 4, 85.
13. Powers, *Introduction to Tibetan Buddhism*, 128.
14. Roerich, *Blue Annals*, 40-41.
15. Crystal Mirror 4, 84.
16. Ibid., 87.
17. Yeshe Tsogyal, *The Lotus-Born: The Life Story of Padmasambhava* (Boston and London: Shambhala, 1993), 12.
18. Batchelor, *Awakening of the West*, 64.
19. Ibid., 64-69.
20. Ibid., 67.
21. Bechert and Gombrich, *The World of Buddhism*, 255.
22. Snelling, *The Buddhist Handbook*, 170-171.
23. Powers, *Introduction to Tibetan Buddhism*, 133.
24. Crystal Mirror 4, 94.
25. Bechert and Gombrich, eds., *The World of Buddhism*, 259.
26. Jonathan Landaw and Andy Weber, *Images of Enlightenment: Tibetan Art in Practice,* (Ithaca, New York: Snow Lion Publications, 1993), 156.

27. Crystal Mirror Series, volume 5, *Lineage of Diamond Light* (Berkeley, Calif.: Dharma Publishing, 1991).
28. Powers, *Introduction to Tibetan Buddhism,* 119.
39. Ibid., 136.
40. David Snellgrove and Hugh Richardson, *A Cultural History of Tibet* (New York: Frederick A. Praeger, Publishers, 1968), 129.
41. W. Y. Evans-Wentz, ed., *Tibet's Great Yogi Milarepa: A Biography from the Tibetan Being the Jetsun-Kahbum* (London: Oxford University Press, 1928), 8-10.
42. Powers, *Introduction to Tibetan Buddhism,* 138-139.
43. Snelling, *The Buddhist Hanbook,* 173.
44. Evans-Wentz, ed., *Tibet's Great Yogi Milarepa,* 7.
45. Venerable Khenpo Karthar Rinpoche, *Vajradhara, The Primordial Buddha,* teaching presented at Karma Triyana Dharmachakra (KTD) Center, Woodstock, New York, March 25, 1986, KTD Web site: kagyu.org, 1-7.
46. Venerable Khenpo Karthar Rinpoche, *Teaching on the Life of Tilopa,* KTD Center, Woodstock, New York, March 25-30, 1986, KTD Web site: kagyu.org, page 4 of 6.
47. Ibid.
48. Venerable Khenpo Karthar Rinpoche, *Teaching on the Life of Naropa,* KTD Center, Woodstock, New York, March 25-30, 1986, KTD Web site: kagyu.org, page 2 of 6.
49. Herbert V. Guenther, *The Life and Teaching of Naropa* (Boston and London: Shambhala, 1995), xiii.
50. Venerable Khenpo Karthar Rinpoche, *Teaching on the Life of Naropa,* 5-6.
51. Powers, *Introduction to Tibetan Buddhism,* 355-361.
52. Ibid., 362.
53. Lama Ole Nydahl, *Teaching on the Mahamudra,* Mahamudra Retreat, November 26-30, 2000, Marble Falls, Texas.
54. Powers, *Introduction to Tibetan Buddhism,* 362-363.
55. Batchelor, *The Awakening of the West,* 118.
56. Powers, *Introduction to Tibetan Buddhism,* 363.
57. Guenther, *The Life and Teaching of Naropa,* xiv.
58. Ibid., xiii-xiv.
59. Powers, *Introduction to Tibetan Buddhism,* 348.
60. Ibid., 350.
61. Snellgrove and Richardson, *A Cultural History of Tibet,* 132.
62. Evans-Wentz, *Tibet's Great Yogi Milarepa,* 87.
63. Ibid., 131.
64. Batchelor, *The Awakening of the West,* 109.
65. Evans-Wentz, *Tibet's Great Yogi Milarepa,* 217.
66. Ibid., 286.
67. Nydahl, "The Tantric View of Life" (videotape).
68. Powers, *Introduction to Tibetan Buddhism,* 350.

69. David Snellgrove, *Indo-Tibetan Buddhism: Indian Buddhist and Their Tibetan Successors,* volume 2 (Boston: Shambhala, 1987), 493-503.
70. Ibid., 513.
71. Ibid., 502-503.
72. Ibid., 493.
73. Powers, *Introduction to Tibetan Buddhism,* 352.
74. Ibid., 349.
75. Lama Ole Nydahl, *Ngondro: The Four Foundational Practices of Tibetan Buddhism* (Grass Valley, Calif.: Blue Dolphin Publishing, 1990), 31.
76. Landaw and Weber, *Images of Enlightenment: Tibetan Art in Practice,* 57.
77. Nik Douglas and Meryl White, *Karmapa: The Black Hat Lama of Tibet* (London: Luzac and Co., 1976), 34.
78. Powers, *Introduction to Tibetan Buddhism,* 349.
79. Douglas and White, *Karmapa: The Black Hat Lama of Tibet,* 35.
80. Ibid., 34-37.
81. Yeshe Dronma, *The Kunzig Shamarpas of Tibet: The Reincarnations of The Kunzig Shamarpa, The Red Crown Lama of Tibet* (N.c.: Dorje and Bell Publications, 1992), 12.
82. Batchelor, *The Awakening of the West,* 113.
83. Powers, *Introduction to Tibetan Buddhism,* 139-140.
84. Ibid., 119.
85. Bechert and Gombrich, *The World of Buddhism,* 261.
86. Ibid., 162.
87. Snellgrove and Richardson, *A Cultural History of Tibet,* 149.
88. Douglas and White, *Karmapa: The Black Hat Lama of Tibet,* 44.
89. Snellgrove and Hugh Richardson, *A Cultural History of Tibet,* 153.
90. Douglas and White, *Karmapa, The Black Hat Lama of Tibet,* 62.
91. Fields, *How the Swans Came to the Lake,* 328.
92. Batchelor: *The Awakening of the West,* 102.
93. Douglas and White, *Karmapa: The Black Hat Lama of Tibet,* 63-64.
94. Shamar Rinpoche, "Statement Regarding the Holy Religious Items of the 16th Karmapa in Rumtek," E-mail: karmapa-issue.org, September 22, 2000.
95. Powers, *Introduction to Tibetan Buddhism,* 143.
96. Ibid., 143-144.
97. Douglas and White, *Karmapa: The Black Hat Lama of Tibet,* 86.
98. Ibid., 87.
99. Powers, *Introduction to Tibetan Buddhism,* 145.

100. Fields, *How the Swans Came to the Lake*, 280.

Chapter 3
   1. Karma Triyana Dharmachakra: Web site, www.kagyu.org/karmapa/kar/kar02lhtml, "How the Karmapa's Lineage Came to the West," part 1, 1998, 1-2.
   2. Batchelor, *The Awakening of the West*, 114.
   3. Julian Gearing, "Struggle for Tibet's Soul," *Asiaweek Magazine,* October 20, 2000, at Web site: Asiaweek.com, page 2 of 8.
   4. Karma Triyana Dharmachakra, "How the Karmapa's Lineage Came to the West."
   5. Fields, *How the Swans Came to the Lake*, 278.
   6. Chogyam Trunga Rinpoche, *Born in Tibet* (Boston and London: Shambhala, 1995), 25.
   7. Ibid., 26.
   8. Ibid., 252.
   9. Fields, *How the Swans Came to the Lake*, 282.
   10. Batchelor, *The Awakening of the West*, 104-105.
   11. Ibid., 105.
   12. Snelling, *The Buddhist Handbook*, 212.
   13. Chogyam Trungpa Rinpoche, *Born in Tibet*, 256.
   14. Ibid., 258-262.
   15. Fields, *How the Swans Came to the Lake*, 327.
   16. Kalu Rinpoche, *The Dharma: That Illuminates All Beings Like the Light of the Sun and the Moon* (Albany: State University of New York Press, 1986), 7.
   17. Fields, *How the Swans Came to the Lake*, 327.
   18. Lama Ole Nydahl, *Riding the Tiger: Twenty Years on the Road: The Risks and Joys of Bringing Tibetan Buddhism to the West* (Nevada City, Calif.: Blue Dolphin, 1992), 90-91.
   19. Chogyam Trungpa Rinpoche, *Born in Tibet*, 216.
   20. Fields, *How the Swans Came to the Lake*, 330.
   21. Karma Triyana Dharmachakra, "How the Karmapa's Lineage Came to the West," part 2, 1998, 1-5.
   22. Alf Evers, *History of an American Town* (Woodstock, New York: The Overlook Press, 1987), 670.
   23. Karma Triyana Dharmachakra Web site, www.kagyu.org/kar/kar02.html, Khenpo Karthar Rinpoche, part 1, information drawn from *Densal,* "Biography of Khenpo Karthar Rinpoche," by Eleanor Mannikka, 1-5.
   24. Ibid., part 2, 1-5.
   25. "A Brief History of the Rigpe Dorje Foundation," sangha publication of the San Antonio Karma Kagyu Rigpe Dorje Center, 1-2.
   26. Ibid., 1.
   27. Tomek Lehnert, *Rogues in Robes: An Inside Chronicle of a Recent Chinese-Tibetan Intrigue in the Karma Kagyu Lineage of*

Diamond Way Buddhism (Nevada City, Calif.: Blue Dolphin Publishing, Inc., 1998), 72.

28. "A Brief History of the Rigpe Dorje Foundation," 1-2.
29. Lama Ole Nydahl, *Entering the Diamond Way: My Path Among the Lamas* (Nevada City, Calif.: Blue Dolphin Publishing Inc., 1985), 10.
30. W. Y. Evans-Wentz, *Tibetan Yoga and Secret Doctrines* (London: Oxford University Press, 1958), 39.
31. Nydahl, *Entering the Diamond Way*, 63-83.
32. Ibid., 1-203.
33. Ibid., 216.
34. Ibid., 219.
35. Ibid., 229.
36. Paul Sherwood, *Falling Silent: A Seeker's Journey*, 311-312.
37. Nydahl, *Entering the Diamond Way*, 231.
38. Nydahl, *Riding the Tiger*, 9.
39. Ibid., 18-19.
40. Ibid., 239.
41. Ibid.
42. Ibid., 264.
43. Ibid., 456.
44. Ibid., 183.
45. Ibid., 167.
46. Ibid., 389.
47. Ibid., 190-191.
48. Batchelor, *The Awakening of the West*, 115.
49. Chogyam Trungpa, *Born in Tibet*, 5-6.
50. Nydahl, *Riding the Tiger*, 199-202.
51. Ibid., 205.
52. Lama Ole Nydahl, personal correspondence to Dewitte Lindsey, August 17, 1998.
53. Chogyam Trungpa Rinpoche, *Shambhala: The Sacred Path of the Warrior* (Boston and London: 1988), 202.
54. Ibid., 198.
55. Batchelor, 106.
56. Ibid., 106-107.
57. Shambhala Sun, July 1995, "The Sakyong's First Address," Halifax, Nova Scotia, May 15, 1995. Page 4.
58. Ibid., 6.
59. Jesper Jorgensen, personal correspondence, E-mail, June 6, 1998.
60. Marilyn Kinsey, personal correspondence, E-mail, January 3, 2001.

Chapter 4

1. Lawrence Wells, personal interview, June 8, 1998.

2. Betty Kelen, *Gautama Buddha in Life and Legend* (New York: Avon Camelot, 1967), 71.
3. Lawrence Wells, personal interview, June 8, 1998.
4. Ibid.
5. Ibid.
6. Ibid.
7. Ibid.
8. Ibid.
9. Ibid.
10. Ibid.
11. Ibid.
12. Elsa Gonzalez, personal interview, July 2, 1998.
13. Ibid.
14. Ibid.
15. Ibid.
16. Ibid.
17. Celeste Budwit, personal interview, June 3, 1998, Houston, Texas.
18. Ibid.
19. Ibid.
20. Ibid.
21. Ibid.
22. Ibid.
23. Ibid.
24. Joan Klein, personal interview, June 14, 1998.
25. Beth Condrey Kennan, personal interview, June 14, 1998.
26. Ibid.
27. Ibid.
28. Ibid.
29. Beth Kennan, personal correspondance, E-mail, August 1, 1999.
30. Beth Kennan, personal interview.
31. Ibid.
32. Ibid.
34. Lama Dudjom Dorje, personal interview, June 14, 1998.
35. Ibid.
36. Ibid.
37. Jan Puckett, personal interview, July 2, 1998.
38. Ibid., 151.
39. Connie White, personal interview, July 2, 1998.
40. Jan Puckett, personal interview.
41. Ibid.
42. Connie White, personal interview, July 2, 1998.
43. Marilyn Kinsey, personal correspondance, E-mail: February 15, 2000.
44. Ibid.

45. Marilyn Kinsey, personal interview, April 19, 1998.
46. Pattie Holestein, personal interview, February 1, 1998.
47. Ibid.
48. Ibid.
49. Ibid.
50. Ibid.
51. Tore Fossum, personal interview, May 2, 1998.
52. Mike Savage and Mary Anne Fields, personal interview, February 1, 1998, Houston, Texas.
53. Carol Boethel, personal interview, July 30, 1998.
54. Tore Fossum, personal interview, 81.
55. Ibid.
56. Donna Russell, personal interview, July 28, 1998.
57. Ibid.
58. Ibid.
59. Ibid.
60. Ibid.
61. Carol Boethel, personal interview.
62. Ibid.
63. Ibid.
64. Ibid.
65. Bonnie Cooper, personal interview, May 4, 1998.
66. Ibid.
67. Ibid.
68. Mike Savage and Mary Anne Fields, personal interview.
69. Ibid.
70. Ibid.
71. Ibid.
72. Ibid.
73. Dylan Carter and Justin Coody, personal interview, June 1, 1998.
74. Ibid.
75. Ibid.
76. Ibid.
77. Ibid.
78. Sergio Ayala, personal interview, June 26, 1999.
79. Nathaniel Rich, personal interview, June 14, 1998.
80. Ibid.
81. Ibid.
82. Ibid.
83. Ibid.
84. Ibid.
85. Ibid.
86. Beth Harrison, personal interview, November 27, 2000.
87. Ibid.
88. Ibid.

89. Ibid.
90. Ibid.
91. Ibid.
92. Marilyn Kinsey, personal interview,: November 27, 2000.

Chapter 5
1. Karma Triyana Dharmachakra, "His Holiness the 17th Gyalwa Karmapa," at Internet site: Kagyu.org/Karmapa, page 6 of 10.
2. Ibid.
3. Ibid., 3.
4. Gearing, "Struggle for Tibet's Soul," page 2 of 8.
5. His Holiness Kunzig Shamar Rinpoche, "The Reincarnation and Recognition of the 17th Karmapa Thinley Thaye Dorje," at Web site: www.karmapa-issue.org/intex_recognition, September 22, 2000, page 1 of 4.
6. Ibid.
7. Lehnert, *Rogues in Robes*, 224.
8. Shamar Rinpoche, "The Reincarnation and Recognition of the 17th Karmapa," 2-4.
9. Tenzin Geyche Tethong, "Letter to the Office of his Holiness the Dalai Lama," at Web site: www.Diamondway-buddhism.org, August 7, 2000.
10. Gearing, "Struggle for Tibet's Soul," 2-4, 6-8.
11. His Holiness Kunzig Shamar Rinpoche, "The Truth About the Karmapa Controversy," at Web site: www.diamond.org, February 28, 2000, pages 1-2.
12. His Holiness Kunzig Shamar Rinpoche, "Statement Regarding the Holy Religious Items of the 16th Karmapa in Rumtek," at Web site: www.Karmapa-issue.org, September 22, 2000, 1-3.
13. Gearing, "Struggle for Tibet's Soul," 3.
14. Ibid., 4.
15. Lehnert, *Rogues in Robes*, 238-246.
16. Michel Nesterenko, *The Karmapa Papers* (France: privately published, 1992), 16-17.
17. His Holiness Kunzig Shamar Rinpoche, "Statement to all Kagyupa Members of October, 1999," at Web site: www.diamondway-buddhism.org/news/4-2000.htm, 1-2.
18. Beth Kennan, personal interview.
19. Amy Lavine, "The Development of American Vajrayana," in Prebish and Tanake, eds., *Faces of Buddhism in America*, 108.
20. Tenzin Geyche Tethong, "Letter to the Office of His Holiness the Dalai Lama," August 7, 2000, at Web site: www.karmapa-issue.org, 1-3.
21. Shamar Rinpoche, "Statement to all Kagyupa Members of October 14, 1999," 1.
22. Gearing, *Struggle for Tibet's Soul*, 5.

23. Shamar Rinpoche, *The Truth about the Karmapa Controversy,* 1.
24. Tashi Wangdi, Response to Terry Sullivan's letter to the editor of *Asiaweek,* at Web site: www.karma-issue.org, September 22, 2000. 1-2.
25. Shamar Rinpoche, *The Truth About the Karmapa Controversy,* 1.
26. Ibid., 2.
27 Charles S. Prebish and Kenneth K. Tanaka, ed., *The Faces of Buddhism in America,* Tibetan Buddhism in America: "The Development of American Vajrayana," Article by Amy Lavine, (Berkeley: University of California Press, 1998) 99.
28. Richard Hughes Seager, *Buddhism in America* (New York: Columbia University Press, 1999), 190-222.
29. Ibid., 234.
30. "Toward the Mainstreaming of American Dharma Practice," Dr. Jon Kabat-Zinn, in Brian D. Hotchkiss, ed., and Al Rapaport, comp., *Buddhism in America: Proceedings of the First Buddhism in America Conference* (Rutland, Vt.: Charles E. Tottle Company, Inc., 1998), 479- 481.
31. Ibid., 521.
32. Seager, *Buddhism in America,* 192.
33. Ibid., 211.
34. Prebish and Tanaka, eds., *The Faces of Buddhism in America,* "Epilogue" by Tanaka," 293.
35. Ibid., 194; Jan Nattier, "Landscape of Buddhist America."
36. Charles Prebish, *Luminous Passage: The Practice and Study of Buddhism in America* (Berkeley: University of California Press, 1998), 258-259.
37. Robert A. F. Thurman, "Toward an American Buddhism," in Hotchkiss and Rapaport, eds., *Buddhism in America: Proceedings of the First Buddhism in America Conference,* 460.
38. Jon Kabat-Zinn, "Toward the Mainstreaming of American Dharma Practice," 516.
39 Fields, *How the Swans Came to the Lake,* 60.
40. Ibid., 61-69, 73, 129.
41. Ibid., 62-69.
42. W. W. Newcomb Jr., *The Indians of Texas: From Prehistoric to Modern Times* (Austin: University of Texas Press, 1993), 272.
43. Frank Glover and Sherry, e-mail, March 3, 1998.
44. Venerable Kamburagalle Nanda, president of the Texas Buddhist Council, personal interview, March 3, 1998.
45. Keith Kachtick, "Let It Be," *Texas Monthly Magazine* 29, March 2001: 120.
46. Nanda, personal interview.
47. Ibid.
48. Sangha statistics derived from personal interviews.

Bibliography

Abhayadatta. *Buddha's Lions: The Lives of the Eighty-Four Siddhas* Berkeley, Calif.: Dharma Publishing, 1979.

"A Brief History of the Rigpe Dorje Foundation," sangha publication of the San Antonio, Texas, Karma Kagyu Rigpe Dorje Center.

Batchelor, Stephen. *The Awakening of the West: The Encounter of Buddhism and Western Culture.* Berkeley, Calif.: Parallax Press, 1994.

Bays, Gwendolyn. *The Lalitavistara Sutra: The Voice of the Buddha: The Beauty of Compassion,* vol. 1. Berkeley, Calif.: Dharma Publishing, 1993.

Bechert, Heinz, and Richard Gombrich, eds. *The World of Buddhism: Buddhist Monks and Nuns in Society and Culture.* New York: Facts on File Publishing, 1984.

Bercholz, Samuel, and Sherab Chodzin Kohn, eds. *Entering the Stream: An Introduction to The Buddha and His Teachings* Boston: Shambhala, 1993.

Conze, Edward. *Buddhism: Its Essence and Development.* New Delhi: Munshirma Manodarlal Publishers, 1997.

———. *A Short History of Buddhism.* Oxford, England: Oneworld, 1980.

Cook, Elizabeth. 1992. Crystal Mirror Series, Vol. VIII, *Light of Liberation.* Journal of the Tibetan Nyingma Meditation Center, Berkeley: Dharma Publishing, 1992. Crystal Mirror Series, Volume IV, Berkeley: Dharma Publishing, 1975.

Dronma, Yeshe. *The Kunzig Sharmarpas of Tibet: The Reincarnations of the Kunzig Sharmarpa, the Red Crown Lama of Tibet.* United States: Dorje and Bell Publications, 1992.

Douglas, Nik, and Meryl White. *Karmapa: The Black Hat Lama of Tibet.* London: Luzac and Co., 1990.
Durant, Will and Ariel. *The Age of Voltaire: A History of Civilization in Western Europe from 1715 to 1756, with Special Emphasis on the Conflict between Religion and Philosophy,* New York, 1965.
Eliot, T. S., *The Complete Poems and Plays: 1909-1950.* New York: Harcourt, Brace & World Inc., 1971.
Evans-Wentz, W. Y., ed. *Tibet's Great Yogi Milarepa: A Biography from the Tibetan Being the Jetsun-Kahbum.* London: Oxford University Press, 1928.
———. *Tibetan Yoga and Secret Doctrines.* London: Oxford University Press, 1958.
Evers, Alf. *History of an American Town.* Woodstock, New York: The Overlook Press, 1987.
Feuerstein, Georg. *Tantra: The Path of Ecstasy.* Boston: Shambhala, 1998.
Fields, Rick. *How the Swans Came to the Lake: A Narrative History of Buddhism in America.* Boston: Shambhala, 1992.
Gearing, Julian. "Struggle for Tibet's Soul," *Asiaweek Magazine,* 26:41, October 20, 2000.
Govinda, Lama Anagarika. *Foundation of Tibetan Mysticism.* York Beach, Maine: Samuel Weiser, 1969.
Greene, Brian. *The Elegant Universe: Superstrings, Hidden Dimensions, and the Quest for the Ultimate the Ultimate Theory.* New York: Vintage Books–Random House, 1999.
Guenther, Herbert V. *The Life and Teaching of Naropa.* Boston: Shambhala, 1995.
Hixon, Lex. *Mother of the Buddhas: Meditation on the Prajnaparamita Sutra.* Wheaton, Illinois: Quest Books–Theosophical Publishing House, 1993.
Hotchkiss, Brian D., ed. *Buddhism in America: Proceedings of the First Buddhism in America Conference.* Al Rapaport, comp. Rutland, Vt.: Charles E. Tottle Company, 1998.
Jung, C. G. *The Archetypes and the Collective Unconscious.* New York: Princeton University Press, 1959.
Kachtick, Keith. "Let It Be," *Texas Monthly* 29, March 2001.
Kalu, Rinpoche. *The Dharma: That Illuminates All Beings Like the Light of the Sun and the Moon.* Albany: State University of New York Press, 1986.
———. *Profound Buddhism: From Hinayana to Vajrayana.* San Francisco: Clear Point Press, 1995.
———. *Secret Buddhism: Vajrayana Practices.* San Francisco: Clear Point Press, 1995.
Karma Triyana Dharmachakra. "His Holiness the 17th Gyalwa Karmapa," Web site: Kagyu.org/Karmapa.
———. "How the Karmapa's Lineage Came to the West." KTD Web site: www.kagyu.or/karmapa/kar/kar02.htm., 1998.

Karthar, Khenpo, Rinpoche. *Teaching on the Life of Naropa.* Teaching presented at the Karma Triyana Dharmachakra Center, Woodstock, New York, March 25-30, 1986. KTD Web site: www.kagyu/org.

———. *Teaching on the Life of Tilopa.* Teaching presented at the Karma Triyana Dharmachakra Center, Woodstock, New York, March 25-30, 1986. KTD Web site: www.kagyu.org.

———. *Vajradhara, the Primordial Buddha.* Teaching presented at the Karma Triyana Dharmachakra Center, Woodstock, New York, March 25-30, 1986. KTD Web site: www.kagyu.org.

Landaw, Jonathan, and Andy Weber. *Images of Enlightenment: Tibetan Art in Practice.* Ithaca, New York: Snow Lion Publications, 1993.

Lehnert, Tomek. *Rogues in Robes: An Inside Chronicle of a Recent Chinese-Tibetan Intrigue in the Karma Kagyu Lineage of Diamond Way Buddhism.* Nevada City, Calif.: Blue Dolphin Publications, 1998.

Light of Liberation: A History of Buddhism in India, Crystal Mirror Series, Volume VIII, Berkeley: Dharma Publishing, 1992.

Mannikka, Eleanor, "Biography of Khenpo Karthar Rinpoche," Information drawn from *Densal Magazine,* Karma Triyana Dharmachakra Website: www.kagyu.org.

Moacanin, Radmila. *Jung's Psychology and Tibetan Buddhism: Western and Eastern Paths to the Heart.* Boston: Wisdom Publishing, 1986.

Nesterenko, Michel, "The Karmapa Papers," privately published, 1992.

Newcomb, W. W., Jr., *The Indians of Texas: From Prehistoric to Modern Times.* Austin: University of Texas Press, 1993.

Nydahl, Lama Ole. *Buddhism, The Way and the Goal,* Lecture: Houston, Texas, April 26, 2000. (Videotape)

———. *Entering the Diamond Way: My Path Among the Lamas.* Nevada City, Calif.: Blue Dolphin Publishing, 1985.

———. *Ngondro: The Four Foundational Practices of Tibetan Buddhism,* (Grass Valley, Calif.: Blue Dolphin Publishing, 1990.

———. *Riding the Tiger: Twenty Years on the Road—The Risks and Joys of Bringing Tibetan Buddhism to the West.* Nevada City, Calif.: Blue Dolphin Publishing, 1992.

———. "The Tantric View of Life." Lecture, Houston, Texas, November 18, 1998 (videotape).

———. Teaching on the Mahamudra, "Wishes for the Attainment of Mahamudra by the 3rd Karmapa." Lecture: Mahamudra Retreat, November 26-30, 2000, Marble Falls, Texas

Powers, John. *Introduction to Tibetan Buddhism.* Ithaca, New York: Snow Lion Publications, 1995.

Prebish, Charles S. *Luminous Passage: The Practices and Study of Buddhism in America.* Berkeley: University of California Press, 1999.

Prebish, Charles S., and Kenneth K. Tanaka, eds. *The Faces of Buddhism in America.* Berkeley: University of California Press, 1998.

Roerich, George N. *The Blue Annals.* Delhi, India: Motil Banarsidass Publishers, 1949.

Seager, Richard Hughes. *Buddhism in America.* New York: Columbia University Press, 1999.

Shamar, His Holiness Kunzig Rinpoche. *The Reincarnation and Recognition of the 17th Karmapa Thinley Thaye Dorje.* Web site: www.karmapa-issue.org, September 22, 2000.

———. "Statement Regarding the Holy Religious Items of the 16th Karmapa in Rumtek." Web site: www.karmapa-issue.org, September 22, 2000.

———. "Statement to All Karma Kagyu Members of October 1999." Web site: www.diamond-buddhism.org, October 14, 1999.

———. "The Truth about the Karmapa Controversy." Web site: www.diamondway-buddhism.org, February 28, 2000.

Shambhala Sun Magazine. "The Sakyong's First Address, Halifax, Nova Scotia, May 15, 1995, Volume Three, Number 6. July, 1995.

Shaw, Miranda. "Everything You Always Wanted to Know About Tantra ... but Were Afraid to Ask." *What Is Enlightenment Magazine*, 13, spring/summer 1998.

Sherwood, Paul. *Falling Silent: A Seeker's Journey.* Published privately by Mildred Sherwood, 1998.

Snellgrove, David. *Indo-Tibetan Buddhism: Indian Buddhists and Their Tibetan Seccessors,* volume 2. Boston: Shambhala, 1987.

Snellgrove, David, and Hugh Richardson. *A Cultural History of Tibet.* New York: Fredrick A. Praeger Publishers, 1968.

Snelling, John. *The Buddhist Handbook: A Complete Guide to Buddhist Schools, Teaching, Practice, and History.* Rochester, New York: Inner Traditions, 1991.

———. *The Elements of Buddhism.* Shaftesbury: Element, 1990.

Tethong, Tenzin Geyche. "Letter to the Office of His Holiness the Dalai Lama." Web site: http:www.karmapa-issue.org/letter_new.htm.

Thomas, Jeremy and Francis Bouygues, producers. *Little Buddha.* Miramax Home Entertainment, distributed by Buena Vista Home Video, 1993.

Trungpa, Chogyam Rinpoche. *Born in Tibet.* Boston: Shambhala, 1995.

———. *Shambhala: The Sacred Path of the Warrior.* Boston: Shambhala, 1988.

Tsogyal, Yeshe. *The Lotus Born: The Life Story of Padmasambhava.* Boston: Shambhala, 1993.

Wangdi, Tashi. "Response to Terry Sullivan's following letter to the editor of *Asiaweek.*" Web site: http.www.karmapa-issue.org/response_asiaweek.htm, September 22, 2000.

Yeshe, Lama Thubten. *Introduction to Tantra: A Vision of Totality.* Somerville, Mass.: Wisdom Publications, 1987.

Index

A—
Abhidharma, 20, 38
Adams, Jerry, 121
Adams, Kay, 121
Akong Rinpoche, 160
Akong Tulku, 81, 165-166
Altan Khan, 75-76
Amitabha, 47
Amitayus, 22
archetypes, 6-7, 19
Arnold, Sir Edwin, 176
Aronoff, Carol, 103
Asoka (emperor), 15, 40
Atisa (teacher), 52-53
Ayala, Sergio, 148, 157

B—
Bahadur Shah, King, 165
Bardor Tulku, 121
Bedi, Freda, 79, 80, 81, 85
Black Hat Lamas, 75
Boethel, Carol, 134, 135, 138-140
Bon (folk religion), 44-45
Born in Tibet (Chogyam Trungpa Rinpoche), 83, 99
Bowa, Leigh, 133
Buddha, 2-4, 12, 14, 15-16, 22, 26, 29, 33, 39, 47, 54, 69

Buddha Laxmi, 91
Budwit, Celeste, 116-119, 121, 125

C—
Carter, Dylan, 144, 145-148, 150, 157
Chogi Lodro, 61
Chogyal Tashi Namgyal, 78
Chogyam Trungpa Rinpoche, 70, 79-86, 95, 96, 106, 108, 119, 177
Choying Dorje, 72
Clear Lake Center, 128-33
Coody, Justin, 144, 145-148, 153
Cooper, Bonnie, 140-141, 157
Cross, Allen, 115
Cummins, Gaye, 156, 157
Cutting through Spiritual Materialism (Chogyam Trungpa Rinpoche), 83, 112

D—
dakinis, 32
Dalai Lama, 68-69, 76-77, 167-169
Dallas Karma Thegsum Choling center, 119-124
Darma Wangchuk, 67
Dazey, Bob, 138
Dechen Wangmo, 160-161

Deer Hunter, The (film), 7
Deng Shegpa, 73-74
Deng Xiaoping, 165
Densatil (monastery), 67
dependent origination, 6
Deshung Rinpoche, 176
Dhamcho Yongdu, 163
Diamond Way Buddhism, 128-133:
   Austin Center, 145-148
   Clear Lake Center, 128-133
   Friendswood Center, 133-135
   Houston Center, 141-144
   Texas A&M University Buddhist Association, 148-152
   Texas Diamond Way Buddhist Retreat Center, The, 155-157
   Unitarian Universalist Church Center, 135-140
   University of Houston Center, 152-155
Dolmert, Wally, 128
Dorje Chang, 54, 66, 68
Dorje Khyung Dzong, 83
Driver, John, 80-81
Drupon Dechen Rinpoche, 160
Dudjom Rinpoche, 168
Dusum Khyenpa, 67, 69, 74, 77
Dzongchen Ponlop, 89

E—
Eightfold Noble Path, 4, 11
Eliot, T. S., 28
energy, 27, 28

F—
faith, 21
Ferguson, Corey, 148
Fields, Mary Anne, 134, 139, 141-144, 154, 157
Five Treasuries of Knowledge, 89
Fossum, Tore, 133-135, 144, 145, 166
Four Noble Truths, 3-4

G—
Gampo Abbey, 114
Gampopa, 49, 64-67, 69

Gautama, Siddhartha. *See* Buddha
Geshe Wangyal, 176
Gibbons, Edward, 136
Glover, Frank, 177
Glover, Sherry, 177
Godan Khan, 71
Goenka, S. N., 39
Gonzalez, Elsa, 111-116, 117, 125
Goshir Gyaltsap Rinpoche, 70, 163
Greenleaf, Netam, 106
Gushri Khan, 71, 76
Guterias, Dorea, 115
Gyalo Thondup, 168
Gyaltsap Rinpoche, 92, 165
Gyaltsen Norbu, 163
Gyalwa Karmapa, 76, 81, 86, 91, 93, 160, 169

H—
Harris, Tom, 106
Harrison, Beth, 144, 145, 152-155
Hartung, Caty, 103
Hayes, Mark, 146
Hollestein, Pattie, 130-135, 136
Hoshang Mohoyen, 49

J—
Jamgon Kongtrul Karma Lodro Chokyi Senge. *See* Jamgon Kongtrul Rinpoche
Jamgon Kongtrul Khyentse Oser, 89
Jamgon Kongtrul Lodro Thaye, 88
Jamgon Kongtrul Rinpoche, 88-89, 92, 115, 125, 126, 163-164
Jamgon Kongtrul Tulku, 70, 80, 81
Jesus Christ, 60
Jetsun Milarepa. *See* Milarepa
Jiang Zemin, 164
Jigme, Doctor, 91
Johnstone House, 81
Jorgensen, Jesper, 102-103, 129, 131, 136, 145, 146, 147, 150

Jung, Carl Gustav, 6-7, 19

K—
Kalu Rinpoche, 12, 84-85, 91
Kamalasila (student), 49
Kamburagalle Nanda, 177-178
Kampo Nesnang (monastery), 70
Karma Gon (Kagyu center), 70
Karma Pakshi, 72
karma, 6-9, 11
Karma Triyana Dharmachakra (KTD):
    Dallas Karma Thegsum Choling (KTC), 119-124
Karmapa War, 95, 102, 159-170
Karme Choling. *See* Tail of the Tiger
Kennan, Beth Condrey, 119-123, 167
Khenpo Karthar Rinpoche, 86-88, 97, 108-109, 120, 121
Khenpo Tsultrim Gyamtso Rinpoche, 89, 119
Kinsey, Marilyn (Parrish), 103, 128, 133, 155-157
Klein, Anne, 110
Klein, Joan, 119
Kublai Khan, 70, 72, 73
Kunzig Shamar Rinpoche, 103, 161, 163, 164, 168, 169

L—
Ladonna, Linda, 114
Lama Caffasan, 133-134
Lama Dudjom Dorje, 120, 122, 123-124
Lama Ole Nydahl. *See* Nydahl, Ole
Lama Sherab Rinpoche, 161
Langdarma (king), 50-51
Lehnert, Tomek, 129
Lhatotori (king), 41, 42
Light of Asia (Arnold), 178
Little Buddha (film), 4
Lobzang Trakpa, 75
Lopon Tsechu Rinpoche, 91, 92-93, 95, 134, 140, 142, 146, 161, 169

Lupton, Susan, 156

M—
Mahamudra, 59-60
Maitri Institute, 83
mantras, 34-36
Mantrayana, 23, 24
Marpa, 61-63, 66
Mazhang (minister), 46
Meditation in Action (Chogyam Trungpa Rinpoche), 83
meditation, 4-5, 31-33
merit, 21-22
Middle Way, 15-16, 17
Milarepa, 25, 62-64, 65, 66
Mipham Rinpoche, 160-161
Mune Tsenpo, 50

N—
Nagabo Jigme, 166
Nagarjuna (founder of Vajrayana), 24
Nagarjuna (philosopher), 15-16, 18, 20
Nalanda (university), 26
Nalanda Foundation, 83
Naropa, 55-58, 59, 60, 61, 62, 65-66,
Naropa Institute, 83
Ngawang Losang Gyatso, 77
Ngondro (purification process), 59-60
Ngorpa Lagen, 161
Nipahm Rinpoche, 109
Nirvana, 11, 12, 20
Nydahl, Hannah, 89-93, 94-95, 99, 146, 166
Nydahl, Ole, 89-103, 109, 128, 129, 133, 146, 147, 150, 153, 170

O—
Osel Tendzin, 100-101
Owens, Rami, 156, 157

P—
Padmasambhava (tantric master), 39, 47-48, 49-50
Pakmodrupa Dorje Gyelop, 67

204 TIBET TO TEXAS

Pali Canon, 2
Parrish, Dudley Boysen, 103
Pema Chodron, 113-114
Penor Rinpoche, 168
Peters, Roland, 102, 193
Ponlop Rinpoche, 126
Prajnaparamita Sutra, 13-14
projection, 18-19
Puckett, Jan, 114-115, 124-127
Pybus, Diana, 82

R—
Ralpachen (king), 44, 50
Rangjung Rigpe Dorje, 68, 77, 78, 84, 162
reincarnation, 7-10
Rich, Nathaniel, 148-152, 155
Rich, Thomas, 101
Riding the Tiger (Nydahl), 100
Rigpe Dorje Foundation, 88, 124-128:
    San Antonio Rigpe Dorje Center, 124-127
Rocky Mountain Dharma Center, 83
Rocky Mountain Shambhala Center, 107
Rogues in Robes (Lehnert), 129
Rowe, Bruce, 122
Ruiz, Samuel Rosa, 129
Rumtek (monastery), 75, 78, 166
Russell, Donna, 135-138, 139, 140, 147

S—
Sacks, Bob, 142
Sakya Lama Phagpa, 70
Samye Ling Meditative Center, 81, 82
Sangha del Corazón, 114
Santaraksita (professor), 46-47, 48
Savage, Michael, 133, 134, 139, 141-144, 157
Sawang Osel Rangdrol Mukpo, 101, 119
Schneider, Karola, 156
Shambhala International:
    Austin Center, 105-111
    Dallas Shambhala Study Group, 119
    Houston Shambhala Center, 116-119
    San Antonio Center, 111-116
Shang Tselpa, 67
Shen, C. T., 85, 86, 95
Shen, Nancy, 85
Sherab Tarchin, 160
Shiva, 23
Siddhartha (Hesse), 119
Six Perfections, 58
Sonam Gyatso, 75
Songtsen Gampo, 42, 43-44
Swanson, Bill, 122

T—
Tai Ming Chen, 73-74
Tai Situ Rinpoche, 70, 86, 92, 125, 160, 163, 165, 166, 167
Tail of the Tiger (meditative center), 82, 83, 114, 119
tantrism, 25, 26-27, 29, 30-33, 36-37, 38
Teachings on the Nature of Mind (Nydahl), 145
Templeton, Melody, 156, 157
Tenzin Gyatso, 165
Thaye Dorje, 102, 103, 147, 162, 164, 166, 169, 170
theism, 19
Thich Nhat Hanh, 127
Thogden Amdo Palden Rinpoche, 159-160
Thoreau, Henry David, 176
Thrangu (monastery), 87
Tibetan Book of Living and Dying, The (Sogyal Rinpoche), 136
Tibetan Yoga and the Secret Doctrines (Evans-Wentz), 90-01
Tilopa, 54-55, 56, 57, 59, 60, 65-66
Toghan Temur, 75
Tolpe Dorje, 75
Tonmi Sambhota, 43
Topga Yulgyal Rinpoche, 166
Tripitaka, 2
Trisong Detsen, 44, 45, 46-47, 49

Trungpa Rinpoche, 98-99, 100, 109-110, 170
Trungpa Tulku, 81
Tsenpo Khore, 52
Tsong Khapa Lo Sang Draka, 11
Tsurphu (monastery), 67, 68, 69, 77
Tusum Khyenpa, 67

U—
Ugyen Trinley, 102, 109, 160, 164, 165, 166, 167, 169, 170
Ugyen Tulku, 169

V—
Vairocana (translator), 50
Voltaire, 19-20

W—
Wallace, Terri, 121
Wells, H. G., 135
Wells, Lawrence, 105-111, 127
Wenzel, Carolyn, 128, 130
Wharton, Jo, 120, 121
White, Connie, 126, 127-128
Williams, Michael, 157
Winn, Steve, 115
Wong Ho, 127

Y—
Yellow Hat Lamas, 75
Yeshe O, 52
yoga, 24-25
Yogacara sect, 17-18, 20-21, 23, 39
Yung-lo (emperor), 75

About the Author

Dewitte Lindsey was a "domestic missionary" for thirty years—that is, a Texas classroom teacher of history, government, and the dramatic arts; a football and basketball coach at the junior high school level; assistant principal; and most recently, the director of a GED program. He has recently retired and is living in a state of semi-bliss.

Mr. Lindsey's interest in the spiritual world began abruptly in 1961 when, as a college freshman lying in bed after a long evening of intense study, he had a remarkable spontaneous visionary experience. He could find no one at all to talk to about the event and its meaning. But the intervening years have led him to search for deeper understanding of that episode and ultimately led to the writing of *Tibet to Texas*.

A resident of Huntsville, Texas, Mr. Lindsey has traveled extensively.